The Wars of the
ROSES

ABOUT THE AUTHOR

Anthony Goodman was, until his recent retirement, Professor of Medieval History at the University of Edinburgh. His other books include *John of Gaunt*, *Richard II: The Art of Kingship*, *War and Border Societies in the Middle Ages*, *The Wars of the Roses: Military Activity and English Society, 1452-97*, and *History of England from Edward II to James I*. He lives in Edinburgh.

The Wars of the ROSES

THE SOLDIERS' EXPERIENCE

ANTHONY GOODMAN

TEMPUS

oodman, R.E. and
R.A.

Cover illustrations:

Front: The battle of Barnet, MS.236, fol.2r. University Library of Ghent, (Belgium)

Back: Evocative portrayal of the rout of the Lancastrians at the battle of Towton in 1461. Courtesy of Jonathan Reeve (JR643b13p689 14501500)

This edition first published 2006

Tempus Publishing Limited
The Mill, Brimscombe Port,
Stroud, Gloucestershire, GL5 2QG
www.tempus-publishing.com

British Library Cataloguing in Publication Data.
A catalogue record for this book is available from the British Library.

ISBN 0 7524 3731 3

Typesetting and origination by Tempus Publishing Limited
Printed and bound in Great Britain

Contents

Preface

The Wars of the Roses have been frequently refought in print over the last few decades, in a variety of historical contexts. My excuse for entering the fray – for a second time – is that I am curious about the ordinary soldiers who took part in them, about their attitudes and experiences. Those of us blessed with not having experienced warfare are likely to be constantly surprised by the recollections of veterans. I remember General Essame once saying that the overwhelming impression he had received from talking to veterans of the Boer War was their boredom in the immensity of the veldt. Far removed from the excitement of Deneys Reitz's *Commando*! Alas, writers of the fifteenth and early sixteenth centuries were uninterested in recording the bowmen's and billmen's recollections either of frantic activity, or of relaxation round the campfire. These common soldiers' mentalities have left no clearly defined imprint. I have tried to give them some sort of background, by roaming over a wider geographical area and timespan than that occupied by the Wars. Hopefully, this will conjure up faint outlines of the English and Welsh 'goddams' (as Joan of Arc allegedly termed them) and will help towards positioning the Wars in a context of later medieval and early modern conflicts, particularly other civil wars. In providing this context, I have rashly strayed into early modern English history, fortified by the insistence of the late Denys Hay, my mentor, guide and friend, that the year 1485 should not be regarded as a historical barrier.

I owe thanks for advice and/or references, received over many years, to Professor Christopher Allmand, Professor Michael Bennett, Dr Nicholas Bennett (Vice-Chancellor and Librarian of Lincoln Cathedral), Professor David Carpenter, Owen Dudley Edwards, Professor Ralph Griffiths, Dr Michael K. Jones, Dr Simone Macdougall, Professor Angus Mackay, the late K.B. McFarlane, Dr Maureen Meikle, Mrs Katherine Parker, Harry Schnitker and Andrew Wheatcroft.

I have benefited over the years from the expertise of Dr Jeremy Crang, Assistant Director of the Centre for Second World War Studies in the University of Edinburgh.

Luis Pablo Martínez and Jorge Saiz Serrano made it possible for me to use the Villena collection in the Archivo del Reino de Valencia.

I have benefited from the help of many librarians and archivists, in particular that of Dr Norman Reid, Keeper of Manuscripts and Muniments at the University of St Andrews, Ms Susan Maddock, Principal Archivist at Norfolk Record Office, and keeper of the borough archives at King's Lynn, and Miss Esther Ormerod, archivist at Somerset Record Office.

I owe a special debt of gratitude to Geoffrey Wheeler, for allowing me to select illustrations from his extensive and remarkable library of photographs illustrating the Wars of the Roses and the age of Richard III.

My wife Jackie has saved me from many grammatical errors and infelicities of style, and has contributed shrewd and valuable points of argument.

Finally, I am heartily grateful to Jonathan Reeve of Tempus, for his faith in the book, and his constant help and encouragement.

Abbreviations

'Annales Ricardi Secundi et Henrici Quarti', *Johannis de Trokelowe Chronica et Annales*, ed. Riley, H.T., R.S., 1866.

Arrivall: Historie of the Arrivall of King Edward IV, ed. Bruce, J., Camden Soc., London, 1838.

Blood Red Roses: Fiorato, V., Boylston, A. and Knüssel, C. ed., *Blood Red Roses. The archaeology of a mass grave from the Battle of Towton AD 1461*, Oxford, 2000.

CCR: Calendar of Close Rolls.

CP: The Complete Peerage of England, Scotland, Ireland and Great Britain and the United Kingdom, ed. G.E.C., new edtn by Gibbs, V. et al., London, 1910–59.

CPR: Calendar of Patent Rolls.

CSP: Calendar of State Papers.

Commynes: Commynes, Philippe de, *Memoirs. The Reign of Louis XI 1461–83*, trans. and ed. Jones, M., Harmondsworth, 1972.

Dodds: Dodds, M. H. and R., *The Pilgrimage of Grace 1536–1537 and the Exeter Conspiracy 1538*, 2 vols, Cambridge, 1915.

EHR: The English Historical Review.

Foedera: *Foedera, Litterae… et Acta Publica* (etc.), ed. Rymer, T., 20 vols, London, 1704–35.

Froissart: Froissart, Jean, *Oeuvres*, ed. Lettenhove, Kervyn de, 25 vols, Brussels, 1867–77.

Gesta Henrici Quinti: Gesta Henrici Quinti. The Deeds of Henry V, trans. and ed. Taylor, F. and Roskell, J. S., Oxford, 1975.

Hall: Hall, Edward, *The Vnion of the Two Noble and Illustre Famelies of Lancastre and Yorke* (etc.), London, 1548 – edtn London, 1809.

Knighton: *Knighton's Chronicle 1337–1396*, ed. Martin, G. H., Oxford, 1995.

Paston Letters: The Paston Letters 1422–1509, 4 vols, ed. Gairdner, J., Edinburgh, 1910.

PRO: Public Record Office (The National Archives).

R.S.: Rolls series, London.

Westminster Chronicle: The Westminster Chronicle 1381–1394, ed. Hector, L.C. and Harvey, B.F., Oxford, 1982.

Whethamstede: Whethamstede, John, 'Register', *Registra quorundam Abbatum Monasterii S. Albani*, ed. Riley, H.T., 1, R.S., 1872.

Worcestre: Worcestre, William, *Itineraries*, ed. Harvey, J.H., Oxford, 1969.

Introduction:
The Wars of the Roses Today

*One of the rules in the Wars of the Roses was that nobody was ever
really King but that Edmund Mortimer really ought to be: any Baron
who wished to be considered King was allowed to apply at Warwick the
Kingmaker's, where he was made to fill up a form...*

*9. How do you propose to die? (Write your answer in BLOCK
CAPITALS.)*

W.R. Sellar and R.J.Yeatman, *1066 and All That*, 1930

From a modern viewpoint, the Wars of the Roses are
easy to send up. They appear like bull-headedly repetitive exercises in mutual self–destruction by ruthlessly
ambitious and singularly unattractive nobles. The tally of twelve
important battles between 1455 and 1485, involving a gradually
shifting cast of nobles, and ostensibly concerning variations on
a couple of leading issues, is unique in English medieval history.
An illumination in a manuscript of Edward IV's official account
of his recovery of the kingdom in 1471, in which his principal
Lancastrian opponents are depicted as nonchalantly queueing
up after his victory at Tewkesbury to have their heads cut off,
now appears grimly comic. The Wars do not resonate with and

connect to future debates about the liberties of the English and Welsh in the ways in which the Great Civil War of the seventeenth century was to do, and still does today. The issues raised in the Great Civil War, about forms and freedom of worship, the legitimate basis, locus and operations of secular authority, and the rights of common folk to have their say in the formulation of policy, were to remain central matters of debate and legislation among the English–speaking peoples. Today's republicans can look upon themselves as the heirs of seventeenth–century radicals, arguing in favour of the revival of the Long Parliament's abolition of the Monarchy, and, notably in the case of Tony Benn, the replacement of the elective dictatorship of Prime Ministers, who wield a still potent royal prerogative, by a more fully democratic system of government.

It is understandable that Edward Short (Lord Glenamara), Secretary of State for Education and Science in Harold Wilson's first administration, once held out the Wars of the Roses as an example of the sort of subject in history that he hoped to see being taught no longer. Simon Schama, in his *History of Britain*, suggests that one can see the repetitive tergiversations of the Wars either 'as one of the great epics of English history', or as a story with a somewhat numbing effect. 'If the latter, the temptation is to write off the entire sorry mess as the bloody bickering of overgrown schoolboys, each with their miniature armies or "affinities", whacking each other senseless on the fields of Towton, Barnet and St Albans; a dance of death to a tune played by the Earl of Warwick, "the Kingmaker"'. The former interpretation is the traditional one, first fully adumbrated by the early Tudor historian Edward Hall, and dramatised by Shakespeare. This, I suspect, is what Lord Glenamara objected to as being an example of a narrow and now threadbare sort of political history, concentrating on the enmities and plots of nobles. Incidentally, it is one which ignores the facts that the Wars were an epic of Welsh history, that they became enmeshed in conflicts in Ireland, and led to sieges in France. The second interpretation smacks of the bemused hilarity of Sellar and Yeatman. Finally, Professor

Schama suggests the importance of one underlying issue: 'to make the English monarchy credible again and resolder the chain of allegiance that had once stretched from Westminster to the justices of the shires and the jurors of the villages and that had been snapped by the fate of Richard II'[1]. Richard had been deposed in 1399, and the claim to succeed represented by the young Edmund Mortimer had been passed over in favour of Henry of Lancaster's claim. There is a certain parallelism in Schama's argument to that put forward in the declaration of Edward IV's title to the throne to parliament in 1461, which was to be influential in the classic explanation of the Wars developed in Tudor historiography. This was that there had been lasting divine and human displeasure at Henry of Lancaster's usurpation: consequently, 'this Realm of England... hath suffered the charge of intolerable persecution, punition and tribulation...'[2]. Indeed, Henry IV had had to struggle to resolder all allegiances firmly in the early years of his rule, and faced a much more thorough and long-lasting rejection of them in Wales. In the early years of Edward IV's reign, he fought to impose full control there and in the far north of England, and Richard III and Henry VII both faced major challenges to their rule in their initial years. Yet one remarkable feature of the rule of these three usurping kings was the reverence with which their subjects continued to accept monarchical authority, which had been dragged through the mud – literally at times, in the cases of the fugitive Henry VI, captured in a wood in Lancashire in 1465, and apparently of Richard III's crown, said to have been found in the undergrowth on Bosworth field. Justices and jurors responded to the writs of 'usurpers' with the same alacrity or procrastinations accorded to those of their predecessors. Though the transition to a changed claim to rule was not as smooth in the fifteenth century as it was to be in 1660 and 1688, adaptability to the practicalities of such topsy-turvy situations seems already to have been on the way to becoming as English as roast beef, and as Welsh as toasted cheese. The puritanical republican bureaucrats who reinvented themselves as scambling Caroline courtiers had their earlier counterparts in the Lancastrian household officers who served Edward IV with equivalent zeal, and the former Yorkist councillors who served Henry VII.

The perceived contemporary relevance of the Great Civil War stems from preoccupation with the British constitution and its reform, characteristic public concerns from the age of Earl Grey to that of Tony Blair. Another, related strand in historiography, which reached its apogee in the first half of the twentieth century, stimulated by Victorian concern to reform and expand the civil service, was the study of the development of the central bureaucracy. However, it is notable that there have been no studies of the English constitution and bureaucracy over the fifteenth century on the scale of T.F. Tout's study of administration in the fourteenth century, and Sir Geoffrey Elton's of early Tudor government. Though accusations of 'tyranny' were bandied about in the Wars of the Roses, they were not struggles over the liberties of the subject and the scope of royal prerogative, which, by contrast, link the issues of Magna Carta and the opposition to Richard II's definitions of prerogative to the constitutional struggles of the seventeenth century. The treatise on *The Governance of England* written by Sir John Fortescue to instruct Henry VI's son and heir, but eventually dedicated to Edward IV, sketched broad propositions which were generally acceptable to both Lancastrians and Yorkists. Rebels did not have an agenda to reform the structure of central and local government. Though the Yorkist kings and Henry VII were to be innovators in the administration of royal finance and justice, they strenuously projected themselves as traditionalists, not creators of an institutionally 'new' monarchy set up to reconstruct a failing Crown and disordered society.

Though the Wars of the Roses cannot be easily connected to main strands of constitutional politics and reform, some of the risings, and others in the later Middle Ages, can in some respects be related to another sort of politics, whose importance in modern British history has been expounded in Marxist historiography. This is the politics of the labourer and the artisan. Thanks to the pioneering work of E.P. Thompson, among others, we now have firmly fixed before us the nature and methods of radical popular protest, and the rationale of demonstrations and riots. We can see them as a traditional continuum, significantly interacting with and influencing the politics of elites. As a result of the establishment of this historiographical strand, we can perhaps empathise more than historians who reverenced the state in Victorian style, with the aims and methods of dissidents, and their determination to make public demonstrations against government policies. Also we can do so because, since the march from London to Aldermaston in 1958, organised by the Campaign for Nuclear Disarmament, we have come to accept peaceful forms of mass 'direct action' as recurrent and legitimate parts of the political process.

So we need to put the Wars in the context of the long and notable history of protests in the form of 'direct action' by groups of commons in England, directed against what they perceived as bad government. In this period, these were often made in alliance with or under the leadership of members of the elites. Later medieval English folk had a lexicon of hard-nosed criteria by which they condemned policy, which anticipated or paralleled those of later generations. They hated government by rulers who essentially were thought to flout the moral order; by rulers and their councillors who neglected the adequate defence of the realm and its interests abroad; by those who seemed to undermine without justification the standing of powerful individuals and pressure groups; who conspicuously failed to ensure that the law provided some semblance of indifferent justice to suitors of every status, or who were felt by the poor commons to oppress them with taxes and demands for military service. In the later fourteenth and fifteenth centuries, groups of men (nobles hoping for the support of commoners, commoners looking for noble leadership) were inclined to make vociferous demonstrations in arms, in protest on such matters of public policy – sometimes, indeed, with the direst intent, either to have unpopular royal councillors beheaded or even, though rarely, to have a king deposed. The riot and the march, demonstrations with 'force and arms', became well-established features of English political life, sometimes concerned with highly localised and personal grievances, sometimes with the well-being of all.

In the past half century or so, the study of the Wars of the Roses has been transformed by a new understanding of the motives and socio-political relations of later medieval English magnates. This has been based on the ground-breaking studies of K.B. McFarlane, particularly in the Ford Lectures in the University of Oxford for 1953, and in lectures which he gave in the 1960s.[3] In his hands, as in those of Sir Lewis Namier, studying the members of the House of Commons in the eighteenth century, prosopographical anatomisation of an elite provided a wholly new illumination of their particular and characteristic motivations. Surveying nobles' attitudes to family ties, their use of patronage, their policies for their estates and finances, their roles in regional society, and relations with kings and fellow peers, McFarlane demonstrated the logic of their aims, and the prevalence among them of cogently reflective rather than unthinkingly reflex reactions to political dilemmas and economic problems. In so doing, he retouched and framed them as credible predecessors of successive generations of the higher nobility, such as the great Whig dynasties of the eighteenth century. After McFarlane's new perspectives, the later medieval English nobility could no longer be seen as uncivil, illiterate baronial thugs, at their best consumed by irrational chivalrous fantasies.

There has since been a plethora of works which have reassessed kings and nobles, and the nature and course of national and regional politics, in the era of the Wars of the Roses. Attention has in recent years been focussed on those status groups in the nobility later collectively termed 'the gentry', whose participation or neutrality in the civil wars crucially affected their character and outcome. Among outstanding works which have given a firmer social and political context to the Wars and their leading protagonists are Robin Storey's *The End of the House of Lancaster* (1966), Charles Ross's *Edward IV* (1974), Ralph Griffiths's *The Reign of King Henry VI* (1981), Rosemary Horrox's *Richard III. A Study in Service* (1989), A.J. Pollard's *North–East England during the Wars of the Roses* (1990) and Michael Hicks's *Warwick the Kingmaker* (1998).[4] Recent

work by Dr John Watts and Dr Christine Carpenter has emphasised dynamic and consensual aspects of the relationship between
king and magnates, within the context of a re-examined political
ideology.[5] Professor Colin Richmond, Dr Keith Dockray and
Professor Pollard have illuminated episodes of popular protest
and disturbance in the period of the Wars.[6]

The contemporary fascination with warfare has produced
numerous new studies of battles in the Wars; a model example
is one on the battle of Wakefield (1460).[7] Much ink has flowed
over the battle of Bosworth, much of it concerned with fixing its
site from the literary and documentary sources. A most promising line of enquiry about such sites and the evidence which they
can yield has been opened up by the battlefield historians Tony
Pollard and Neil Oliver in their survey of the site of Edward
IV's victory over Warwick in 1471 at Barnet.[8] However, the
battle which, in some aspects, has recently been vividly brought
to life is one of Edward's other great victories, Towton (1461),
which clinched his usurpation of Henry VI's throne. In 1996 a
mass grave was discovered at Towton Hall. The thoroughgoing
examination of the remains, in which archaeologists from the
University of Bradford were heavily involved, has brought us
face-to-face with the common soldier.[9]

It is with common soldiers, especially English and Welsh ones,
who took part in the Wars of the Roses and in other campaigns of
the later Middle Ages, that the present study is largely concerned.
Indeed, it is difficult to penetrate their mentalities and recreate
their conditions of service – it is only from the Peninsular War
onwards that there is a flow of memoirs by rankers. Here an
attempt is made to view the common soldiers' experiences of
warfare and rebellion in England and Wales, and their attitudes
towards it, over the later medieval and early modern periods, and
to contextualise the Wars of the Roses as part of a sequence of
noble and popular revolts.

At the risk of writing about the Wars in the vein in which
Sellar and Yeatman delighted, which Lord Glenamara scorned,
and which arouses Schama's amusement, let me now give a

brief outline of main events in the Wars of the Roses. They are generally held to have commenced with the rising of Richard, Duke of York, in 1455. Descended from Edward III through both his father and mother, he was a mature, dignified magnate with a distinguished record of service in the 1440s in defence of his close kinsman Henry VI's recently lost provinces in France. The Duke was supported in arms in 1455 by his brother-in-law Richard Neville, Earl of Salisbury, a faithful, hard-working scion of the Lancastrian dynasty, and a leading northern magnate, and by the latter's young son Richard, Earl of Warwick. The allied rebels publicly protested about defaults in government and their own grievances. York felt that his counsel in the affairs of the King's realms had not been given the weight due to him, and that his interests as a magnate had been neglected and slighted at court. The rebels won what was to be the first of two battles at St Albans on 22 May. York's hated rival Edmund Beaufort, Duke of Somerset (who also had a direct line of descent from Edward III) was killed in it, and so was Salisbury's regional rival, Henry Percy, Earl of Northumberland. The King was captured, but treated with respect; York briefly exercised rule as Protector of the Realm.

The Wars are usually held to have ended on 22 August 1485, with the battle of Bosworth. There, the third Yorkist king, Richard of York's younger son Richard III, was killed in conflict with rebellious forces headed by Henry Tudor. In contrast to Richard, who had built himself a reputation as an effective and just ruler of the North of England in his brother Edward IV's reign, Henry was an obscure exile, brought up in alien Welsh and Breton ways. However, he was the late Henry VI's nephew (the son of his half-brother Edmund Tudor, Earl of Richmond), and had a direct descent from Edward III through his mother Margaret Beaufort (niece of the Duke of Somerset killed in the first battle of the Wars). Henry was acclaimed as king on the spot at Bosworth field. Despite his persuasive propaganda that through his subsequent marriage to Edward IV's daughter Elizabeth of York he had terminated the internecine conflicts, his rule was to be challenged by members of the House of York, real and pretended. Nevertheless, Henry VII died in his royal bed in 1509, and his son Henry VIII, though aged only seventeen, succeeded smoothly, wielding full personal authority, and without facing challenges to his title – the first incoming king to enjoy a smooth succession for nearly ninety years.

Between 1455 and 1485 there were numerous rebellions, and from 1460 onwards fighting between partisans of Lancaster and York in Wales, Ireland and France, and at sea too. In 1459, York and his Neville allies, again excluded from power, especially at the determination of Henry VI's forceful queen, Margaret of Anjou, once more staged a revolt, complaining of malicious intentions towards them at court. Salisbury inflicted a sharp defeat on some of the royal forces at Blore Heath, but at Ludlow the Yorkist leaders fled in the face of the overwhelming magnate support which the King fielded against them. York went to Ireland, where he had been royal lieutenant, and the Nevilles, and York's eldest son Edward, Earl of March, fled to Calais. There, Warwick, who had been royal lieutenant of this English enclave, was able to secure support, and fend off the Crown's attempts to regain control. In 1460 these 'Calais lords', though attainted of treason, invaded Kent, rallied popular support by their manifesto against allegedly bad government, gained admission to London, and defeated and captured the King at the battle of Northampton. Henry was once more escorted to London by triumphant rebels.

The Duke of York then returned in equal triumph from Ireland to attend parliament, where he dismayed his peers by claiming the throne, as the descendant, through his mother, Edmund Mortimer's sister Ann, of Edward III's son, Lionel, Duke of Clarence. Henry VI's descent was only from a younger son of Edward III, John of Gaunt, Duke of Lancaster – but he had no females in his line of succession, whereas York had two. The Lords were not prepared to ditch their long-held allegiance to Henry, so the compromise was reached that he would hold the Crown for life, to be succeeded by York and his heirs. This settlement excluded the right of Henry's own son, Edward, Prince of

Wales: it was a recipe for dynastic war, definitively splitting the royal kin between the houses of Lancaster and York.

A substantial number of lords and commons were prepared to rally in arms in Yorkshire to Margaret of Anjou, to support the cause of her son. York and Salisbury hurried up there: they underestimated the opposition, and, at the battle of Wakefield, York was killed and the captured Salisbury was executed by popular demand. The personal venom which events had injected into the tightly knit circles of royal and noble kinsfolk was reflected in the display of defeated nobles' heads on the gates of York. Queen Margaret capitalised on the victory by leading an army southwards in February 1461, which defeated Warwick at St Albans. The King, whom the Earl had taken with him, was reunited with his queen. The mayor and citizens of London prevaricated over the admission of the King and Queen with their apparently unruly army. Just over a fortnight before the battle of St Albans, York's son and heir Edward, Earl of March, had defeated a Lancastrian force at Mortimer's Cross, near Leominster (Herefordshire). Welshmen were heavily involved on both sides. This turned out to be the decisive battle in the Wars as regards Wales. Though the Lancastrians long continued to fancy their chances of maintaining resistance there, most of Wales remained in Yorkist control until Henry Tudor advanced through it, after landing with his invasion force in Pembrokeshire in 1485. March, after his victory in 1461, had hastened to meet the defeated Warwick – and they were admitted to London. Henry VI and Margaret withdrew their ragged forces to Yorkshire. Edward had himself acclaimed king by his supporters, and sat regally attired in Westminster Hall.

The new king and the experienced military men around him did not waste time, soon concentrating the resources and manpower of southern shires and towns for a push northwards. In March Edward's army forced the passage of the River Aire at Ferrybridge (Yorkshire). Next day the Yorkists attacked Henry's army, which included probably the largest number of English peers ever assembled on a battlefield, drawn up at Towton, just south of Tadcaster. Edward won a hard-fought and bloody victory – a striking judgement of God in favour of his upstart kingship. The Lancastrians were too demoralised to hold York. Henry VI, his queen and his son Edward soon fled to Scotland. From then onwards, the Lancastrian cause was heavily dependent on the support of foreign princes – especially the rulers of Scotland and France – who wished to embarrass English kings, and hobble any threatening diplomatic or military initiatives they might contemplate.

Nevertheless, the Lancastrian cause was maintained for the next few years on the margins of the realm, in the Anglo-Scottish Borders and remote parts of Wales, where royal armies could not operate for long without logistical problems and heavy costs. With the surrender of Bamburgh Castle in Northumberland in 1464, the capture of Henry VI in 1465, and of Harlech Castle in Gwynedd in 1468, the Lancastrian cause seemed doomed. Queen Margaret and her son maintained their pretensions in exile on the continent, with the faint hope that Louis XI of France might find it politic to give significant backing to the cause of his English and Angevin kinsfolk. It was perhaps a measure of Edward's complacency, and a sense of the stability of Yorkist rule, that Henry VI was allowed to live on, a prisoner in the Tower of London, and even receive visitors, though he and his chamber seem to have been in need of a good scrub. There appears to have been Yorkist unconcern about the Lancastrian court in exile, and about young Henry Tudor, who was being honourably educated in the household of Edward's staunch supporter William Herbert, Earl of Pembroke. By contrast, Henry VIII was to be greatly concerned about the machinations abroad of a defiant Yorkist claimant to the throne, Richard de la Pole ('the White Rose'), and rejoiced heartily at his death in the battle of Pavia in 1525.

What breathed new life into the Lancastrian cause in 1470 was the disintegration of the Yorkist regime. The previous year, Warwick, supported by his brothers John Neville, Earl of Northumberland and George, archbishop of York, ranged themselves against Edward and other newly elevated Yorkists, notably his queen Elizabeth's kinsmen, the Wydevilles and Greys, and the leading Welsh Yorkist, William Herbert, Earl of Pembroke. Moreover, Warwick was joined by one of the King's brothers, George, Duke of Clarence – though the youngest brother, Richard, Duke of Gloucester, was to remain remarkably loyal to Edward throughout his hair-raising vicissitudes of the next few years. Warwick and his allies instigated risings in Yorkshire, and invaded the realm from Calais. Their northern supporters defeated a loyalist Welsh army commanded by the Earl of Pembroke, at Edgcote (near Banbury, Oxfordshire). Edward, reacting sluggishly, was soon taken – in his bed! However, public opinion apparently found the notion of obeying him as yet another puppet king, like Henry VI, unendurable. When some unreconciled Lancastrians took advantage of Yorkist disarray, by raising revolt in the Marches towards Scotland, Warwick found that he had to release the King in order to raise sufficient support to crush the rebels.

Early in 1470, Warwick and Clarence (now his son-in-law) once more plotted risings in the North, but one of them, composed mostly of Lincolnshire peasants, seems to have been launched prematurely, in reaction to Edward's more sprightly military preparations. He easily swept away the commons, at Empingham in Rutland ('Losecoat Field'), and set off northwards in pursuit of Warwick and Clarence, who engaged in a long and circuitous retreat, finally fleeing by ship from Exeter. Repulsed at Southampton and by the English garrison in Calais, they landed in Normandy. This was, in fact, a diplomatically opportune moment for them to do so. Louis XI of France was desperate to disrupt the alliance between his perennial opponent Charles the Bold, Duke of Burgundy (ruler of much of the Low Countries) and Edward IV. Louis effected an astonishing reconciliation of Clarence and Warwick with Margaret of Anjou and her son the Prince of Wales. With French assistance, in September, these former pillars of the Yorkist establishment landed in the West Country, and, proclaiming Henry VI, advanced into the Midlands. Edward had recently succeeded in suppressing a revolt in the Neville interest in Yorkshire, but his attempts to rally support against the invasion were undermined by the sudden treachery of Warwick's brother John Neville (disgruntled at his demotion from Earl of Northumberland to Marquess Montague). Edward fled to his brother-in-law Charles the Bold's county of Holland, and a few days later Clarence and Warwick were among the lords who escorted an unimpressively attired Henry VI from his prison in the Tower of London, once more proclaimed king.

The England of the restored King Henry, in contradiction to its traditional stances and predominant commercial interests, was soon at war with the Low Countries, as an ally of the French Crown. Charles the Bold, in retaliation, funded a small force for Edward to attempt to reconquer his realm. He landed somewhat tentatively in Yorkshire, and was allowed in wary sufferance within the walls of York. Hostile magnates and commons alike showed a reluctance to attack him – perhaps his past victories had earned him a formidable reputation as a field commander. Marquess Montague, the diehard Lancastrian Earl of Oxford and even Warwick himself rejected opportunities to confront him – enabling his former retainers to join him with their contingents. Clarence was reconciled with Edward, and they were admitted to London, with the outmanoeuvred Warwick hard on their heels. At Barnet (Middlesex), the armies clashed fiercely, and sacrilegiously, on Easter Day. Warwick and Montague were killed in the rout. God's blessing on the rashly impious Edward's title had been remarkably confirmed. Henry was once more confined in the Tower.

Yet Margaret of Anjou, her son, and faithful Lancastrian lords landed at Weymouth (Dorset). They set out to roll up support in the West Country and Wales, but Edward was determined to intercept them as soon as possible, pushing his men on to catch up with the exhausted Lancastrian soldiers at Tewkesbury. There he won the victory which, it was soon clear, had shattered the House of Lancaster's pretensions. Their heir,

Edward, Prince of Wales, was killed in the battle. Margaret of Anjou was captured. The Prince's prospective heir, Edmund Beaufort, Duke of Somerset, the last male Beaufort, was executed after the battle. Henry VI's surviving half-brother, Jasper Tudor, Earl of Pembroke, charged with raising forces in Wales, could not resist Edward's supporters there, and fled to the duchy of Brittany with his nephew Henry Tudor. Edward, in the aftermath of Tewkesbury, had not been able to rest. William, Bastard of Fauconberg (a member of the Neville family), with some of Warwick's former soldiers and sailors, and commons from Kent and Essex, in May launched belated, powerful but unsuccessful assaults on London. Edward had to secure the capital (where Henry perished on the night of his arrival), and advance into Kent, to suppress the embers of rebellion.

That should have been the end of the Lancastrian story. The dynasty owed its resurrection, in the guise of the Tudors, to Edward's loyal brother, Richard, Duke of Gloucester, whose machinations were to cause the second great disruption of the Yorkist establishment. After Edward's death in 1483, he was apparently accepted without demur as Protector of the Realm for the minority of the former's son Edward V. Gloucester's rapid and extreme measures against the King's maternal relatives and some eminent Yorkist supporters were the actions of a man unsure of his authority, and in a hurry to consolidate it. He had good reason to be anxious; the authority of Protectors had been contentious, sometimes brief. During Henry VI's minority, his uncle Humphrey, Duke of Gloucester, had constantly complained of the restrictions placed on his authority as Protector. Richard's father had been unable to consolidate his political authority during his two brief Protectorates in the 1450s. If precedents were followed, Edward V's minority would be formally ended in two or three years' time. In assuming a slippery, short-term eminence, Richard was risking his loss in the long term of his exceptional dominance in the North, an obvious target for erosion by a youthful king jealously flexing regal muscles. Why then did Richard decide to mount an even more fragile eminence

– the throne? As he must have been only too aware, it had taken his brother over ten years to consolidate a novel dynastic authority. Maybe the allegations of the illegitimacy of Edward V and his brother, Richard, Duke of York, shocked him deeply, preying on the mind of this pious prince, who in his rule and judgements as Lieutenant in the North, and as king, showed fair-mindedness and, indeed, compassion. God had given his family the throne because the rule of the Lancastrians was unrighteous. Would He not deprive the House of York if it, too, maintained an unlawful succession? Richard may have assumed the terrible burden of seizing the Crown in the hope that God would reward his rectitude, but with clear-eyed political forebodings that he would have to act with harshness against dissidents, and that his actions would stir up the regal pretensions of every Tom, Dick and (Tudor) Harry.

Such soon proved to be the case. In the autumn of 1483 there were risings of gentry and commons, notably in parts of southern England. They failed. The Duke of Buckingham, distrusted as Richard's recent accomplice, proved an incompetent rebel leader. Richard and his captains efficiently nipped the buds of rebellion. His soldiers were even on the beach where the unknown Henry Tudor's ships hove to. Henry wisely declined invitations to land. However, the legacy of the rebellion was profound, since well-reputed knightly leaders of it sought refuge with Henry in Brittany. Their support for his kingship gave it a new credibility: now he had a reputable 'government in exile', composed not only of the familiar Lancastrian suspects, but also of shrewd former councillors and soldiers of Edward IV. In 1485 the government of Charles VIII of France was in a situation comparable to that of his father Louis XI in 1470. The French Crown wanted to unsettle an English king who supported its opponents, and had to hand for the purpose some formidable Lancastrians and disgruntled Yorkists, this time already allied. It is, indeed, puzzling that in 1485 Richard's army, superior in size, put up such an indifferent performance against Henry Tudor's French-backed force at Bosworth. It was certainly the case that

Richard's reordering of the political landscape had not had time to become embedded, to be widely regarded as the stable norm considered to be worth sustaining.

The same, indeed, was true of Henry VII's wavering rule in his early years. It faced no lack of challenges. There were foreign powers willing to fund more dynastic attempts, and there were popular grievances in England, especially over taxation. Yet the two did not link up to form a strong dynamic for revolt, as had happened sometimes in the recent past. No rebellious noble leader emerged with the prestige of Richard, Duke of York, or the charisma of Warwick. And there was a lack of credible alternative candidates for the throne – hence the resort of Henry's opponents to supporting impostors. He had a more plausible candidate under lock in the Tower of London, until executed on a trumped-up charge in 1499. This was Clarence's son, Edward, Earl of Warwick – bearer of a dangerously famous title, but an unknown and apparently rather vacant youth. Moreover, less than two years after Henry's victory at Bosworth, God had again shown him remarkable favour. In 1487 Henry decisively defeated a challenge by invaders which in some ways replicated his own in 1485, at the battle of Stoke (Nottinghamshire). There, it was the leading rebel magnate, Richard's nephew John de la Pole, Earl of Lincoln, who was slain. The impostor whom he was supporting, the obscure Lambert Simnel (supposedly the young Earl of Warwick) was captured. The battle effectively ended the major campaigns of the Wars – first formally termed as 'of the Roses' in the nineteenth century. Yet generations of folk in the Tudor age were to grow up keenly aware of their shadow – and even the young Henry VIII was not sure that the old dynastic strife was over. Among the concerns of the present study are the character of the memories of the campaigns which survived, the traditions about them which crystallised in families and communities, and the possible effects which these traditions had on political attitudes in the sixteenth century.

2

Attitudes to War

With fire and sword the country round
Was wasted far and wide.
And many a childing mother then
And new–born baby died:
But things like that, you know, must be
At every famous victory

Robert Southey, 'After Blenheim'

A t the courts of France and Burgundy, the dynastic revolutions, the numerous battles, the slaughter of nobles and soldiers, and, by contrast, the lack of depredations in the Wars of the Roses were matters of wonder and puzzlement, tinged at times with scorn. Charles the Bold, Duke of Burgundy, said in 1475 that English soldiers who had been reined back from fighting in France by Edward IV might just as well stay with him and fight the French as massacre each other in England.[1] Philippe de Commynes, a noble from Flanders who had been a councillor of Louis XI of France (d.1483), in his *Memoirs* frequently mused about the significance of the frequency and ferocity of the Wars. However, he noted that 'the realm of England enjoys one favour above all other realms, that neither the countryside nor the people are destroyed nor are the buildings burnt or demolished. Misfortune falls on soldiers and on nobles in particular'.[2] Such comments by foreigners had a good deal of truth in them. Why did the Wars of the Roses have apparently distinctive, even odd characteristics? To view the conundrum in its settings, let us examine such subjects as conventions in general about warfare in the later Middle Ages, English perspectives on war and peace, the ways in which campaigning was characteristically carried on in other lands, and the peculiar English cult of rebellion.

STATES OF WAR AND PEACE

In the later Middle Ages, elites in England and Wales subscribed, at least nominally, to ecclesiastical doctrines and chivalrous conventions about the circumstances in which war was justifiable, and the rules under which it should be waged. They held these views in common with other elites in Western Christendom with whom they shared cultural attitudes and had close social ties – notably the French, the Netherlanders, the Lowland Scots and the Anglo-Irish. In the twelfth and thirteenth centuries, the Church's laws about war were refined by canonists. They insisted that war was justified only as a means of procuring a rightful peace, restoring rights which had been usurped, whose violent abrogation had perpetuated wrongdoing. The supreme continuing example of usurpation was the occupation by Muslims of Christs's patrimony, the Holy Land. Participation in a crusade aimed at restoring the Holy Land to its rightful place in Christendom was a holy task for warriors, especially as those whose blood they would shed were infidels. Crusades against Muslims, and other persistent offenders against God (such as heretics, the enemies within Christendom) were authorised by God's vicar on earth, the Pope. Otherwise, war ought only to be declared and waged by the authority of princes, the rulers to whom the exercise of temporal sovereignty was delegated.

In England and in like-minded societies, the effusion of Christian blood by co-religionists was generally deplored. It was regarded as the last resort as a way of enforcing justice, but it was all too frequently part of the general condition. However, sensibilities to the horrors of war were not entirely dulled among participants. Buonaccorso Pitti, a Florentine, recalled in his memoirs how, as a bright young blade, he had served as a mercenary in the army with which Charles VI of France had driven an English force out of Flanders in 1383. The English evacuated a town by night and at first light the French entered unopposed:

> Inside we found most of the houses on fire and heaps of dead English and townsfolk. I saw one cruelly horrifying sight: a woman, who appeared from her clothing to be of good class, was sitting with a two year-old child in her arms, a three-year-old clinging to her shoulders and a five-year-old holding her hand, by the door of a furiously burning house. She was pulled up and moved some distance away to prevent herself and the children from coming to harm but, as soon as she was let go, rushed back to the door of the house, despite the great flames which were billowing from it, and was finally burnt inside with her three children. In the end, the whole town was burnt and destroyed.[3]

The anonymous chaplain who wrote *The Deeds of Henry V*, and who was present at the King's victory over the French at Agincourt in 1415, described the reactions of the victors at the sight of heaps of the slain. There was compunction and pity at the deaths of so many warriors at their hands, 'famous and most valiant had only God been with them'. Many of the English, he says, were in grief and tears, moved by 'the terrible deaths and bitter wounds of so many Christian men', fully revealed by their nakedness.[4] An English soldier, John Page, who took part in Henry's siege of Rouen (1418–19), in a poem about the siege, which he drafted when on active service, showed his sensitivity and that of his fellows to the horrors of war.[5] In wintertime, the defenders of Rouen expelled poor folk. Crowds of women with children in their arms and old men were thrust out at the gates:

And all they said at once then
'Have mercy upon us, ye Englishmen'.
Our men gave them of our bread.

However, the English soldiers, in obedience to their orders, pushed these wretches back into the city ditches, and would not let them pass by the watch. Page recalled their plight, poorly clothed, starving in the cold:

There men might see so great pity,
A child of two years or three
Go about to beg its bread.
Father and mother both were dead.
Under some the water stood :
Yet lay they crying after food.
And some starved unto death,
And some stopped of their breath,
Some crooked in the knees,
And some all lean as any trees,
And women held in their arms
Dead children in their bosoms,
And the children sucking in their pap
Within a dead woman's lap.
There ne was no man, I understand,
That saw that but his heart would change,
And [if] he considered that sight
He would be pensive and no thing light.

When Page describes Henry's triumphant entry into his recalcitrant city, after its surrender, his eye is caught by the emaciated state of the inhabitants:

Of the people, to tell the truth,
It was a sight of great routh [sorrow],
Much of the folk that were therein,
They were but bones and bare skin,

With hollow eyes and visage sharp,
Hardly they might breath or carp:
With wan colour as the lead,
Unlike to living men but unto dead.

Page's awkward and simple verses vividly conjure up a scene of the kind all too familiar from images of the victims of the twentieth century's wars. Indeed, Page was writing a panegyric on Henry V's conquest of Rouen. As a soldier, he knew his duty, and he considered Henry's treatment of the people of Rouen during the siege to have been legally correct, tempered with mercy. Yet clearly he could not get out of his mind the hellish scenes of desperate civilians he had witnessed, and felt compelled to describe them.

Rulers sometimes proposed heroic expedients to their opponents, which it is perhaps too facile to dismiss merely as propaganda exercises, in order to demonstrate their ardent desire to avoid the effusion of Christian blood. The warlike Edward III did so, though with some prudence on his part, when he challenged Philip VI's right to the throne of France in 1340. He suggested that Philip should have himself shut up in a lion's cage. If Philip emerged unscathed, Edward implied that he would accept him as the rightful king of France. Philip sensibly eschewed such undignified and fraught posturing.[6] In 1383, with an appearance of more boldness, Edward's grandson Richard II fulsomely challenged Philip's great-grandson Charles VI to settle the issue by single combat, as one alternative to battle – perhaps confident that the challenge would be declined.[7] Neither of these royally anointed lads had made a name for himself in the jousting lists.

However, these sorts of attempts at point-scoring were unusual. Rather, diplomatic processes were busily and very publicly undertaken, in order to persuade opinion at home and abroad that the search for peace had been pursued exhaustively. English kings, through communications to parliaments and to great councils (solemn assemblies of the king with selected nobles), and through proclamations, earnestly and piously sought to justify their belligerence, outlining their efforts to avoid war. As a result of such propaganda exercises, monastic sources are often mines of information (or misinformation) about diplomacy. Taxpayers, clerical and lay, all avid to avoid paying subsidy, needed to be convinced that God favoured their giving in a righteous cause. Soldiers needed to be reassured that their souls would not be imperilled by fighting in an unjust one. In respect of the soldiers' morale, the commander's mien in the field and address to the troops before battle might be crucial factors. Such continues to be the case in modern warfare. The Duke of Wellington may have been contemptuous of histrionics, but in the Second World War General Montgomery was following medieval precedent when he addressed gatherings of soldiers in his Western Desert campaign, wearing his distinctively odd array of cap badges, and speaking with studied simplicity. Medieval kings and nobles had to display themselves confidently to their troops. One wonders whether Henry V's facial scar, the consequence of what would have often been a fatal arrow wound, received at the battle of Shrewsbury, was regarded as a talisman by his soldiers. Commanders needed to be preachers, as well schooled in forensic skills as friars, in order to move the hearts of the people so that they would unleash deadly fury on their brethren in Christ. The contemporary emphasis in noble education on knowledge of the liberal arts had warlike applications.

The development of conventions and ceremonies marking stages up to the outbreak of war emphasised that it was a princely prerogative to wage it, as still is the case in Great Britain, though the right is now devolved by the Crown to the Prime Minister. In the later Middle Ages, heralds were dispatched to make public declarations of war at the opponent's court. Royal banners were raised to signal a state of war. Subjects who rode in arms without authority, especially once the king's standards were displayed, risked condemnation as rebels and traitors. A group of magnates known as the 'Lords Appellant', who rose in armed protest against Richard II's policies in 1387, were furious when one of his knights, Thomas Trivet, 'advised the king to take the field and unfurl his standard against the insurgents'. Eventually the King commissioned his friend Robert de Vere, Duke of Ireland, to do just that – but when the armies met, the unpopular and undistinguished Duke's unfurling of the standard of the lions and lilies and one of St George failed to dash the hearts of the rebel soldiers.[8] By contrast, Richard Horkesley *alias* Ramkyn, a soldier in the army of Sir Henry Percy and his uncle the Earl of Worcester, confronting Henry IV near Shrewsbury in 1403, 'seeing the king's standards refused the rebels and came to fight with the king against them', according to the royal pardon he received.[9]

An apologist for the Yorkist lords who had fled precipitately from the threat of Henry VI's army at Ludlow (Shropshire) in 1459 tried to make a virtue out of their necessity by casting their decision in terms of obedience to lawful authority and reverence for Christian precept. According to 'Bale's Chronicle', the 'Duke [of York] and the Earls [of Salisbury and Warwick] left the field because the king [Henry VI] was in the vaward [vanguard] and displayed his banner to fight, therefore and in eschewing of his death and the shedding of great blood', the lords meekly left the field![10] Sir Robert Welles, leading a rebellion of potentially flaky Lincolnshire commoners against the formidable Edward IV in 1470, was made of sterner stuff. The King 'took the field, where he understood the said Sir Robert Welles to be in arms with banners displayed against him, disposed to fight' (at Empingham). The Lincolnshiremen were speedily crushed – the battle became known as Losecoat Field for the thoroughness and speed with which the fleeing rebels discarded their impedimenta. The captured Welles was executed for his temerity.[11]

Thus in England particularly sharp distinctions were made between the states and tokens of war and peace. Elsewhere these might be blurred. In English sources from this period there are references to Ireland as, contrastingly, a 'land of war', where the King's peace and authority were habitually flouted by the

practice of private warfare, and by attacks on the King's lieutenant or deputy and loyal lieges, as a result of the weakened state
of English royal authority. In this respect, indeed, Ireland closely
resembled the state of much of Western Europe earlier on in the
Middle Ages. Gaelic chiefs and Gaelicised lords of Anglo-Irish
lordships waged endemic warfare, seizing cattle from neighbours,
and enforcing submission and the provision of tribute, hospitality and military aid on them. Insecurity in Ireland is reflected
in the widespread and dense distribution of later medieval
tower-houses.[12] There, ancient notions of the heroic nature of
warfare were strongly expressed in the recitation by bards of
verses recalling great deeds, and their composition of new ones
casting patrons in the same mould.

Indeed, resort to private warfare without the sanction of sovereign authority was to be found in much of later medieval
Europe. The practice of feud was widespread. In Germany royal
authority was in many regions weak or bewilderingly shared out
between a variety of authorities, ecclesiastical, noble and civic.
War between private parties (*Fehde*), as distinct from public war
(*Krieg*), conducted by king or prince, was an accepted custom,
with its own rules of engagement.[13] In Scotland feud was
endemic too. Royal powers of justice were exercised fitfully by
kings and their justiciars, and in many parts were delegated to
the perpetual control of landowners. Feuds were sustained not
just in Gaelic society in the Highlands, but in the Lowlands,
despite the more vigorous assertions of royal authority there.
Lowland and Border regions were dotted with tower-houses,
which continued to be built there as domestic defences – the
mark of insecure living – throughout the sixteenth century.

In Wales feuding practices lingered in the fifteenth century, and
in England in the shires near the frontier with Scotland. However,
generally in England disputes over property rights, a prominent
feature of landowning society, led only to trespass, and more
occasionally to violence, when aggrieved parties failed to get the
cumbersome procedures and often venal proceedings of the
common law tweaked in their favour. They might then be

minded to pursue their claims with force and arms, aided by friends and tenants, and covertly protected by influential patrons and 'well-willers'. The English elites certainly paid plenty of lip service to the general importance of upholding the king's peace, but from mere gentleman to quasi-princely duke, when they believed that the honour and profit of their family were in jeopardy, they were prepared to resort to force. The strong personal exercise of kingship was needed to ensure that central and local institutions of government were used to contain the potential for factious partisanship and disorder, rather than being exploited to abet or condone it, recipes for rebellion and civil war.

The first decade of Henry VI's personal rule, from 1437 onwards, was ominous for his failure to contain quarrels among the nobility, and for increasing outbreaks of large-scale domestic violence.[14] Henry's rule was, indeed, a disaster. His personality remains mysterious. He was physically robust, surviving vicissitudes into middle age. He was of reasonable height, and, according to humble former subjects who recognised his miracle-working apparition after his (probably violent) death in the Tower of London in 1471, he cut a regal figure, resplendent in a gown of blue velvet. He was highly literate and was well aware of the duties of kingship. He was to inspire intense loyalties, and was long reverenced even by his leading opponents. Yet he failed singularly to govern with intelligence and the necessary modicum of fair dealing with his nobles, perhaps because of his eccentric absorption in religious studies, perhaps because of mental weaknesses. Some of the anecdotes recorded by his former chaplain and hagiographer, John Blacman, suggest that he may have bestowed or withdrawn favour according to a puritanical code. For instance, he humiliated a duke with a display of truly Plantagenet wrath for bringing in a troupe of topless ladies to dance for him.[15] Pope Pius II (d.1464), who had a closer knowledge of the English political scene than most popes, and might have been expected to appreciate Henry's piety, described him as 'a man more timorous than a woman, utterly devoid of wit or spirit, who left everything in his wife's hands'.[16]

The rule of such an unusual king was likely to induce anxiety in English society, where people rejoiced in living in a 'land of peace'. In the early fifteenth century, a chronicler at St Albans Abbey described in detail a spiked metal ball, maliciously inserted in Henry IV's bed. The usually well-informed monk did not even know a name for it. Yet it sounds like an obstacle commonly used to impede horses in battle, a caltrop.[17] In the decades before the Wars, fulfilment of customary expectations that English life would continue to be relatively peaceful were reflected in the general neglect of the fortifications of royal and private castles, and of city and town walls. Exceptions were to be found mainly in the far north, where some landowners maintained garrisons. The constables of the bishops of Durham's castle at Norham, on the frontier line of the River Tweed, contracted to keep a garrison there. In these frontier regions, even some rectors and vicars lived in ruggedly defensive tower-houses.[18] In the 1460s diehard Lancastrians were confident enough in the defence capabilities of principal royal and private castles in Northumberland to garrison them, and, in some cases, to hazard being besieged in them.[19]

Yet Sir John Norreys (d.1465), former keeper of Henry VI's wardrobe, built a great timbered house at Ockwells (Berkshire), which appears to have lacked castellated defences.[20] Caister Castle, near Great Yarmouth (Norfolk), was, exceptionally, a new castle, built by a veteran of the French wars, Sir John Fastolf (d.1459), who was well acquainted with the latest trends in fortification on the continent. Its brick walls and moat provided good defence against casual sea-raiders and local trespassers; a rakishly tall tower gave a field of observation over the flat countryside.[21] The dilapidated state of the defences of so many English castles – and many towns – helps to explain why siege warfare was marginal in the Wars of the Roses. Why, then, were so many of them defended with ardour, and some success, during the Great Civil War of the seventeenth century? There was then, for instance, the epic siege of the Marquis of Worcester in his castle of Raglan (Gwent), in 1646. This was probably the most formidable castle built in Wales or England during the fifteenth century, an expression of the new territorial power of Sir William ap Thomas (d.1445) and his son Edward IV's leading Welsh supporter, the grim warrior William Herbert, Earl of Pembroke (d.1469).

However, traditionally tall towers, gatehouses and curtain walls were in this period vulnerable to the use of rapidly advancing gunpowder technology, and did not provide sufficiently effective platforms for the deployment of heavy artillery. What was to facilitate the military reactivation of antique fortresses in the seventeenth century was the revolution in methods of fortification which had started with the evolution of the bastion in the fifteenth century. Low-level polygonal bastions which acted as revetments to earthen banks were more resistant to bombardment, and provided more effective platforms and casemates for artillery, with comprehensive angles of fire. Such fortifications could be thrown up speedily and at low cost, when wholly constructed as earthworks. In this form, they could be used to mantle older stone fortifications, and to provide them with outworks and circumvallation in emergencies.

There were two notable instances of private warfare erupting briefly during the Wars of the Roses. One was a siege and the other a small-scale battle. In 1469 John Mowbray, Duke of Norfolk, took advantage of the control which the Earl of Warwick had imposed by rebellion over Edward IV to mount a siege of Caister Castle (then owned by the Paston family). The Duke was supported by a distinguished company of gentry from the shire. Surrender was negotiated after artillery breached the walls; the Duke forcibly took possession of the residence he coveted.[22] The following year, other lords took advantage of Edward's campaign against the rebellion of his brother, George, Duke of Clarence, and the Earl of Warwick, by blatantly conducting private warfare. Thomas Talbot, Viscount Lisle and Lord Berkeley, who had a furious dispute over possession of the manor of Wotton (Gloucestershire), formally arranged to settle the issue by battle on Nibley Green, nearby. It actually took place. Lisle was killed, his force put to flight, and the victors ransacked and occupied the

manor house at Wotton.[23] Instances of violent opportunism in
private disputes, while major campaigns of the Wars were in train,
could doubtless be multiplied, but one does not have the impression that they escalated notably in the period. It may be that
private opponents tended to join in the public campaigns,
hoping to secure estates they coveted as a result of forfeiture
of their defeated rival and the favour of a victorious prince.
Perhaps, then, the Wars channelled and contained propensities
for domestic violence. Yet they multiplied the numbers of dispossessed and forfeited nobles, giving some of them motives
for joining in renewed dynastic uprisings, and contributing to
the perpetuation of large-scale and bloody civil strife which so
bewildered foreigners.

ENGLAND EMBATTLED: FEAR, CRUELTY AND MERCY

What views did the English and Welsh have on how warfare
should affect and involve society, and how did they actually
behave towards civilians? Lay as well as clerical members of the
elites were, it is to be presumed, generally aware of the 'canonical truce', by which the law of the Church gave protection to
clergy and other civilians, and to their possessions, if they were
not engaged in acts of war. Clerics, because of their avoca-
tion, were forbidden to shed blood.[24] Nevertheless, the Crown
ordered military arrays of the clergy in England in order to
repel anticipated invasions by the French and the Scots in the
fourteenth and fifteenth centuries, and it is likely that on some
occasions clerical contingents actually fought the Scots. John
Barbour, archdeacon of Aberdeen, in his epic verse-poem *The
Brus* (1375) recalled the black humour evoked by the casualties
inflicted by his fellow countrymen in their victory at Myton on
Swale (Yorkshire) in 1319:

Tharfor that bargane callit was
The chaptour of Mytoun, for thar
Slayn sa mony prestis war[25]

Thomas Walsingham, monk-chronicler of St Albans Abbey (Hertfordshire), applauded the abbot of Battle (Sussex) for boldly commanding the defence of the port of Winchelsea against French raiders in 1377, and saving it from the fate of the neighbouring ports of Rye and Hastings, which the French burnt, plundering, and killing local people.[26] A royal messenger was dispatched to Cornwall and Devon with letters of privy seal directed to knights there, the abbots of Tavistock, Buckfast and Torre, the prior of Plympton and a couple of esquires. All alike were instructed to array with their men and stay on the coasts to resist any attempt at landing from the enemy fleet at sea.[27] Recounting warfare on the northern Borders in 1379, Walsingham indignantly related atrocities supposedly committed by Scottish raiders on the populace of Northumberland. As a divine punishment, he said, they contracted the plague currently afflicting the English, their prayers for protection from it to their patron saints (which he painstakingly and gleefully reproduced) proving inefficacious.[28] Walsingham's remarks were in a well-established monastic genre about the horrors of invasion, and they and their like help to explain why clerical opinion endorsed the Crown's and laity's determination that clergymen ought to flout the canonical prohibition on taking up arms in face of threats of invasion. In the summer of 1386, people in south-east England fearfully anticipated the arrival of the huge fleet and army which Charles VI of France was assembling in Flanders. At Westminster Abbey, the monks in chapter debated whether it was lawful for them to fight in defence of the realm. They decided that it was, and that Abbot Litlington (a man of mature years who died soon afterwards) and two of the brethren (one of them reputed to be the tallest man in England) should proceed to the coast in full armour.[29]

However, fighting men in military retinues recruited for service abroad were laymen. The chaplain who wrote such a vivid account of Henry V's campaign in France in 1415 mentions only his religious duties. Before the battle of Agincourt, Henry arranged that the priests accompanying the army to say the divine offices should stay with the baggage at the hamlet where he had encamped.[30] Maybe in the eyes of soldiers (and in their own), their vital spiritual role would have been compromised if they had fought too. Priorities in 'outward' warfare were different from those for the defence of the realm. The special sacredness of 'this blessed plot' encouraged the overriding of canon law in its defence. By the later fourteenth century, England was considered by some of its denizens to be the special possession of the Blessed Virgin Mary, defended by her knight, St George.[31]

No mention has been found of clerical contingents in the Wars of the Roses, like that which Archbishop Melton led to disaster at Myton, or the force which his aged successor Henry Bowet had organised in 1417 to counter a Scottish invasion; the invaders withdrew before the priests caught up with them.[32] Distinguished clerics sometimes accompanied armies in the Wars, and sometimes raised retinues to engage in them, but these companies are likely to have been composed, in the same way as those of secular nobles, of lay officers of their households, tenants and 'well willers', including such well-set-up, tall yeomen, fellows skilled in archery, as they could recruit. In 1487 John Morton, archbishop of Canterbury and Richard Fox, bishop of Exeter both led companies to join Henry VII's army, as it moved north to oppose the rebels headed by the Earl of Lincoln. The bishops took their leave of Henry long before there was likely to be an engagement, handing over command of their companies to laymen.[33] In 1489, when Henry set out from Hertford to deal with a rebellion in Yorkshire, Fox was again in his company, and Morton was soon to join him.[34] Nevertheless, there seems to have been a reluctance among the clergy to break the canonical prohibition by participating in arms in civil war, and lay opinion approved of this.

Fears of invasion in southern England, such as had led to the abbots of Devon being called to arms in 1377, had been allayed by Henry V's conquests in France, but they revived in the 1440s and 50s as a result of the crumbling of English control in Normandy and its loss in 1450. In 1448 Rye and Winchelsea were burnt by the French, and in 1457 a force led by Pierre de Brézé, *grand sénéchal* of Normandy, a fine soldier, sacked Sandwich and killed many of the townsmen. When Henry VI's formidable queen, Margaret of Anjou, landed in Northumberland in 1462, intent on reviving her deposed husband's fortunes, it could hardly have been reassuring to English folk that she was accompanied by Brézé and about 2,000 French soldiers![35] The recurrent English fears of invasion in the later Middle Ages are likely to have been reinforced, not only by news of occasional bloody pinpricks on the margins of the realm, but by knowledge of the deplorably unchristian ways in which English soldiers habitually behaved abroad on the king's service, the like of which God might visit on the English for their sins. English clerics in their chronicles recorded burning and destruction abroad by their compatriots routinely, without condemnation, and sometimes with approval. A monk in Yorkshire (author of the 'Anonimalle Chronicle') described how Edward III's columns on his invasion of France from Calais in 1359 'destroyed the whole country' in Picardy and Artois, 'destroyed' the country of Laonnais, and acted similarly elsewhere.[36] The poet Geoffrey Chaucer, then a relatively humble *valettus* (yeoman) in princely service, and still probably in his teens, took part in this expedition, and experienced the shock of being captured.[37] This was his only known military service: years later, in his vivid description of the decorations illustrating violence in the Temple of Mars (*The Knight's Tale*), he may have recalled dreadful sights on the expedition:

> The stable burning with the black smoke...
> The open war, with wounds all bleeding...
> The carrion in the bush, with throats cut;
> A thousand slain...
> The tyrant, with prey seized by force;
> The town destroyed, there was nothing left.[38]

There were, indeed, 'legitimate' cruelties which could be wreaked on civilians. Edward had considered the burgesses of

Calais deserving of execution, after his siege of the town in 1347. From the English viewpoint, the sufferings which they inflicted in besieging distressed and agonized townsfolk were the consequences of refusal to accept the king of England's rights in France: all such could be lawfully treated as traitors rather than civilians.

However, some monastic chroniclers noted favourably the leniency to civilians shown by Edward III's son John of Gaunt, Duke of Lancaster, and by Gaunt's son Henry IV on their respective invasions of Scotland in 1384 and 1400.[39] Henry V's chaplain-biographer was impressed by an example of his enforcement of the 'canonical truce', giving protection to churches, which Henry had published in his Ordinances for War for the campaign of 1415:

> And there was brought to the king in that field [outside Corbie] a certain robber, an Englishman who, in God's despite and contrary to the royal decree, had stolen and carried off from a church (perhaps thinking it was made of gold) a pyx of copper-gilt in which the Host was reserved... And in the next hamlet where we spent the night, by command of the king, who was punishing in this creature the wrong done to the Creator... after sentence had been passed, he met his death by hanging.[40]

Yet, within a day or so, when the inhabitants of hamlets near Nesle refused to pay ransoms to Henry,'he ordered these places... to be set on fire and utterly destroyed'.[41] For the cool-headed commander, however respectful of the deity, however humane, the needs of policy have generally in all ages overidden compassionate considerations. Sir John Keegan has noted how, in the American Civil War, the Union commander Ulysses S. Grant ordered the destruction of livelihood in Confederate regions. During his siege of Vicksburg (1863), his subordinate, Blair, was ordered to scour the area for supply, being 'instructed to take all of it. The cattle were to be driven in for the use of our army, and the food and forage to be consumed by our troops or destroyed by fire'. Keegan makes a comparison with the Duke of Marlborough's despoiling of Bavaria in 1704.[42]

There were, indeed, some less harsh conventions practised in warfare between later medieval nobilities with shared courtly as well as religious values, embodied loosely in the codes of conduct, 'the laws of war', some aspects of which might be the subject of litigation in the court of the constable and marshal of England, the 'court of chivalry'. This concerned itself especially with accusations of treasonable conduct in warfare, and disputes about the right to bear a particular coat of arms and about the ownership of ransoms.[43] In the heat of battle, nobles who surrendered were supposed to be treated humanely and courteously. Even common soldiers in this respect adhered to chivalrous canons, like the small fry who apparently captured a great prize, Alfonso marques of Villena, during the Black Prince's victory at Nájera in Castile in 1367.[44] This was sensible as well as honourable behaviour – a dead noble could not be ransomed, and one whose wounds were not staunched, or who was imprisoned in harsh circumstances, was a doubtful long-term investment. It took Villena over two decades to pay off part of his ransom, for which his son the count of Denia was held as a hostage in England.[45] The youthful Denia, of the blood royal of Aragon, and a future possible claimant to its throne, apparently became so attached to his lowborn 'masters' that he connived in their concealment of him from the King's officers. Thomas Walsingham praised the boy's conduct, but his father complained furiously that 'they made of him whatever they wanted, as if he were mature wax (*com de cera macrada*)'. Could it be that the lad, like Shakespeare's Prince Hal, came to revel in the tavern company of old soldiers and their wenches, rather than studying at his desk and practising in the tilting yard? His often doleful and perhaps sometimes demeaning adventures among the slippery English and Gascons do not seem to have turned him into a degenerate. Though in later life he fell out with his irascible father, he was a proper Spanish noble, and conducted himself bravely at the siege of the English in Balaguer in 1413.

In contrast to the treatment of Denia in English captivity, the young Earl of Pembroke, captured by the Castilians in a sea battle off La Rochelle in 1372, may not have been treated gently. Released in 1375, he died on the way home, reportedly as a result of the poor conditions in which he had been imprisoned. He left behind some of the knights and esquires captured with him, gaoled uncomfortably. One of them, Sir John Harpeden, accepted Henry II of Castile's offer of a combat with visiting Africans. They were muscular twins, who had scandalised the King's court by their heretical beliefs. Harpeden stipulated that, first, he should be let out of prison and allowed to take the air for three weeks. He needed to recuperate after being held in constricted conditions. His convalescence worked wonders: he slew the twins.[46]

Other instances of poor treatment of prisoners, noble as well as common, can be adduced. Walter Ferrefort seems to have been on an expedition to Brittany in 1375, and to have acted as a hostage for the payment of a certain John More's ransom. He wrote to a knight whom he had served, probably the Northumberland landowner Sir John Strother, who was in the retinue of Edmund Mortimer, Earl of March. Ferrefort, imprisoned at St Brieuc, pleaded for the knight to deliver forty francs to his 'master', John de Comman. 'I… am bound hand and foot. And know that I am at very much trouble and expense for the said John More since he went away… So I beg you to remedy this, my dear lord, and to free me and remove me from this detention…'. Ferrefort refers to his companionship with and service to a certain William Doget. The latter had contracted in 1374 to serve Strother on the expedition. Presumably Ferrefort was with Doget, as his archer or menial servant. If this is so, it suggests that a humble member of a retinue could hope for the captain's help, if in dire straits as a prisoner – an incentive for a prisoner's master to turn the screws, whatever the polite conventions! A later instance alleging poor treatment of a prisoner, this time a distinguished one, was preserved in the Wyatt family's traditions. They related that in the 1490s Sir Henry Wyatt, captured by the Scots, was held with less than chivalrous consideration, enduring 'two yeres and more imprisonment in Irons and Stoks'.[47]

Precepts provide flimsy protection in warfare. The Church signally failed to modify the age-old custom that, when castles and towns were taken by storm, the lives of the inhabitants were at mercy. According to one of the most famous episodes described by the doyen of chivalrous chroniclers, Jean Froissart, the Black Prince ignored the pleas for mercy of men and women of all ranks and ages after his soldiers had taken Limoges by assault in 1370. However, when three French knights surrendered after fighting valiantly, and one of them asked his opponent, the prince's brother John of Gaunt, 'to act according to the law of arms', Gaunt replied, 'Sir John, we do not intend to do otherwise, and we accept you for our prisoners'.[48] The prince's cruel attitude encouraged the wholesale slaughter, but it is doubtful if a restraining ordinance would have been wholly effective. Such episodes of urban massacre have recurred in warfare. After British soldiers took huge losses in scaling the walls of Badajoz in Spain in 1812, they wreaked a terrible vengeance on the inhabitants, which their officers were unable to restrain; they even ignored their appalled commander, the future Duke of Wellington.[49] Moreover, in some battles in our period, commanders sometimes set out to spurn Christian and chivalrous convention. The order that no quarter was to be given was issued before the battle of Crécy by Philip VI of France, belatedly and retrospectively by Henry V during the battle of Agincourt, and by the Scottish lords fighting in Charles VII of France's interest before they attacked the army led by Henry's brother John, Duke of Bedford, the infant Henry VI's Regent in France, at Verneuil in Normandy in 1424.[50] When the French defeated the Bretons and English at St Aubin-du-Cormier in 1489, those wearing as a badge the cross of St George were not spared.[51]

At Limoges it had been three of the 'officers' who were spared for their gallantry: the French common soldiers presumably shared the dire fate of the townsfolk. Common soldiers were in any sort of fight more at risk of not receiving quarter, since they generally lacked the tempting assets which made it worthwhile to ransom nobles. However, as we have seen, their captains might feel an obligation to help redeem their men, especially if they were long-term servants, or had proved their military worth. In 1360 Edward III made gifts to help with the ransoms of a variety of non-noble servants captured on his campaign besides young Chaucer – such as the King's carter and seven of his fellows, two purveyors of poultry attached to the royal household, the King's palfreyman, his master of the smiths, some archers and two boys (*garciones*).[52] Common soldiers were especially at risk when they were captured at sea, since the large number of them assigned to man a sizeable sailing ship's defences could not be easily penned in the hold and victualled . When knights in Pembroke's service were captured in the battle off La Rochelle in 1372, 'their men were also in great danger, but their lords, when taken, desired they [the Castilians] would cease the slaughter, as they would pay a proper ransom for them'.[53]

Chaucer's Shipman, in *The Canterbury Tales*, made his prisoners walk the plank: 'If that he fought, and had the higher hand, / By water he sent them home to every land'. However, Chaucer implied that he was a pirate, giving as his provenance the port of Dartmouth, notorious for that lawless kind.[54]

We have been focussing on English perceptions about war with foreigners and the conventions under which they customarily waged it. What about the conduct of English domestic broils? In these, they shrank from behaving as they did abroad. When girding on their harnesses against one another, they acted in a topsy-turvy way. Civilians and common soldiers might hope for mercy, but nobles were fortunate to be given quarter, and, if it was granted, fortunate not to be led off either for summary execution or to await more of a holiday death before assembled soldiers or an urban crowd. Different rules applied. A Yorkist partisan, recording the deaths of the Duke of York and the lords supporting him during and after the battle of Wakefield (1460) complained about this. They died because a truce of the kind the English made with their foreign foes had been breached by their opponents: they 'were traitorously and against law of arms by taking of Treaties granted, murdered and slain'.[55] Yet there are indications that commanders were often anxious for some canonical rules and secular conventions to be observed. In order to highlight further the social characteristics of English domestic warfare, let us consider some examples of how warfare was conducted and affected society in some other western European countries.

SOME CONVENTIONS OF WARFARE ABROAD

The often cruelly unchristian behaviour of English and Welsh soldiers abroad in the later Middle Ages, both on their commanders' orders and at their own will, was characteristic of many indigenous armies in Western Europe. The torture and killing of prisoners, maltreatment and ransoming of civilians, theft of their stock and goods, destruction of dwellings and looting of churches were often routine occurences during rebellions and civil wars as well as in conflicts between sovereign powers. Harshness might be applied as deliberate policy, for instance, as an expression of what many regarded as the right of princes to display anger. It was reported that after John the Fearless, Duke of Burgundy, had defeated the army of the city of Liège at Othée in 1408, when he was asked if they ought to cease from killing the Liègeois, he replied that they should all die together, and that he had no wish for them to be taken and ransomed.[56] The Duke, characteristically of medieval princes, had been involved in close combat in the battle, circumstances which may have typically aroused in him, and them generally, the urge which can flare up among soldiers to massacre the surrendered as well as the haplessly fleeing. Such intents can surface in the best disciplined modern armies, when involved in heavy infantry fighting, but their usually more detatched and often distant commanders are better equipped and motivated to curtail them.

Duke John's grandson Charles the Bold (d.1477) eventually metamorphosed from a mild campaigner into a harsh one, according to the memorialist Commynes, his former servant. When Charles invaded France in 1472, Commynes says, he 'marched towards Nesle in Vermandois and began to wage a more vicious and evil type of war than he had ever used before – he set fire to everything he passed' (rather like that great English hero Henry V had ordered to be done thereabouts within living memory). The Duke's soldiers killed everyone who had borne arms in defence of Nesle – but Commynes admits that this happened before he arrived there.[57] In a letter to his ally, the Duke of Brittany, Duke Charles (indeed, a more obsessive warrior than most fifteenth-century princes) actually boasted about his severity in Normandy (perhaps to cover up his limited military achievement): 'I have burned and ravaged the whole Pays de Caux so that it will not cause any trouble either to you or us for a long time'.[58] In his wars in the Holy Roman Empire in the 1470s, occasions when Charles ordered the massacre of captured garrisons were well known. His pitilessness was matched by his German and Swiss opponents. The Swiss customarily took hardly any prisoners in battle. However, their sack of Estevayer-le-lac (on Lac de Neuchâtel) in 1475 was so savage that the civic government of Bern reprimanded its captains for permitting cruelties 'which might move God and the saints against us in vengeance'.[59]

Prior attempts to define or delimit acceptable ravaging often fell on deaf ears. When Charles ordered Liège to be razed after capturing it in 1468, his stipulation that the churches should be inviolate was widely disobeyed. There, as at other places said to have been put to the torch in medieval warfare, destruction of property is likely to have been less complete than chronicle sources suggest – but the pilfering of goods was probably accomplished with deft and impoverishing expertise. The common soldier was more interested in breaking open chests in churches than in the unrewarding, back-breaking toil of hooking down gables and demolishing walls. For all groups in society, it was the soldier's fundamental urge to strip foodstuffs, stock and goods, rather than the desire of lords to have dwellings branded with symbolic scorch-marks and rooflessness, which held the potential for family and communal disasters. Perhaps it was a relief to layfolk when their churches held the promise of superior loot. Though the trampling of local cult-objects was grievous to communities, it was the impious soldiers who risked divine punishment for their temerity. In 1346, when David II was about to invade England, St Cuthbert appeared to him in a dream, mildly requesting him not to invade or damage his lands. David ignored this, and, as a result, was defeated and captured.[60]

In 1465, before Charles the Bold had inherited the duchy of Burgundy from his father Philip the Good, he and other French princes had rebelled against Louis XI; he advanced towards Paris. The youthful Commynes was serving in his household contingent, and in later life vividly recalled the terrors and muddles of being on his first campaign – his account of the engagement at Montlhéry gives a much better impression of the confusion of the battlefield than that of any other medieval soldier. He presents the Burgundian treatment of opponents and civilians on this campaign as different from that in Charles's later campaigns. He alleges that Charles kept his soldiers under strict restraint in 1465, and was merciful in his dealings with Nesle and other places he was to unleash them on in 1472. 'All along the route the count [i.e. Charles] refrained from acts of war and his men never took anything without paying for it. The towns of the Somme as well as others allowed his men to enter them in small numbers and gave them what they wanted for their money.' At Lagny-sur-Marne he had all documents dealing with *aides* and taxes burnt. He forbade them to be levied, and had salt distributed from the royal warehouse without payment of the gabelle.[61] Particular circumstances favoured the success of this mild princely policy – the soldiers were paid, the campaign was short, and Charles was domineering, a 'hands-on' commander, who was in his element in the campaign, cajoling, cursing and cuffing the soldiers.

The contrasts between the behaviour of Burgundian soldiers in 1465 and in the 1470s remind us that we must not overemphasise the degree of uniformity in the normal conduct and impact of warfare in later medieval society. The behaviour of soldiers was conditioned by the aims of princes and nobles, the character of military organisation and by cultural factors. A campaigning *tour d'horizon* will illustrate this. Scotland provides a good starting-point, since it was the polity neighbouring England most akin to it (as far as the Lowlands were concerned) in language, culture and institutional structure. The former English judge, Sir John Fortescue, in his treatise *The Governance of England*, drafted in the 1460s, asserted the similarity of Scotland to England in having a constitution in which the community of the realm had a significant input in the exercise of sovereignty.[62] In the occasional conflicts between Scottish kings and nobles, however, harsh ravages were sometimes perpetrated without apparently provoking a general backlash in opinion. In 1444 the lords controlling government during James II's minority attacked the estates of Bishop Kennedy of St Andrews – 'ane richt gret herschipe [ravaging] maid in Fyff [Fife]'. This embraced 'nocht only the bischopis lands bot also the haill landis adjacent thairto'.[63] In 1452, after James and his companions murdered William, Earl of Douglas at supper in Stirling Castle, the earl's kinsmen sacked and burned the burgh. The King, on his retaliatory punitive campaign in the Borders, failed to discriminate between the lands of enemies and friends.[64] Contrastingly, there had been stronger condemnation of this sort of behaviour when in 1390 Alexander Stewart, Earl of Buchan, ('the Wolf of Badenoch') had sacked Elgin. His men had burnt the cathedral, parish kirk, hospital and the houses of canons and chaplains.[65]

General opinion may have been habitually more tolerant of acts of violence against civilians in domestic warfare in Scotland than in England. As we have seen, endemic feud produced a higher level of violence in Scotland. The Borders and parts of Lothian had traditionally endured with stoicism harsh English incursions. Scottish kings and nobles needed to be coercive in order to enforce law in a society in which the judicial system was less institutionalised and more fragmented than in England. Scottish civil wars in the fifteenth century were tolerable because, like the Wars of the Roses, they were brief, but, unlike them, not recurrent. However, in the many burghs within easy reach of the Highlands, the incursions of clansmen were especially feared and resented. A monastic chronicler blamed the sack of Elgin on 'wyld wykked Heland-men'.[66]

The growing perception among Lowlanders in the fourteenth century of the significance of linguistic, social and cultural distinctions between themselves and the Highlanders encouraged mutual antipathies which militated against constraint in internecine warfare. English folk did not recognise regional domestic contrasts with such intensity. The nearest parallel to the Scottish situation was tension between English and Welsh. English communities in shires bordering the Marcher lordships of Wales feared customary raiding, and remembered the devastating incursions carried out by Owain Glyn Dŵr's forces early in the fifteenth century, during his revolts against Henry IV, and his attempt to set up an indepedendent Welsh principality. Such fears surfaced more widely when William Herbert, Earl of Pembroke, led a predominantly Welsh army in 1469 into the English Midlands, in support of Edward IV against the rebellion of Clarence and Warwick. Its defeat was greeted with relief and rejoicing.[67] It is not clear whether similar apprehensions were felt when Henry Tudor emerged from Wales with a goodly number of indigeneous recruits, to confront Richard III in the Midlands in 1485, and, if so, whether they turned out to be justified. Indeed, the campaign in England was very brief. Henry was doubtless anxious to discharge his soldiers, and English writers were disinclined to highlight any smudges on his triumph.

Within Wales, traditions of waging war in especially destructive ways persisted. Though language, law and the itineracy of bards and minstrels reinforced a high degree of cultural unity, Welsh society was strongly localised, focussed on the intricate relations within and between extended kin-groups. Wales lacked the unitary institutions of government and the concept of a common identity as a 'community of the realm', reified in parliaments, which in England, and, to a lesser extent in Lowland Scotland, produced common opinions and sympathies which tended to ameliorate the conduct of domestic conflict. In Wales, traditions of feud and stock raiding inclined men to violence. The fragmentation of authority, especially among the many Marcher lordships, encouraged thieves in the hope of evading punishment. These warlike habits, together with the ruggedness and unproductiveness of much of the terrain, and the difficulties of communication by land, had determined the savage nature of warfare during Edward I's conquest of Gwynedd in 1281–2. Welsh guerilla tactics were countered by English destruction of livelihood. Owain Glyn Dŵr engaged with Henry IV and his commanders in the same sort of 'total' war (which Henry had refrained from using against the Scots in 1400). Both sides sacked religious houses considered to be hostile. The war inflicted long-lasting damage on the Welsh economy. This was the bleak environment in which the King's son and heir, the future Henry V, gained his military training: the background helps to account for the steely treatment he sometimes meted out to civilians when on campaign in France.[68]

Memories of the terribly destructive campaigns in Wales in the first decade of the fifteenth century (in which Welshmen fought on both sides) must have remained vivid there in the period of the Wars of the Roses. The horrors did not entirely mute the new conflicts. Some of the War's eruptions had the same dire character, distinctive in their deleterious effects from the more 'civil' contemporary campaigning between Englishmen. After Edward IV had crushingly defeated the Lancastrians in England in 1461, the fugitive Henry VI's half-brother Jasper Tudor, former Earl of Pembroke, for several years organised and encouraged resistance to the Yorkist regime in Wales, headed by William Herbert. Lancastrians held out in some of the of the strong and inaccessible Welsh castles; their most prolonged resistance was centred on Edward I's great castle of Harlech in Gwynedd. The 'tenants and commons of North Wales' (the northern part of

the Principality), in a rare display of apparent communal unity,
petitioned king and parliament for remedy against the depredations of the Lancastrian garrison at Harlech, alleging that many
of them had 'been daily taken prisoners and put to ransom as it
were a land of war; and many and divers of them daily robbed
and spoiled of their goods and cattle'.[69] In 1468 Herbert, veteran of the savage wars in France, like some of his opponents,
led a considerable army which enforced the surrender of the
castle, but on his campaign carried out devastations – presumably on the grounds that there had been widespread collusion
with the men of Harlech. The conduct of his army gained him
his reputation for pitilessness in England. The bard Guto'r Glyn,
in a poem composed within weeks of their surrender, in praise
of his military successes in Wales, wrote in awe of his ferocious
treatment of Gwynedd, but entreated him to follow a merciful
policy there from now on:

> All your host, they're brave,
> Are dragons through forests.
> Where livestock wouldn't go, your steeds climbed
> The core of Yr Wyddfa [Mount Snowdon].
> Your traces [of burning] are over the rocks,
> you made Eryi [Snowdonia] ploughed land.
> Your men broke in three divisions
> through moors and the wild land.
> If you kindled a fire for a time
> by killing and fighting all,
> it was a blow for disobedience,
> tearing apart Gwynedd and thrashing it.
> If the land, noble Herbert, was
> without faith, as Paul was,
> whoever may be in flight, a foe of faith,
> if he stop, he'll be baptized.
> And you, do not now be
> cruel with men by fire.
> Do not kill hawks of Gwynedd who made a feast for us

as Peter the bees.
Do not impose a tax on the region there
that cannot be collected.
Do not reduce Gwynedd to fallow,
do not surrender Môn [Anglesey] to anger.
Let not the weak complain
of betrayal or theft from now on.[70]

Welsh warfare was of a cruel kind more often found on the continent than in England.

Let us return to the continent, and to that shrewd, if heavily biased, observer of war and society, Philippe de Commynes. Writing about Charles the Bold's later campaigns, he remarked that in most respects 'our wars... are more cruel than the wars in Italy and Spain'. However, as regards Germany, he declared that, generally, 'there are so many strongholds and so many people inclined to do wrong, to pillage and rob and to use force and violence against each other on the slightest pretext, that it is almost incredible'.[71] An earlier memorialist who also knew parts of Germany well, Pope Pius II, commented on the pitilessness of warfare in conflict over tenure of the archbishopric of Mainz – a war waged in 1461, the year of Towton, the biggest battle of the Wars of the Roses. The English campaign, as far as we know, did not inflict such hardship and destruction on civilians.[72] Warfare was endemic in Pius's native Italy, involving popes, kings, communes and *signori*. He tends to describe campaigns there, including ones which he instigated, in milder terms than the war over Mainz, admitting to the destruction only of property. When, also in 1461, a papal force stormed the town of Montorio al Vomano (Marche), held by a *signore*, a papal vassal who was defying him, he says that it was plundered, and that his soldiers set fire to townsmen's houses and the town walls. He does not say that their persons or those of the defending force were maltreated, simply that the garrison was made captive.[73]

A means of bringing well-defended communes to heel was to destroy the resources of the *contado*, the surrounding area which they controlled and on which they depended for military manpower, foodstuffs and other supplies. In 1463 Pius's army, invading the region around Sora, 'devastated the country far and wide, ruining the ripening grain everywhere. The people of Isola [Isola del Liri, near Sora], after suffering the destruction of their fields were the first to surrender'.[74] Maybe Pius minimised the suffering wrought by his armies, but if he was tailoring his narrative in this way, at least it reflects on Italian susceptibilities in the matter. Indeed, warfare in Italy in this period did tend to be less destructive than in some other parts of Europe. Venice, one of the leading states which contracted to employ companies of *condottieri*, increasingly did so on a long-term basis, regulating and stabilising their behaviour.[75]

Other communes and *signori* employing mercenaries wanted to curb their predatory habits, especially when they were quartered in the contractor's territories. In the sixteenth century, the Florentine historian Francesco Guicciardini looked back on past warfare in Italy through spectacles which were not just rose-tinted: 'the soldiery… lived for the most part on their pay, and their licentiousness was restrained within tolerable grounds'.[76] For in the previous century, the objectives of war there had generally been to secure the submission and subordination of other communes, gaining control of their urban manufacture and trade, their rural resources, their strategic strength and communication networks. Some of these objectives might be prejudiced if the *condottieri* were allowed to plunder wealth, destroy the means of livelihood, and alienate elites and populace, whose often well-developed sense of urban patriotism needed to be cultivated by the new ruler rather than snuffed out. There are some parallels between the objectives and methods of warfare in Italy and England in the period. A smooth takeover was in both cases much to be desired.

There are some striking parallels between the polities of England and Castile in the fifteenth century, and both similarities and contrasts between the ways in which civil wars were conducted. In both realms, vigorous central administrative and consultative mechanisms had been developed to facilitate royal control of justice and taxation. However, in Castile, domination of lordships and towns by hereditary and ecclesiastical lords was much more widespread and thorough-going. As in England, these lords jostled for royal grants of offices and lordships, partly as a means of satisfying and augmenting their 'affinities' of clients, built up among lesser nobility and urban oligarchies. A coincidental similarity for long periods in the century was that they were ruled by kings who were incapable of managing pressures from magnates skilfully. The Castilian rulers looked to a more able favourite to do so, whose own ambitions inevitably created tensions with other nobles. John II (d. 1454), Henry VI's kinsman, and John's son and successor Henry IV (d. 1474) were not unlike the English king in such respects. Yet, however feebly, the two Spaniards upheld a traditional exaltation of monarchical power. Richard II of England would have approved John II's statement in 1438 that 'the king has all the laws under him, having them not from men but from God whose place he holds in all temporal matters; he is not bound to judge by the opinions of men but... according to his conscience... I cannot and ought not to be judged in this by any person'.[77]

King John was responding in this statement to a manifesto from discontented nobles urging him 'to rule your realms in your own person... without the interference of any other person'. They aimed to undermine the ascendancy at court of Alvaro de Luna, as had John's kinsman Alfonso V of Aragon, when years before, in support of the opposition of his brothers (great landowners in Castile) to Luna, he had denounced him for 'usurping and appropriating to himself the administration and government both of the king's person and of his kingdoms'. That had similarities with the Lord Appellants' denunciation of Richard's leading favourites in 1387. Both English and Castilian rebels posed as the true upholders of royal power. They certainly did not wish to dismember it. Characteristically, they proclaimed that they wanted it to function more effectively and justly, with the unspoken caveat (a challenge to their ostensible concern for the commonwealth) that it should do so in their particular interest.

In Castile, as in England in the later Middle Ages, nobles strongly asserted traditions of protest against 'bad' government, likewise issuing public statements of grievances, with proposed remedies, in order to excuse resort to force, and to win allies. There was a strand of Castilian political discourse which promoted arguments that kings were accountable to their subjects as well as to God. The royal councillor and historian Mosén Diego de Valera wrote pointedly to John II and Henry IV that some Old Testament kings had been deposed, and that some Gothic ones had been killed by their subjects because of misgovernment. The Castilian nobleman Gutierre Diaz de Gamez, in his chivalrous life of his master Pero Niño, count of Buelna, completed in the 1430s, envisaged a scene in which Richard II of England had in 1399 been ceremonially deposed by the deprivation of his symbols of office. In 1465, at Avila, rebel nobles deposed Henry IV by treating an effigy of him in this way, finally knocking it off its chair.[78]

The prelude to this scene was that in 1464, as in England in 1460, a dynastic issue had been raised by an alliance of nobles. Juan Pacheco, marques of Villena, was the would-be kingmaker. Henry VI had been forced to recognise the Duke of York as his heir, disinheriting his own son. Henry IV was forced to recognise his young brother Alfonso as heir to the throne, disowning his own daughter, Juana, whose real father, it was rumoured, was the favourite, Beltran de la Cueva. The subsequent deposition of both kings (one in effigy) resulted from their repudiations of these settlements. In both realms the consequence was several years of civil war. When Alfonso died in 1468, the rebels intended to switch their allegiance to Henry's sister Isabella. She preferred to reach an understanding with her brother, but, when relations broke down between them, in 1470, he reignited dynastic conflict by recognising Juana as his true heir. Foreign intervention was to ensue. A year after Henry's death in 1474, the King of Portugal, Afonso V, betrothed to Juana, invaded Castile in her interest, but was decisively beaten in 1476 by Isabella's husband, Ferdinand of Aragon, at Toro. That effectively ended the dynastic strife. The self-styled 'Queen Juana' stayed in a convent in Lisbon till her death in 1530 – not the sort of peaceful fate unsuccessful candidates to the English throne might have anticipated.

Though it is possible to make parallels between the motives and political conventions animating noble rebels in Castile and England, the dynastic wars in the two realms, despite some superficial similarities, had marked differences. The Castilian ones lasted for just over a decade; they were not punctuated by many ferocious battles, or by regular cold-blooded killings of princes and nobles. Henry IV, like his father, died peacefully in his bed – three English kings of the period did not. Castilian kings and rebellious nobles seem to have been more inclined to bargain and compromise. In the small and internally demilitarised landscape of England, members of a highly militarised nobility could speedily mount a formidable challenge in the field to a king. If they were defeated, the king had the institutional means to sweep away their hereditary power-bases practically within weeks. Kings and nobles consequently came to behave in the later fifteenth century with a ruthlessness and disloyalty which makes the mindset of their Castilian contemporaries appear moderate and honourable. In England, domestic conflict was a more desperate business. For English folk in general, it took the form of short, uncomfortable showers. In Castile, the rain of disorder was characteristically more prolonged and desultory. There, the civil wars and invasions of the later fourteenth century had enhanced the fortification of castles and towns, and the country's long frontiers with powerful principalities necessitated their maintenance. Such strongpoints could be centres of continuing rebellion, in lordships which the Crown was sometimes ill-placed to prise from their rulers. The price paid by the population, on a much more serious scale than in England, was the continuance over years of disorders instigated by factions of lesser nobility and urban oligarchs.

The general picture of social effects of warfare in later medieval Western Europe is one of sometimes contrasting and sometimes comparable light and dark hues. Policy played a part; it might be expedient for princes and nobles either to attempt to enforce Christian and chivalrous precepts, or to condone their flouting. In some regions the growing power of the state and its elaboration of military organisation enabled rulers to be more effective in controlling the behaviour of soldiers. They might egg them on to demonstrate harshness, in order to undermine opponents' morale and end a campaign quickly, before the usually limited resources and credit from which to cover costs ran out. After Charles the Bold's death in battle with the Swiss at Nancy in 1477, Louis XI of France equalled his ruthlessness in his hasty attempts to take over the Burgundian inheritance. When his soldiers invaded Artois, southern Flanders, Hainault and the Cambrésis, they were accompanied by thousands of labourers drafted to harvest the grain and transport it to France. In these highly urbanised regions, the resistance of cities and towns would be weakened if they could not garner the already precariously sufficient regional agrarian resources. As a result of Louis' strategy, the peasants in these regions were harshly pillaged by the invading French.[79] This strategy, and, as we have seen, Duke Charles's in the 1470s, contrasted starkly with that of the princely coalition in rebellion against Louis in 1465. The princes, proclaiming themselves as the 'League of the Public Weal', had set out to win 'the hearts and minds' in their campaign against royal 'tyranny'. The conduct of their troops towards the opposing soldiery and towards civilians, as described by Commynes, was much like that of armies in domestic campaigns in later medieval England.

PILLAGE IN ENGLAND

In England the conventional abstention from massacring, injuring and pillaging was rarely broken. An exception was the ravaging of parts of the county palatine of Chester by Henry of Bolingbroke's army during his rebellion in 1399. Cheshiremen seem to have been sometimes regarded in England as predatory and disruptive; in recent years resentment against them had been stoked up by the favours which Richard II showered on them, including their recruitment to his novel guard of archers. As Henry's army approached the Welsh Marches, there were expectations among the rank and file of opportunities to plunder. Henry became inclined to mercy. The chronicler Adam Usk says that it was through his mediation that peace was made between Henry and the lordship of Usk, Adam's birthplace. Henry had wanted to ravage the lordship, because its ruling lady, the King's niece Eleanor Holand, had been planning to resist him. At Shrewsbury, he says, Henry issued 'a proclamation that the army would head for Chester, but that since they [the men of Chester] had sent messengers to offer their submission to him he would spare the people of that region and their land; whereupon a number of people who had been hoping to plunder the area for their own profit now returned to their own homes'.[80] However, during the advance through Cheshire, mutual acts of hostility between soldiers and civilians led the former to disregard the ordinance and commit depredations. Adam witnessed the effects: 'I went to Coddington church hoping to celebrate Mass but I found nothing there except doors and chests broken open, and everything carried off'.[81]

There is remarkably little solid evidence for such behaviour in England in the Wars of the Roses. Propagandist allegations were bandied about, playing on fears that opponents intended to spoil and rob. On some occasions common soldiers were massacred, dwellings pillaged, corn and chattels stolen. Much of these sorts of mayhem were doubtless unrecorded. However, the usual policy of commanders was to try to keep soldiers on a strict leash. This was one reason why they favoured short campaigns, when there was less likelihood that wages and commodities would run out, and soldiers alienate opinion by perforce battening on the populace.

There was one campaign in the Wars in which a chorus of, indeed, biased writers alleged that an army ravaged through whole regions – from Yorkshire down the strategic spine of England to the outskirts of London. In February 1461, a Lancastrian army, accompanied by the queen, Margaret of Anjou, set off southwards with the objectives of seizing the capital and rescuing the King from the hands of the Yorkists. The depredations of this army became a mantra of pro-Yorkist chroniclers – but no firm documentary evidence has been found for them. Elements of this army certainly seem to have caused alarm in Yorkshire before it set off. The men of Beverley procured a copy of a proclamation from Lord Neville's camp ordering that they were not to be plundered. The testimony of Abbot Whethamstede of St Albans about outrages after the Lancastrian victory, not far from his abbey cannot be dismissed lightly.[82] It is inherently likely that, whatever the strictures of their captains, the soldiers acted with unusual harshness. They were campaigning at an unseasonable time of year, when grain stocks were low. The northerners among them are likely to have nourished resentments against southerners which reciprocated with popular southern prejudices against them. Rumours spread in the south of depredations on their advance; after their victory, the common people in London were more vociferously opposed to the admission of their soldiers into the city than even its harassed governors were. The following year, Yorkshiremen similarly felt at the mercy of Edward's army after his victory at Towton. The burgesses of Beverley gave presents to Yorkist lords, and 20 shillings to Henry Awger, captain, 'that no one should plunder'.[83]

It was the Lancastrian army's evil reputation which had facilitated and precipitated the crucial change of dynasty from Lancaster to York. The recently deceased Duke of York's son and heir, the Earl of March, fresh from his victory at Mortimer's Cross, was speedily admitted to the city. His supporters rightly judged that opinion in the south would in the circumstances accept this little-known, strapping youth of nineteen as king. For kings under threat and their would-be supplanters over the next few decades, the lesson of this sequence of events must have been writ large – conforming to civilians' hopeful expectations of soldierly conduct was more persuasive about dynastic right than a cartful of cunningly drawn genealogical rolls of the kings of England.

REBELLIOUS ENGLISH HABITS

Consideration of rebellion in general in later medieval England may help in understanding the conventions which appear to have governed the conduct of the Wars of the Roses, and the sometimes surprisingly 'laid back' reactions to their occurrence among contemporaries – a mindframe which, if anticipated by those planning to take up arms, may have given them encouragement. In the second half of the fifteenth century – if we can judge from the long memories there were to be of the Wars[84] – there must have been vivid ones about the risings of Richard II's and Henry IV's reigns. Some of these memories may not have been encouraging for those minded to raise or participate in new stirs. Weighty precedents suggested that those who took up arms and raised unauthorised banners in the realm, threatening mayhem and disturbance, risked the dire fate of traitors. There were awesome examples of the fall of the powerful and distinguished, and the tainting of their blood. In 1403 Sir Henry Percy ('Hotspur'), a hero of the nation for his fights with the Scots and French, died rebelling against Henry at the battle of Shrewsbury. His uncle Thomas, Earl of Worcester, royal councillor and distinguished veteran of the French wars, was captured there and swiftly executed. Hotspur's body was scarcely cold in the grave before it was dug up and exhibited, before being carved up, as was his uncle's, for display in different parts of the realm. In 1408 Hotspur's father, the Earl of Northumberland, a towering figure in government and the defence of England since the 1370s, invaded the north from exile: his death in battle against the arrayed men of Yorkshire completed the downfall of the House of Percy. Rebel heads and body parts became familiar features of urban street furniture in the early years of Lancastrian rule.[85]

Rebels, not surprisingly, vociferously denied that they were engaged in treasonable activities. The leaders of the Pilgrimage of Grace in Yorkshire in 1536 and of Kett's Rebellion in Norfolk in 1549 followed time-honoured traditions when they insisted that their unauthorised armed assemblies were loyal demonstrations aiming to achieve the reform of government. The argument was grudgingly accepted by rulers only when it was expedient for them to do so, in order to spin out negotiations and secure the dispersal of rebels. In 1405 Richard Scrope, archbishop of York, put himself at the head of a protest movement in Yorkshire, petitioning for the reform of government, without the intention of overthrowing Henry's rule motivating the Earl of Northumberland's coincidental plotting. Scrope hesitated about initiating conflict, and was persuaded by the King's brother-in-law Ralph Neville, Earl of Westmorland, to surrender. That did not save him or his youthful supporter Thomas Mowbray, Earl Marshal, from summary execution. Government propaganda attempted to blacken their cause, by alleging that it was part of the undoubtedly treasonable Percy conspiracy.[86]

Under Henry IV, the miscalculations, hesitations and different agenda of rebels, and the vigilance of the King and his supporters nipped major risings in the bud. By championing the claim to the throne of the youthful Edmund Mortimer, Earl of March, the Percys anticipated the principal dynastic issue of the Wars of the Roses, raised by Edmund's nephew and heir Richard, Duke of York in his claim to the throne in 1460. The Percy family, however, seem to have taken on board the painful lessons of the effects of treason – ultimately with dire consequence for some of them. Hotspur's son Henry, recalled from exile in Scotland by Henry V and restored to the earldom of Northumberland in 1416, died fighting for Henry VI at St Albans, and his son the third earl died in the same cause at Towton in 1461. Edward IV copied Henry V by restoring the Percy heir to the earldom in 1470. The family misfortunes of this Henry Percy had taught him to be a resolute trimmer. During the dynastic revolutions of 1470–1 he prudently stayed at home, and at the battle of

Bosworth, whatever personal 'kingmaking' ambitions may have been stirring in him, he kept his soldiers, a substantial contingent in the royal army, picknicking, watching to see the outcome. That earned him a short spell of imprisonment from the victor.[87]

The extent to which nobles were deterred from rebellion by the hazards exemplified in Henry IV's reign is unclear, especially as, by contrast, the risings against Richard in 1387 and 1399 had succeeded brilliantly in attaining their objectives, at least in the short term. In the case of common folk, the lessons are even more opaque. Whereas under Henry a rebellious archbishop and earl were executed honourably with axes, some common rebels suffered the terrible and degrading fate of hanging, drawing and quartering. The huge loss of life in the battle of Shrewsbury came as a shock: nothing like it had been experienced in inter-necine conflict since Henry III's reign. Yet the campaigns against Lancastrian rule had been short, localised, to some extent con-ducted on the margins of the realm. The disruption they had caused had been unremarkable. Memories of their unwelcome lessons may have been to some extent countered by traditions about previous defiances and rebellions. Widescale support for risings had been a recurrent if occasional feature of English politics. The Anglo-Norman kings had developed a system of government which was precociously centralised and often regarded as oppressive. Its functioning had provoked the develop-ment of remarkably sophisticated movements for constitutional reform under King John and Henry III. They provided respected precedents for armed protests against 'tyrannical' kingship, which might achieve a wide spectrum of social support.

In some circumstances, indeed, plotters realised that wide-spread and popular support for their cause was lacking, and perforce resorted to an 'un-English' *coup de main*. Richard II's friends, who schemed to restore him soon after his deposition, plotted to seize Henry IV. They intended to gain entry into Windsor Castle as the court celebrated Twelfth Night there, disguised as a group of entertainers ('mummers'). Their plot was betrayed, and furious common folk seized and assassinated fleeing ringleaders in Gloucestershire and Essex. A few years later, as we have seen, persons unknown attempted to make Henry inadvertently impale himself in his nightshirt on a nasty spiky metal object. In 1413 Lollard heretics (mostly artisans and peasants) plotted to seize their persecutor Henry V and his brothers. Their plan perhaps owed something to the 'Epiphany Rising' of 1400. Armed companies converged on London. It was planned that a group disguised as mummers would gain entrance to Eltham palace as the court partied there soon after the Christmas season of 1413–14. As in 1400, the rising was easily crushed by the King, because it had been leaked. Two years later, Richard, Earl of Cambridge, (Richard, Duke of York's father) and a few other nobles, who favoured March's claim to the throne, plotted to assassinate Henry and his brothers at Southampton, where they were engrossed in organising the invasion of France. Once again, the plotters were betrayed.[88]

It is notable that in the Wars of the Roses, there was an absence of attempts to assassinate kings. Richard, Duke of York, surely had opportunities to dispose of Henry VI when he was in his power; Edward IV kept Henry imprisoned in the Tower of London for several years, accessible to the public, and only apparently had him killed in 1471 after his brief reoccupation of the throne.[89] York and his son may have been anxious to eschew the shameful precedent of Richard II's convenient demise under Henry IV, and, even more, the example of York's father the Earl of Cambridge, best remembered for his treason in trying to kill Henry V, whose reputation as a great warrior-king remained undimmed in the later fifteenth century. It is surprising that no attempts were made on Edward IV, Richard III and Henry VII, all of whom aroused deep personal hatreds. Towards the end of the century, indeed, royal apartments may have been less accessible and better guarded by henchmen. Henry Beaufort, Duke of Somerset, still a covert Lancastrian, had tried to organise a widespread rebellion against Edward IV in 1463. Since the King had made a bosom companion of Somerset and even invited him into his bed, one might have thought that the inwardly seething Duke had intimate opportunities to effect the demise of the genial usurper. However, such behaviour, he may have been convinced, would forever besmirch his family honour, shock the exiled Henry VI and cast shame on his cause. There had been the notorious example of how James I, King of Scotland, had been horribly slain by noble plotters who had in 1437 been treacherously admitted to his apartments in Perth. They had done the deed in the presence of the queen, Duke Henry of Somerset's aunt Joan Beaufort, whom they manhandled. Afterwards the eminent plotters were regarded with horror. They were soon hunted down, and were executed in exemplary fashion. An Englishman, John Shirley, wrote an account of these events, *The Dethe of the Kynge of Scotis*, before 1456, purportedly translated from a Latin original. It has been suggested that Shirley's version was written for the young Henry VI's edification.[90] In 1483, Henry Stafford, Duke of Buckingham, according to his son Duke Edward, had wanted to kneel before Richard III and stab him. If this was not a somewhat maladroit attempt by the son to distance his father's memory from his close association with Richard's usurpation, it seems that *in extremis* one English noble's thoughts turned to the neglected example of Brutus as a remedy for tyranny.[91]

English tradition favoured open rebellion over covert plots, as chivalrous, manly and honourable. Though rebellion carried the risks of dishonour, death and material loss, it opened an alternative vista of splendidly augmenting both reputation and fortune. Failed attempts did not necessarily entail lasting historical infamy, such as was visited on the killers of James I. After forfeiture, opinion often favoured the restoration of innocent noble heirs in blood, estates and titles. Families often honoured forbears condemned for treason: that could be regarded as a malign turn of Fortune's wheel. Moreover, as far as literary traditions were concerned, rebellions were not generally remembered for their devastating effects on the populace – until the rhetoric of sixteenth-century writers about the wars between Lancaster and York, whose doleful interpretation had telling contemporary relevance. An exception to later medieval apparently roseate memories of rebellion was, as far as London was concerned, the Great Revolt of 1381. It seems that in the memory of its elites, the brief occupation of the city by the commons of Kent and Essex was a time of mayhem and destruction. The ruinous site of The Savoy, John of Gaunt's fine palace, which the rebels had sacked and set on fire, was a reminder, for generations travelling along The Strand or on the river between the city and Westminster, of the horrors of popular disorder. The site remained derelict until Henry VII built his great hospital there. The name of a leader of the Revolt, Jack Straw, became a byword for disruption. In Lincoln's Inn, over the Twelve Days of Christmas, social inversion ruled, as in other institutions, with the apprentices at law lording it over their masters. (A relic of this sort of inversion today is the custom in the British Army of superiors serving Christmas dinner in the mess to lower ranks.) Over the Twelve Days in 1516–17, 'Jack Straw' and his followers broke down doors and invaded rooms in the Inn (just as within living memory students at Edinburgh University used to do to tutors' rooms in the battles over Rectorial elections). The governors of the Inn were not amused, and imposed harsh penalties. In 1593 there was published a play by George Peele, *The Life and Death of Jack Strawe*, denigrating him and his companions, and exalting the opposition to them of the mayor in 1381, William Walworth, as the saviour of social order. The historiographical tradition about the Revolt developed by the London elite was spread throughout the realm by the chronicles and histories published there.[92]

However, the more usual sort of noble-led rebellion was often welcome and long recalled either with nostalgia or fading rancour. In 1327 Queen Isabella and a small company of exiles landed unopposed at Orwell (Suffolk), intent on confronting Edward II. The queen rolled up support as she traversed the realm, and prudently refrained from testing the patience of her sympathisers in London by attempting to gain entry with her army. She had it proclaimed that her supporters should take what they could from the possessions of her enemies (principally, the Despenser family), but her soldiers were not so discriminating in their plundering. Nevertheless the King could not muster sufficient support to avoid capture and deposition. Some in the later fourteenth century looked back on these precedents with favour – hence Richard II's hankering to achieve the canonisation of his murdered great-grandfather.[93] Rebellion recurred sixty years after Edward II's demise, when the Lords Appellant suddenly appeared with armed retinues at Harringay (Middlesex), and launched their Appeal of Treason against some of the young King's leading councillors. Nobody lifted a finger against them, and they were able to get supplies to maintain their forces, despite a royal prohibition to the Londoners from giving any to them. When the Duke of Ireland led his force from Cheshire through the Midlands to confront them, the support he received was negligible, and the Appellants easily dispersed his supporters at Radcot Bridge (Oxfordshire). The Appellants' numbers had been augmented because they had been joined in their Appeal of Treason by two other magnates, one of them being the King's cousin Henry of Bolingbroke. Fresh from their victory, they advanced on London, whose mayor sent them the keys of the city. There was probably relief that they had seen off an army of northern and provincial 'backwoodsmen', whereas Warwick signally failed to do so in 1461. The ominous precedent of successful rebellion was revived in 1387; on this occasion it did not end in deposition – though Richard may have been threatened with it.[94]

In 1399 Bolingbroke, exiled the previous year by Richard II and deprived by him of his succession to the duchy of Lancaster, landed in arms with a small group of sympathisers at Ravenspur on the coast of the East Riding of Yorkshire. Richard was far distant, campaigning in Ireland. Northern lords and Lancastrian retainers flocked to Bolingbroke's support. The retinues which the Regent, his and the king's uncle, Edmund of Langley, Duke of York (Duke Richard's grandfather) and other royal support- ers tried to rally faded away in face of Bolingbroke's advance across the Midlands to Bristol and then up to Chester. At Bristol some of the leading supporters and councillors of Richard who had taken refuge in the castle were convicted in the Court of Chivalry 'of treason and evil government of both the king and the kingdom', and executed.[95] This was reminiscent of the actions of the rebels in 1327, after Edward II's favourite Hugh Despenser the elder surrendered Bristol Castle to them. He had then been accused of a variety of crimes before the same court, notably that he had usurped royal power, and set aside the laws of the land, causing Thomas, Earl of Lancaster, to be executed without just cause. Despenser had been convicted and executed.[96] Bolingbroke's strategy, designed to cut off Richard's potential sources of support and trap him in Wales on his return from Ireland, had the advantage that it kept his army, strongly northern in composition and hungry for loot, well away from London, where its appearance might have modified the strong goodwill he enjoyed there. Victorious, he was to be ecstatically received in London. Practically universal support for or acquiescence in his rebellion, by commons as well as lords, were doubtless factors in his decision to claim the crown. The sequence of rebellion, deposition and usurpation was to set an unforgettable, fateful precedent for the fifteenth century.[97]

So risings could not have been regarded as novelties in the second half of the fifteenth century, or as *sui generis* manifestly unwelcome and deleterious. There were many alive in 1455 and 1461 who could remember the dramas of 1399, and some, doubtless, who had participated then in the great rides up and down England and into Wales, or whose fathers had. Folklore about the conduct and significance of the risings of 1387 and 1399 is likely to have influenced behaviour in new stirs and reactions to them. When Duke Richard claimed the throne in the wake of rebellion in 1460, some of his steps seem to have been intended as a symbolic reversal of Bolingbroke's moves to dethrone Richard, as whose rightful heir York now presented himself. He set out to undo the great wrong which his grand-father Duke Edmund had vainly tried to prevent. After Richard came into Bolingbroke's hands, through treachery, at Flint Castle, he was ignominiously taken as a prisoner through the Midlands to London. Bolingbroke started to use his own seal to grant royal offices and was to assert his claim to the throne before the assembled estates of the realm, after they had given their assent to Richard's deposition. In 1460 York, like Richard, returned from Ireland (where he had formerly been royal lieutenant). The Duke made a stately progress through the Midlands to London, with a large and distinguished company. In its later stages, the royal banner, undifferenced, was borne before him, as if he were the king, without the mark of cadency appropriate to a cadet line of the royal kin. He broached his claim to the Lords in parliament, to whom it was generally much less welcome than Bolingbroke's had been.[98]

In 1471 Edward IV, who had been forced into exile by Warwick the previous year, making way for the restoration of a bedraggled Henry VI, returned to England with a small armed company. He landed in the same place as Bolingbroke had done in 1399, though he had first tried his luck on the coast of Norfolk, where the commons barred his entry. In Holderness he was met by hostile arrays of the commons. There and subsequently on his progress in Yorkshire, and in especial to gain a grudging admission to York, he employed a ruse which Bolingbroke had used (the latter perhaps at first with more sincerity). Just as the Bolingbroke had asserted that he had only come to claim his rightful inheritance of the duchy of Lancaster, so Edward was vehement in his insistence that he was a loyal subject of Henry VI, whose objective was to receive back his duchy of York. However, Edward's conquest of England was to be much more demanding than Bolingbroke's, with months of hard campaigning and two major battles (Barnet and Tewkesbury) ahead. After ten years of dynastic conflict, in 1471 England was a much more politically polarised society than it had been in 1399. There were not only deeply entrenched rival dynastic and noble allegiances, but divisions between those who felt their interest lay in participation and those intent on remaining observers. Edward had to work hard to get his support out, as was to be the case with leaders of dynastic revolt in 1485 and 1487.[99]

The Wars were diminishing in intensity, because society at large was becoming wary of pinning the expression of their grievances to a dynastic cause. A reversion to concentrating solely on the issue of grievances about defects in the commonwealth seemed to be a more prudent approach. Rebellious Yorkshiremen in 1489, Cornishmen in 1497, and northerners in 1536–7 preferred to present themselves in the traditional mould of protesters who were only concerned with bad governance. These forms of protest, which had fuelled in particular the early stages of the Wars, reasserted their vigour after them.

Many of the commons who donned their harness for the Wars of the Roses – and for earlier and later revolts – doubtless did so primarily in response to their sense of obligation to a lord, as minor officers in his household and estate organisation, as tenants and as recipients of favours and charity. They were often reacting to heavy pressure to participate, to the threat of loss of office or good lordship. Moreover, professional soldiers were often ready to respond to calls to arms in periods when they were starved of other military employment.[100] However, the readiness of large bodies of common folk in the later fourteenth and fifteenth centuries to join in breaches of the peace of the realm needs to be related as well to recent developments in political culture, which encouraged lieges generally to consider themselves as part of an imagined 'community of the realm'. The concept of such a community, which had been used by critics of kingship in the thirteenth century as a radical tool for subverting the arbitrary aspects of its authority, had been adapted by kings as a means of deflecting opposition, and in the fourteenth century became central to political thinking. Edward III and his successors justified their frequent demands for taxation in parliament on the grounds that the threat to this community was not tyrannical government, but destruction by external enemies, such as the French and Scots. The common people, through the demands of subsidy collectors and commissioners of array, felt the weight of central government more fully, as well as the traditionally heavy hands of the officers of manor and borough courts. That gave them common cause with a host of similar communities which they might have traditionally regarded with suspicion and hatred, or of which they were previously ignorant. Moreover, from the mid-fourteenth century onwards, economic and social regulation by Crown and parliaments proliferated, especially in response to disruption and change in the wake of the plague pandemics. The justices of the peace, whose office evolved under Edward III, were made responsible for the enforcement of a growing number of statutes and ordinances, notably ones regulating wages and conditions of employment. In these circumstances, it is not surprising that, in the Great Revolt of 1381, the commons of Kent and Essex focussed their energies on punishing leading royal ministers whom they held responsible for the imposition and harsh collection of a poll tax (granted the previous year in parliament to fund a campaign in France), and for the attempts to bring defaulters in payment to trial. Their leaders also drafted radical proposals to alter general conditions of land tenure and employment.[101] The tensions in late fourteenth-century society reinforced traditions that resort to arms was a legitimate means of redressing the evils plaguing the commonwealth. The rebels from Kent led by Jack Cade in 1450 hoped to rally support by publishing a manifesto which contained a wide-ranging critique of Henry VI's government.[102] The Yorkist lords who invaded Kent from Calais in 1460 made a public appeal against bad government, and so did Clarence and Warwick when they invaded in 1469, protesting against the rule of Edward IV.[103] Such appeals, focussing on the influence of 'evil counsellors', were to remain a respectable weapon in the armoury of rebellion. They were used by the Cornish rebels of 1497, marching towards London in protest against the imposition of a parliamentary subsidy for war with Scotland, and by the Yorkshire rebels in the Pilgrimage of Grace, protesting against Henry VIII's Reformation policies.

GOD, TYRANNY, REBEL SAINTS AND ROYAL SAINTS

It was not just human discomfort with usurped and tyrannical rule that protesters were concerned about. They feared that such discordances between the order of society and the harmony of Creation would bring down on the community at large, which acquiesced in them, the wrath of God. In the Court of King's Bench in 1404, a certain John Sperhauke of Cardiff testified about the remarks a tailor's wife had made in their house in a village near Baldock (Hertfordshire). Allegedly she said that there had been rain and storms throughout Henry IV's reign. There had been only seven good days. The King was not the rightful king, but the Earl of March was. Henry was not the son of John of Gaunt, but of a butcher of Ghent. Henry had not kept the covenant which he had made with the commons, nor did he wish to obey the Pope. Because of that, there had been a terrible tempest for several days recently. Indeed, these accusations against the apparently recklessly garrulous tailor's wife may have been invented. However, they had to be presented as plausible to the court: they provide a valuable insight into the political reasoning of ordinary folk. We may deduce from this story that it was particularly necessary for opponents in domestic conflict to convince their soldiers that their cause had God's approval, and that He would not visit His wrath on them and on their communities. Passages in *The Book of Margery Kempe*, an account of the life in devotion of a woman from a leading family of King's Lynn (Norfolk), whose first part was completed in 1436, suggests that the well-informed as well as the populace in general considered that bad weather, storms and plague were divine punishments for acquiescence in unrighteous behaviour. When Margery and other pilgrims were arrested by the mayor of Leicester in 1417, the people, it was alleged in *The Book*, were fearful that a storm was punishment for the imprisonment of pilgrims in their town.[104]

The readiness of English folk to take up arms, risking God's wrath by defying an anointed king, might derive not from a conviction that he was a usurper, or not from that alone. There were unique traditions, which sanctified a succession of secular nobles, and leading ecclesiastics too, who defied the king, some of whom led rebellions, and were slain in retribution. They were for long regarded as martyrs in a holy cause, their sanctity made manifest to later generations by the miracles performed at their tombs. This political phenomenon had originated with opposition to the 'tyranny' of Angevin kings. Henry II's opponent St Thomas of Canterbury came to be seen as the archetypal English saint, whose cult retained power and popularity until it was abolished by Henry VIII. He was seen as martyred in defence of the liberties of the English Church. In Yorkshire in 1489, protests against a parliamentary subsidy for war with France escalated into full-scale revolt, after Henry VII's local 'boss', the fourth Earl of Northumberland, was killed while trying to suppress a riot. Ringleaders dispatched letters urging men to array in arms to stand up 'for such unlawful points as St Thomas of Canterbury died for'. The appeal must have had some success, as the rebels assaulted York and briefly occupied it. [105]

Simon de Montfort, Earl of Leicester, killed in 1265, became a cult figure for his upholding of the liberties of the community against Henry III. Fifty or so years later, the anonymous contemporary biographer of another king who provoked widespread fury, Edward II, alluded to 'the battle of Evesham... where that noble man Simon de Montfort laid down his life in the cause of justice'. [106] Simon's fame was to be eclipsed by that of Thomas, Earl of Lancaster, Edward II's cousin and relentless critic. He was executed for treason after being taken in arms at the battle of Boroughbridge (Yorkshire) in 1322. Miracles occurred at his tomb in Pontefract priory – it was alleged to have flowed with blood in 1367. A hermitage was founded on the hill nearby where he was executed, and a liturgy was composed for his feast day. The cult retained some potency well into the sixteenth century. The Yorkshireman Sir Hugh Hastings made a bequest in 1482 for wax 'to be burned in the Abbey of Pontefract in the honour of Seynt Thomas of Lancastre', and Leland was to note the 'fine church on the hill where the good Duke [*sic*] of Lancaster was beheaded'.[107]

Some kings worried about the creation of new anti-monarchical cults. In 1397 the Earl of Arundel was executed, convicted for treason committed ten years before as one of the Lords Appellant. Richard II, fearful that a cult would develop at his tomb, insisted that he should be buried in obscurity in the Blackfriars church in London. In this instance, Richard succeeded in stamping out the first sparks of a cult, but Henry IV could not have the remains of Richard Scrope disposed of so neatly in 1405. Since he was archbishop of York, he could not be denied burial in York Minster, where his tomb (much altered) can be seen on the north side of the Lady Chapel. A cult speedily developed, centred on it, which ecclesiastical prohibitions and the erection of timber obstructions failed to snuff out. This cult was to be tolerated after Henry's death.[108]

The only cult produced as a result of the Wars of the Roses was not one of a lost rebel leader, but of a lost king – Henry VI. That is surprising, in view of the deaths in battle of magnates who had emphasised in rebellion their concern for the commonweal. The Duke of York, according to his epitaph 'loved the people and was their defender', and chroniclers stressed Warwick's popularity. However, York's sons did not promote a cult for him; the epitaph composed for him when his remains were translated with great ceremony in 1476 highlighted his virtues as a governor, the man worthy to be king.[109]

The medieval English monarchy was exalted by numerous customary holy phenomena (such as the miracle-working powers attributed to kings), and could invoke the support of long-established royal saints, Edmund the Martyr and Edward the Confessor. Despite the sad deaths of some recent English kings, only one of them had attracted a cult – Edward II, presumed murdered in 1327. His tomb in Gloucester Abbey was accessible – without such an easy focus, it was difficult for a cult to develop. Henry IV made sure that Richard II's body was spirited away after exhibition in St Paul's Cathedral in 1400, to

be buried obscurely in the Dominican friary within the precincts of the royal lodge at Langley (Hertfordshire). Edward V
(a cult about whom might have recalled some features of that
of the Anglo-Saxon boy-martyr St Edward) was buried in lasting obscurity. Enthusiasts for Richard III might ask why his
cult did not flower until the twentieth century. Henry VII had
him buried quite openly in the Franciscan friary at Leicester,
an important town on principal trade routes. Why did not
the murdered Richard (about whose personal devoutness we
have recently become well-informed) appear posthumously, to
bestow holy bounty on his erstwhile subjects? There were plenty
of people around in the early Tudor period, highborn and low,
who had enjoyed Richard's temporal bounty, and might have
been inclined to look for his spiritual favour. The reasons why
a cult did not arise may have been that his rule did not last
long enough to become embedded in popular consciousness as
a norm, and that the dramatic and public way in which it was
untimely cut short appeared like an adverse judgement of God.
Besides, Henry VI had a head start in cornering regional markets
in royal miracle-working.

Henry VI's cult appears to have developed soon after his
sudden and convenient death in the Tower of London in 1471,
though he was buried obscurely in Chertsey Abbey (Surrey).
The cult was to become widespread and to attract devotees from
all social strata. It was regarded as subversive under Edward IV,
but it was not apparently exploited by pro-Lancastrian rebels
in 1473, 1483 and 1485. Nor did Henry's apparition engage in
condemnatory discourse: it specialised in curing the mishaps and
ailments of his faithless former subjects and their accident-prone
children. Richard III recognised Henry as now a docile Yorkist
subject, who could safely be added to the line of English royal
saints. Richard had his remains and cult-centre translated to
St George's Chapel, Windsor Castle. Henry VII was to elaborate
Richard's scheme, bolstering his uncle's cult.[110]

One reason for the mushrooming of this new royal cult may
have been troubled thoughts at the rejections of a long and firmly

held allegiance. In 1460, when Henry's right to the Crown was first challenged, anyone up to the age of thirty-eight had known no other king than him. Some of his devotees interceded with him by bending a penny. As a result of his long reign, a large amount of his coinage was in circulation (a goodly amount still exists), a constant reminder of broken oaths, and a ready-made, handy cult-object.[111]

The cult that emerged from the Wars was one which did not reinforce the sanctification of rebellion, but exalted the battered image of monarchy, when seized on by Henry VII and exploited by him as a way of promoting his dynasty and the honour of the Crown. The failure to turn rebels into martyrs may have been a consequence of their general inclination, from 1460 onwards, to emphasise the dynastic issue at the expense of the traditional aim of reforming government. Yet though Warwick's successes against Edward may have been helped by his continuing emphasis as rebel leader on the needs of the commonwealth, even he did not attract a cult. However, as we have seen, the Wars did not discredit the old ways of rebellion. Despite the new barrage of monarchical propaganda in the Tudor period, with its emphases both on the religious and politic virtues of obedience, some forms of armed protest remained up to the Glorious Revolution (or, perhaps one should say, up to the American Revolution) as English as good ale. Indeed, a certain weariness with bolder forms of protest may have generally characterised society during the lifespans of those who were adult during the risings of the 1480s. In the revived rebelliousness of the sixteenth century, even before the Reformation, the traditions of invoking or creating sanctified leaders seem to have been dormant. The most widely supported Tudor risings, those in the North in 1536, had a different religious focus (as did later rebellions). The visual symbols projected by the 'pilgrims' in the main gatherings in Yorkshire had christocentric messages. Rebel contingents from the Bishopric of Durham as well as Yorkshire paraded banners with various symbols of the Five Wounds of Christ, and similar badges were widely displayed by their fellow soldiers. This was a contrast both to customary invocations of St Thomas or Earl Thomas of Lancaster, and to the wearing of merely secular tokens, such as the bear and ragged staff or the white boar, which their grandsires had presumably borne in the late civil wars. The Wounds of Christ had become one of the most potent cults in recent decades. English archers on crusade in Castile in 1511 had hoisted it as their banner, rather than the crusading cross of St George. The rebels of 1536 were to some extent anticipating the variety of confessional tinctures which were to colour some later risings. However, in the end they were desperate to relinquish their novel and precarious holy status. At an assembly on the hill where Thomas of Lancaster ('St Thomas') had been beheaded at Pontefract, the commons dispersed, after the pardon was read. At Doncaster, in the presence of Henry VIII's commander, the Duke of Norfolk, Robert Aske, their leader, and the other gentry, tore off the badge of the Wounds and cried, 'We will all wear no badge or sign but the badge of our sovereign lord'.[112]

3

Soldiers

*And the soldiers likewise demanded of him [St John the Baptist], saying,
And what shall we do? And he said unto them, Do violence to no man,
neither accuse any falsely, and be content with your wages*

St Luke, Chapter 3, verse 14

What sort of men constituted the rank and file who fought in civil conflict in England and Wales in the later Middle Ages, and in particular in the Wars of the Roses? Where did the recruits come from, and where had they learnt the trade of war? How was it apparently possible, on occasion, to conjure an army up speedily, like warriors sprung from the soil? Such questions are crucial to understanding military organisation and activity in England and Wales, since, as we have seen, in contrast to most continental principalities (and Ireland) for much of the period, domestic warfare was not endemic there. However, the English Crown was notable for the ways in which it routinely projected Anglo-Welsh military power abroad, and organised defences against repeated threats of invasion during the Hundred Years War (conventionally dated from 1337 to 1453). In order to do so, it needed to elaborate on and maintain two discrete, contrasting and mostly distinct military systems Each of them had elements which could be utilised by both parties in civil conflict, but neither of them was ideally geared for it. Kings and nobles who rode off to do battle in England and Wales needed, above all, experienced soldiers about their person and in the vanguard, men proved in the wars in France and Scotland. For warfare abroad, the English Crown often contracted for the services of foreign mercenaries, but it also needed to 'wage' large numbers of native-born soldiers to form its armies, man its fleets and garrison the towns and castles that it strove to control. These needs created pools of English professional soldiers. Some of them banded into companies which, most prominently in the aftermath of Edward III's peace with the French Crown in 1360, maintained coherence and continuity, campaigning then as mercenaries in various parts of the continent, most notably, over several decades, in Italy.[1] Questions arise as to the extent to which English professional soldiers could be utilised in domestic conflicts in England and Wales. It may be that the availablity of numbers of them at times, if willing to participate, provided a stimulus to rebellion. At other times, during repeatedly renewed truces with England's habitual adversaries, Crown and political community eagerly cut back on the huge costs of maintaining soldiers. Questions arise as to whether in these lean times the pool of them shrunk or dried up, in the absence of the previous incentives and opportunities for men to maintain themselves in the profession or learn it. Perhaps continuity of military experience was largely lost in these periods, and the conduct of domestic campaigns characterised by amateurism and unwillingness or inability to absorb innovations. These issues have a particular relevance to the Wars of the Roses, since in their first phase (up to 1461), they were fought in the aftermath of the repatriation of a combat-hardened English military establishment from France, and in their subsequent phases (1469–71 and 1483–87) in one of the longest periods in later medieval and early modern English history when the Crown launched few major expeditions abroad. With such issues in mind, in relation to domestic conflicts, let us touch on the world of the English soldier in the later fourteenth and fifteenth centuries, before going on to consider the roles of foreign mercenaries in English pay, and the participation of husbandmen and artisans called up to join or oppose rebels.

THE ENGLISH AND WELSH PROFESSIONAL SOLDIER AT WORK

Edward I (d.1307), in his Welsh and Scottish wars, and his grandson Edward III (d.1377), in his wars in Scotland and France, established systems of recruitment of English companies for pay and, also, after Edward I's conquest of the principality of Gywnedd in 1282–3, of Welsh ones. Professors Chris Given-Wilson and Michael Prestwich have written, citing Dr Andrew Ayton, that 'what we witness… from the 1290s onwards, is "militarization" of the English gentry resulting in the formation of a military elite with "abundant collective experience and a powerful shared mentality"'.[2] If that is true of the knights and esquires who went abroad in the king's wars, it must in some degree also be true of the native common folk whom they recruited for their retinues. Many of these enrolled commons were probably drawn from the elites in village communities, as Dr Ayton's studies of how they needed to equip themselves for service abroad under Edward III suggest. So they included men whose family standing might give them an authoritative voice, if they survived campaigning and returned home, in the formation of popular opinions about war, peace and the conduct of kings and nobles. The well-to-do commoner marketing his skills with lance, longbow, axe or dagger needed to possess a sturdy horse to ride on most expeditions, besides light military harness.[3] Soldiers with and without mounts were recruited to serve in the permanently maintained garrisons which gave forward protection to England's frontiers, in Scotland and France, as well as in other garrisons mostly in France, at various stages of the Hundred Years War. Standard daily rates of pay were offered by the Crown to men-at-arms and archers, the same for service on expeditions abroad and in garrisons (1s and 6d respectively).

These scales may have eventually become less of an incentive for commoners to serve, except those from poorer parts of the realm and from Wales, as a result of the improving customary conditions for many wage-earners in the aftermath of the plague pandemics. In the 1370s, it was alleged, Robert Archer of Forncett (Norfolk), 'in search of high wages outside that township, leads out of it each autumn six or eight labourers... and he takes for himself and his associates 6d a day and food, and does so against the prohibition of the constable of the township for this year'.[4] For most of the fifteenth century, population levels overall failed to recover to the higher pre-plague plateau, and labour remained in high demand. During the building of Lord Hastings' new castle at Kirby Muxloe (Leicestershire) in 1481–2, overseers of masonry and carpentry were paid 8d a day, most craftsmen 6d, labourers and dikers 3d to 4d.[5] Archer's company, travelling round harvesting in 1379, earned their sixpences more congenially than the soldiers bound for Brittany who were disastrously shipwrecked that year, and the option of working at Kirby Muxloe may well have seemed preferable to that of toiling warily through the hostile Scottish Lowlands on Gloucester's expedition of 1482.

Besides, instalments of military pay were often in arrears. Yet, in some circumstances and particular periods, there were tempting incentives for commoners to enrol for service in France. Not only might they benefit from pardons for crimes, but there were opportunities for substantial gain – prospects of plunder; the reward to which they were entitled for capturing well-heeled opponents, and the possibility of military and social elevation in status. Such prospects were, indeed, dimmer in the generally more barren and bleaker campaigning environments in Scotland – or in Ireland, whither royal lieutenants from England customarily took a small military retinue across to Dublin. Nor were prospects of gain good in the first decade or so of the fifteenth century in Wales, where English armies struggled to make headway against Owain Glyn Dŵr.

Generally, service on the continent offered the hope of better pickings. In 1367 Edward III's son, the Black Prince, recognised the claims of two obscure esquires, William Hauley and John Shakell, to major shares in the ransom of the Marquis of Villena, whose capture in 1367, and giving of his son Denia as a hostage, have been alluded to. The refusal of the esquires many years later to hand over the hostage to the Crown made them celebrated. They were imprisoned in the Tower of London in 1378. Hauley escaped, but was killed by pursuing royal officers, when seeking sanctuary in Westminster Abbey.[6] The actual captor of the Aragonese prince seems to have been a mere menial – Hauley's servant Richard Henry, *alias* Chambirleyn. He colluded, among others, with his master in the concealment of Denia, for which, like Shakell, he was eventually pardoned. In 1380 he was awarded compensation from the Crown of 1,000 marks (£666 13s 4d) for his share in the ransom.[7] Such success stories are likely to have become well known among the populace, as spectacular lottery wins do today. The most remarkable rags to riches tale was that of Sir John Hawkwood (d.1394), son of an Essex tanner, who, after fighting in Edward III's wars in France, commanded the predominantly English White Company, a dominant force in Italian warfare for decades. He amassed a fortune and purchased estates in different parts of Italy.[8]

More ephemeral was the success of the son of a serf from Salle (Norfolk) – Robert Salle. Though somewhat of a brawler, he distinguished himself fighting in France in Edward III's later years. He was knighted, and appointed by the King as captain of the castle of Marck in the March of Calais. During the Great Revolt of 1381, the gentlefolk and citizens of Norwich, according to the leading chronicler Jean Froissart, sent Salle to parley with the companies of commons encamped in arms outside the city walls. Presumably they considered that they would be awed by his military reputation, and that he would speak their language. They overestimated his diplomatic skills. The commons urged him to join them, on the grounds that he was in origin one of them. His reply was absolutely scathing; among other choice insults, he seems to have described them as a load of shit. They promptly lynched him.[9] English chroniclers recorded his death and the indignation it evoked among nobles.[10] In the present context, what is notable about Froissart's story is the implication that Salle's history was well known among the commons of Norfolk. Past individual and collective bonanzas from the French wars may have become part of folklore. Traditions were recorded by the antiquary John Leland in the 1540s about how English castles had been built on the profits of war.[11] Generations of boys were probably excited by stories associated with great soldiers whose impressive tombs were in parish churches, like Sir Matthew Gournay's, by the warlike symbolism of paintings and statues of St George in churches and guild chapels, and by the re-enactment of his triumph over the dragon on his feast day, which seems to have spread as a parochial celebration in the fifteenth century.[12]

They may have aspired to be taken on service abroad by a man-at-arms, a professional soldier such as Jankyn Nowell (like Salle, inclined to violence in civilian life), who in 1380 contracted with Sir Hugh Hastings to bring a company of four other men-at-arms and five archers for service on an expedition to France.[13] Soldiers boasted excitingly of great deeds to come, as at the anticipated drinking bout which the poet Guto'r Glyn suggested that Tomas ap Watcyn Fychan of Llanddewi Rhydderch (who belonged to a branch of the Vaughan family) should hold some time in the 1440s. Guto'r Glyn himself seems to have enrolled in 1441 as an archer of the body to Richard, Duke of York, on an expedition which set out for France and achieved notable success. Other Welshmen enrolled on it – there was a Thomas Vaughan in the Duke's retinue, and there were four Vaughans in the retinue of his esquire Walter Devereux. Guto'r said in his poem that Tomas was intending to serve the Duke in France. The poet proposed that fellow recruits should 'kill' draughts at his expense as if they were the French leaders:

Muster us, O master in the two Gwents,
Like your father beside your tent.

Your poets, nine armies, won't fail
To give attack and broach his wine.
The Dauphin [Charles VII] will have to cower
before the soldiers of the hogsheads.
We'll cry (a righteous convent)
'Saint George' across the land of Gwent.
Your wine will cry, 'Saint Denys'.[14]

Since the demand for large numbers of soldiers tended to be seasonal, veterans and would-be recruits must have spent a lot of time in taverns; presumably the catering tradesfolk of London (and those women who plied their immoral trade in Cock Lane and the 'stews' of Southwark) benefited from the customary presence of large numbers of them there. However, the turn of international affairs for long periods reduced the Crown's demands for military manpower to a trickle: adventurous but sensible lads might then have preferred to join companies of itinerant masons and harvesters. The general truces made by England with its opponents in 1389 and continuously renewed in the next few years, and the long truces made in 1396 (intended to last twenty-eight years) diminished the Crown's frequent and heavy needs for military employment, which had characterised the previous twenty years. The garrisons of Cherbourg and Brest, ports held by the English Crown, were discharged when they were handed back to their owners. Froissart mentions the disgruntlement of English squires in the 1390s who looked to earn their living by warfare. Fear that opportunities would be permanently diminished if a final peace was made with the French Crown seems to have been a factor in a gentry-led rising in Cheshire and Lancashire in 1393. Four years later, according to a French source, soldiers recently discharged from the garrison at Brest were received at dinner by Richard II. His uncle, Thomas of Woodstock, Duke of Gloucester, complained to him that they had been badly paid and did not know what to do. He said that Richard should hazard his life capturing a city before thinking of selling one conquered by his ancestors. His remarks were, not surprisingly, ill received. The author thought that the return of the garrison from Brest was at the start of the troubles in England which ended with Richard's deposition.[15] Discontent probably did escalate in the 1390s at the closure of traditional opportunities for service, augmenting the tensions between the King and his critics. Richard II may have been aware of the problem. His expeditions to Ireland in 1394–5 and 1399 may have been in part aimed to open up another field of service for English soldiers – Ireland was already a fruitful one for professional soldiers from the Hebrides and western seaboard of Scotland, the *galloglach* (galloglasses). However, the English soon grew weary of the problems of campaigning in Ireland. Richard's establishment of a standing royal guard, the archers recruited from Cheshire and North Wales, may have in part been intended to take up some of the slack from regions which had come to depend particularly on soldiering.[16] However, the increasing numbers who swelled the ranks of Henry of Bolingbroke's rebel army in 1399 probably included discontented old soldiers, eager for a new chance of profit.[17]

In times of truce with the usual princely adversaries, there were some opportunities to serve in the garrisons which the Crown maintained at a reduced level in the castles and towns which it customarily held in enemy territory, as 'barbicans' for the forward defence of the realm. The largest concentration was in Calais and its March. In the mid-fifteenth century, in time of truce, the garrisons of the town and castle of Calais had a complement of 450; Guines Castle, 100; Hammes Castle and the Rysbank Tower had smaller garrisons.[18] In 1404 a contract was made for the maintenance in the castle and town of Berwick, in time of truce, of garrisons with a combined strength of 300, and in 1400 Roxburgh Castle was to have 120, reduced in 1421 by two-fifths.[19] It is probable that in peaceful times the English government had a total garrison establishment of less than 2,000 soldiers. In such hard times for professionals, they grasped at opportunities to serve foreign princes and cities as mercenaries. The famed skills of English and Welsh longbowmen led companies of them to be prized as components of armies on the

continent from the mid-fourteenth to the later fifteenth century.[20] In the lean years before Henry V's invasions of France in
1415 and 1417, however, promising openings abroad were mostly
soon dashed. In 1408, John the Fearless, Duke of Burgundy,
alleged that there were 100 archers from England in the army
of the city of Liège fighting his troops; he was soon to conquer
the city.[21] In the last years of Henry IV's reign, English forces
were briefly sent to serve as mercenaries in the bouts of civil
war which erupted in France. In 1411 Henry dispatched a force
of 1,000 commanded by the Earl of Arundel to aid Duke John
(who already employed a small English contingent). Once the
English had broken the blockade of Paris by his opponents,
the Armagnacs, they were sent home. However, the following year Henry's government switched sides, coming to an
agreement with John, Duke of Berry, to send a force of 1,000
men-at-arms and 3,000 archers (a typical size of expedition for
an English invasion of France). Under the command of Henry's
son Thomas, Duke of Clarence, they landed in Normandy and
rode southwards, but before they could engage, the French
dukes had made peace with each other. Clarence led his army
to English-held Gascony.[22]

There he may have plotted to take it across the Pyrenees. In
Aragon, the communities had recently accepted as king a Castilian
prince, Fernando of Antequera. However, one of the disappointed
claimants, Jaime count of Urgel, plotted rebellion in 1412. He
offered Clarence the right to the Sicilian Crown and a royal
marriage, if he led or sent his 1,000 men-at-arms and 3,000 archers
to his aid. It seems doubtful whether Clarence could have afforded
to do so, but some French and English companies prepared to go;
the Spanish sources suggest that the English predominated among
them. They appear to have been commanded by a Genoese captain,
Basilio, and a certain Gracian de Agramonte. Urgel's Aragonese
supporters were speedily defeated; most of the mercenaries prudently failed to cross the frontier, except Basilio's company, which
in 1413 garrisoned Balaguer, near Lerida. There the English put up
a gallant defence, but, without hope of relief, had to surrender.[23]

That ended the opposition to Fernando's rule, though another English magnate, Edward, Duke of York, had tried to fish in these troubled waters. Edward sent an envoy, Sir John Montfort, to air his own alleged claim to the throne of Castile. He was angling for a royal marriage for his nephew and heir (probably Richard, the future Duke of York), and proposed leading an army to Spain in 1413 to co-operate in crusading against the Moorish kingdom of Granada – a cause dear to Fernando's heart. However, Fernando was able to shrug off menacing English embraces.[24] There seems to have been no participation by English mercenaries in the civil wars in the Iberian kingdoms in the fifteenth century. English and Welsh soldiers' highly prized skills made them expensive commodities, and, as the centre of English military activities in France shifted more markedly to the north of the Loire in the fifteenth century, they became distanced from southern Europe. Moreover, in Spain there was hatred for the introduction of foreign mercenaries, prompted by memories of the incursions of the English and others from north of the Pyrenees in the later fourteenth century. In 1413, far south from Balaguer, the city council of Seville recorded the gist of 'the letter of the said lord king [Fernando of Antequera] of the good news that was received of how the *adelantado* [governor] of Castile and other knights of the said lord king had put to flight vasylio, the English captain [*sic*] of certain men at arms and foot soldiers who came to enter into the kingdoms of Aragon to do evil'.[25] In Italy, by the early fifteenth century, native *condottieri* had largely displaced foreigners. There, the recruitment and organisation of companies became big business, sometimes carried out by *signori*, minor rulers for whom the leadership of mercenary bands of their subjects was an honourable source of income. A by now rare instance of recruitment of English mercenaries is the contract which Doge Francesco Foscari of Venice made in 1434 for the service of Sir Walter of England to lead a company of 100 composed of mounted and foot archers, who, it was stipulated, must be from England and Ireland, or otherwise subjects of the king.[26]

The good times had rolled again for English and Welsh professional soldiers in the late 1410s and the 1420s. Henry V's conquests gave them a prolonged boost, since the English were still being strongly opposed at the time of his death in 1422 by the adherents of the Dauphin Charles, and during the regency in France of his brother John, Duke of Bedford (d.1435) for the infant Henry VI. There was the need to organise a multitude of garrisons in Normandy, Maine and the Ile-de-France, to summon contingents from them and England for field operations, and to maintain the defences of Gascony on high alert. However, by the mid-1440s Lancastrian France was under heavy pressure from the resurgent monarchy of Charles VII, which a series of small expeditions from England ultimately failed to reverse. In 1445 Henry VI surrendered the county of Maine, as part of his marriage settlement with Charles's kinswoman Margaret of Anjou, a hoped-for move towards peace. The English garrisons there, to their disgust, were discharged. In 1449–51 the garrisons in Normandy capitulated to the overwhelming strength of Charles's army. Gascony was afterwards swiftly conquered too, but Bordeaux was briefly recovered by an expedition sent out under the command of the veteran John Talbot, Earl of Shrewsbury, in 1453. This attempt collapsed when the Earl was killed and his force soundly defeated while attacking the encampment of the French force besieging Castillon. Shrewsbury's expedition was to be the last opportunity for recruits to participate in large-scale warfare in France for many years.

The speedy fall of Lancastrian France did not just block avenues of customary military employment, as in the wake of the Anglo-French peace (1360) and the general truces in and after 1389. It led as well to the sudden destruction of a vigorous and rich, if small, Anglo-Welsh military society in France. The total garrison strength in Normandy in 1447–8 (much reduced from what it had been previously in the conquered lands in northern France) has been projected as 2,100.[27] Scattered in garrisons formed through contracts with the captains who held Norman lordships, this society lacked the cohesion of the companies of the 1360s, which had facilitated their collective movement to other fields of military activity as mercenaries. It is doubtful whether the garrisons (and remnants of the defeated field forces sent from England) had the organisational coherence and operational flexibility to adapt wholesale to different circumstances. There was little demand elsewhere for mercenaries. In Italy the Peace of Lodi (1454) and the mechanisms it set up between the contracting Italian states produced a considerable reduction in warfare.

After the peace made in 1360, and after the truces of 1389, English, French and Scottish knights had promptly and frequently gone on crusade (the English and French sometimes in combination), but by the 1450s opportunities to do so had diminished. The defeat of the crusading Order of Teutonic Knights, rulers of Prussia, by the Poles and Lithuanians at Tannenberg in 1410 curtailed their power; moreover, Lithuania had already accepted Christianity. John II of Castile showed little inclination to revive the crusade against his client Moorish kingdom of Granada. The fall of Constantinople to the Turks in 1453 was, indeed, a wakeup call for Western Christendom. The following year, Philip the Good, Duke of Burgundy, held the celebrated Feast of the Pheasant at Lille. There, before a glittering assembly of nobility, one of the court chamberlains, the historian Olivier de la Marche, dressed up as a woman (representing the Church), was led in seated on an elephant by the court giant, Hans (= the Turk). 'Lady Church' made a piteous lament about her captivity, asking for help, and reminding the company of the capture of Constantinople. 'She' approached the Duke first; he swore to go on crusade, on God, the Blessed Virgin Mary and the pheasant. A bird had been led in, wearing a necklace studded with precious stones – oaths on birds which symbolised noble qualities had a long history. The other nobles then made crusading vows. The sincerity of Duke Philip and his companions should not be doubted; he was to promote the crusade strenuously. However, the times were not propitious, and his and Pope Pius II's efforts were largely ineffective.[28] The kings of France and England were traditionally regarded as the most important northern promoters of crusades, but Charles VII was intent on consolidating his power in the newly conquered territories, keeping watchful eyes on the English, and checking what seemed to the French royal establishment the overweening power of the Duke of Burgundy. Henry VI, despite his posthumous reputation for piety, and the glorious crusading activities of some of his royal predecessors and Lancastrian forbears, showed a passive indifference to this supreme duty of Christian kings. In hard times for soldiers, lords who had captained them had led them off to holy war. Edward, Duke of York, had planned to do so in 1413, as we have seen, but there is no sign that his nephew Duke Richard or other veteran nobles from the wars in France were thinking along these lines forty years later. In the aftermath of the loss of 'empire', they seem to have become inward-looking, preoccupied with domestic politics. Nobles were probably daunted by the awesome power of the Turks, which Richard III and Henry VIII were to rage at – but it was a Scottish king, James IV, who seriously tried to do something about it.[29]

So there was little alternative military employment for soldiers returning from France; this military establishment faced disbandment. Some soldiers who had made close social connections with the French took the oath of allegiance to Charles VII. The majority are likely to have returned to England, though it was unfamiliar to many of them, its relative peacefulness contrasting with society in a 'land of war', in whose brutal conventions they were past masters. Discharged soldiers always made an unwelcome impact, but especially so in the shameful circumstances of the early 1450s. Their sad state and that of their accompanying wives and children could evoke pity, but the soldiers caused upsets by their unruliness in Kent and particularly in London. Some flocked to the King's household – perhaps loudly proclaiming their plight. Henry ordered that they were to be paid wages for fifteen days. The veteran Lord Scales was commissioned to try to keep order among them.[30] The rebellion of Jack Cade and his Kentishmen provided some temporary employment. Sir John Fastolf, retired soldier and former Norman landowner, stationed 'old soldiers of Normandy' in his house in Southwark, to safeguard it against the Kentish rebels, but he was persuaded that this was unwise, and discharged the soldiers.[31] Scales commanded a garrison of returned soldiers in the Tower of London. With him was the Welsh esquire Matthew Gough (or Goch). He was from Maelor Saesneg, and his father had been bailiff of the manor of Hanmer. Gough had distinguished himself in the French wars, and gained extensive Norman estates. He conducted a much-admired defence of Caen earlier in the year. The soldiers, in a fierce fight for control of London Bridge, repulsed the rebel Cade's attempt to reoccupy London; the distinguished Gough was killed there.[32]

Did the presence of unemployed (and presumably often disgruntled) soldiers provide a source of recruitment which, to an unusual degree, facilitated and encouraged rebellion in the early stages of the Wars of the Roses? Did old soldiers play a significant part in the Wars into the 1460s, and new generations of professionals thereafter? It is likely, indeed, that the military capabilities of many unemployed veterans soon deteriorated, as they found alternative employment or sank into criminality and vagabondage. Thomas Beaufort, Duke of Exeter (d. 1426), one of his nephew Henry V's most trusted commanders, anticipated such circumstances: 'if anyone who had served with him as a soldier in France came to poverty, he caused him to have daily food, fuel, and candles'.[33] In default of wages, the necessity may soon have arisen to sell off horses, harness and weapons. When the able-bodied men of Bridport (Dorset) were mustered in 1457, their arms and equipment were listed in detail. Some of them had impressive personal armouries. Typically of the better-equipped, one man had, besides a bow and sheaf of arrows, and the fairly standard salet (helmet) and jack (protective jacket), a sword, buckler, spear and pavis (a large, probably standing shield). Two men equipped as archers had pairs of gauntlets – presumably from suits of armour, as was another archer's 'leg harness'. Surely these appendages would have impeded archers in action – but they were status symbols. One Bridport man was listed simply as having a 'Whyte harnys with a basnet', i.e. a complete suit of plate armour and vizored helmet.[34] Possibly such arms and armour could be cheaply acquired from veterans. Could it have been that England was, comparatively speaking, awash with weaponry returned from France in the 1450s? If so, that facilitated the cheap and adequate equipment of servants and shire levies for domestic broils, with the expectation of less grumbling from them at the high cost of serving.

A high proportion of veterans may have been disabled as a result of wounds, disease and poverty. Preparing to go on campaign in Scotland in 1482, Sir Hugh Hastings recognised the likelihood of casualties among his men. He ordered his executors to reward at their discretion anyone who was 'hurted or maymed' in his service on the expedition.[35] A passage in Sir Thomas More's *Utopia*, published in 1516, is relevant:

> We shall say nothing of those who often come home crippled from foreign or civil wars, as recently with you Englishmen from the battle with the Cornishmen and not long ago from the war in France. They lose their limbs in the service of the commonwealth or the king, and their disability prevents them from exercising their own craft, and their age from learning a new one.[36]

The campaigns alluded to were those of the Cornish insurrection of 1497 and Henry VIII's invasion of France in 1513. They were both short campaigns, yet they had generated sufficiently conspicuous amounts of vagabondage to support a political point. Presumably, More was recalling the beggars he was accustomed to see congregating on the streets of London.

However, given the opportunity, even badly disabled men might have been keen to fight rather than beg or starve. Contemporary surgery (for those with access to it) could induce remarkable recoveries from head wounds.[37] Such a case was one of the casualties whose remains have been found at the battle site of Towton. 'Towton 16' 'displayed a great deal of evidence of having led a relatively long and active life and had fought in previous battles, as evidenced by the well-healed sword cut on the left side of his lower jaw'. Other features of his remains suggest that he may have habitually practised archery and horse riding. Possibly he had been a mounted archer in French or Scottish campaigns, who had not been incapacitated from giving further service. He may have been recalled to the colours as a captain of archers, experiencing once more the soldier's sense of comradeship and anticipatory buzz of action in the field. He was aged forty-six or over, among the older in the gravepit whose remains can be assessed for their age.[38] Another, more extreme case of service by the disabled was to be found among the motley crew of professional soldiers with whom John Paston the younger reinforced his servants and local 'valets' for the defence of Caister Castle in 1469. There were two or three foreigners – 'Ducheman' Matthew, and Raulyns ('extraneus') Mundynet, 'born in France', besides Lancashireman J. Jakson, William Peny, soldier from Calais, John Lofe, also from Calais, John Chapman, a soldier of the Duke of Somerset, and 'Thomas Stompys, handless, and wishing to shoot for a noble' (6s 8d).[39] The last may have been a handgunner or artilleryman who had been the victim of an explosion. His employment could indicate his high reputation for devices in siege warfare – or Paston's desperation to recruit mercenaries.

The magnates and lords who led the armies of the Wars of the Roses in 1455 and 1459–61 were, for the most part, veterans of the French wars – or of campaigning on the frontiers with Scotland. So were many of their subordinate captains. When in 1461 the youthful Edward, Earl of March, (soon to be Edward IV) defeated the Welsh Lancastrians at Mortimer's Cross, his captains included knights who had served in France – Walter Devereux, Roger Vaughan, and William Herbert.[40] Sir John Fastolf's former secretary and biographer, William Worcestre, who had a particular interest in veterans of the French wars, noted the participation of some in the battle. On the Lancastrian side fought members of the local Scudamore family, including Sir John and Sir William, 'brothers, knights in arms in France'; Sir John, ' the most valiant' of his family, seems to have brought a contingent of thirty men. Worcestre listed fourteen esquires who fought for Edward. Among them, he described Richard Haclethes as 'of war', Mr. Harper of Wellington and Henry Apgryffyth as men 'of war', and John Mylewater (son of the Duke of York's receiver), Walter Mutton, and Philip Vaughan of Hay as men 'of the war of France'. Vaughan, he said, 'the most noble esquire of lances among all the rest, was slain at the siege of Harlech Castle by a gunshot'. Worcestre was interested in the continuation by sons of their father's military traditions; Reginald Brygges's father was 'a man of war', and James Assh's father Hopkin, 'a handsome man', had fought in France.[41] It seems probable that commanders and captains who fought at Mortimer's Cross and in the intense campaigning of 1459–61 would have been keen to season novices and raw recruits with old archers who claimed they were 'of war', especially if they reminisced convincingly about the good times in France. Even in the late 1460s there may have been veteran rankers as well as veteran commanders. In 1468 William Herbert, now Earl of Pembroke, (former garrison captain in Maine and subordinate on campaign to Gough) took the surrender of Harlech from Dafydd ap Ieuan ap Einion, who had a long record of service in France.[42] However, the price of civil war as well as the toll of time had thinned the ranks of veterans by then, doubtless lowborn as well as high. In the wars of 1459–61 many famous commanders, some of them once regarded as English heroes for their deeds against the French, were killed or executed, their blood sometimes besmirched with treason – the Dukes of Somerset, Buckingham, and York, Lord Scales, Sir Thomas Kyriel, Andrew Trollope, Osbert Mountford.[43]

We may conclude that one reason why some lords confidently resorted to rebellion in the 1450s and others as confidently opposed them was because there was a conspicuous pool of unemployed veterans in England and Wales with no foreseeable employment prospects, embittered at their losses, and keen to serve again under their old commanders and captains alongside former comrades. The recruitment of ageing ex-professionals, eager to prove that the skills of their prime were undiminished and to recoup their finances, and the eagerness of younger, unproved men to learn their skills and win their approval, may help to explain the ferocity and tenacity with which some of the battles were fought. The civil war of 1459–61 may, indeed, have slightly augmented the pool of habitually unemployed ex-professionals, for James II of Scotland took advantage of it to besiege Roxburgh Castle, resulting in its surrender in 1460, and the following year Henry VI, fleeing into Scotland after the disaster of Towton, handed over Berwick to the Scottish Crown. However, though domestic conflict lingered on in the Anglo-Scottish Borders till 1464, and in Gwynedd till 1468, it did not provide a permanent boost to English professional soldiering. In the civil wars of 1469–71, some 'old soldiers of Normandy' were, as we have seen, conspicuous, but they were the last generation of a diminished profession. Commynes was to observe that the army with which Edward IV invaded northern France in 1475, though well equipped, lacked experience: 'these were not the Englishmen of his [Edward's] father's day and the former wars with France. They were inexperienced and raw soldiers, ignorant of French ways'. He went on to remark, 'I tell no lie when I say that Edward's troops seemed to be very inexperienced and new to action in the field as they rode in very poor order'.[44] Indeed, Commynes had axes to grind – he wished to glorify his old master Louis XI, and condemn Edward's ally Charles the Bold for folly in not stiffening the English army with a substantial body of experienced Burgundian troops. However, he recognised the potential of the English, and elsewhere in his *Memoirs* was second to none in his praise for the combat and tactical skills of English archers in Charles's service.[45] Edward's army undoubtedly had a predominance of raw recruits, for it was one of the largest English armies to have invaded France, with over 11,400 combatants.[46]

THE CALAIS OPTION

The one remaining permanent training ground and area of concentration for English troops, after the loss of Berwick in 1461, was the March of Calais – whose garrisons were well placed to invade south-eastern England. However, they had played no role in English rebellions since the port capitulated to Edward III in 1347. In November 1387, when the Lords Appellant rose in arms against Richard II, Sir William Beauchamp, brother of one of them, the Earl of Warwick, was lieutenant of the March. He was sympathetic to their cause, but kept the garrisons passive.[47] The Appellants did not need their military support. For when news of the rebels' appearance in arms in the vicinity of London spread through the country, 'huge numbers of gentlemen came flocking from all directions to join them'.[48] It is likely that they were able to attract soldiers who had served in their retinues on major expeditions in recent years – the invasion of Scotland in 1385, the defence of London against threatened French invasion in 1386, and the Earl of Arundel's naval expedition in 1387.[49] In 1399 Henry of Bolingbroke, in exile in France, embarked to raise rebellion in England. The Calais garrisons remained loyal to Richard, though Henry may have hoped to subvert them: he sailed from Boulogne, nearby, with the help of English merchants and their shipping.[50]

Under Lancastrian rule, discontent sometimes occurred in the Calais garrisons when pay fell into arrears, especially in the 1450s when the Duke of Somerset (killed at St Albans in 1455) was lieutenant. The Earl of Warwick, subsequently appointed as lieutenant by York (Protector of the Realm as a consequence of his victory), 'politicised' the garrison and gained a long-lasting hold over the loyalties of the soldiers. As Dr David Grummit has demonstrated, he did this, after gaining entry into the port in 1456, by arranging for the Company of the Staple (merchants with a royal monopoly to export English wool through Calais) to pay arrears of the garrisons' wages, and by appointing his own men as captains and officers in the March. He cultivated relations with merchants and soldiers, doubtless displaying his well-known affability with the commons. Unusually for magnates who held the captaincy, Professor Hicks points out, he resided in person. His privateering (he was appointed keeper of the seas in 1457) probably profited some of the soldiers and was widely popular. The strong anti-court sentiments in Kentish ports (which had close ties with Calais) and their hinterlands are likely to have boosted his popularity too.[51]

Nevertheless, Warwick's first attempt to embroil Calais soldiers helped to bring near-disaster to the Yorkist cause. In 1459, when York and his allies felt threatened by a resurgent court party, Warwick led a few hundred men from the Calais garrison to England, passing through London and the Midlands to link up with the Duke of York and his own father, the Earl of Salisbury, in arms at the Duke's castle and town of Ludlow (Shropshire). The campaign which the Yorkists launched thence into the Midlands quickly turned into a retreat to Ludlow in face of the superior numbers of Henry VI's army, which pursued and confronted them nearby at Ludford Bridge, over the River Teme. There York's army disintegrated: among the deserters who submitted to the offer of royal pardons were the veteran Andrew Trollope, who held the office of Master Porter of Calais, and soldiers from the garrison.[52] Warwick, fleeing England with Salisbury and March after the debacle, took refuge in Calais. The bulk of the soldiers there actively supported their rebellion; expeditions were launched across the Channel in December 1459 and June 1460, which dislodged forces mustered at the port of Sandwich (Kent) for the invasion of the March of Calais. This left the one Lancastrian force which had succeeded in establishing itself in the March isolated at Guines Castle. It was commanded by the young third Duke of Somerset, with Trollope among his captains. In this crucial miniature civil war on both sides of the Channel, fought probably mostly by professionals, Somerset and Trollope alone had some success for King Henry. They had nuisance value in harrying the environs of Calais, but were too weak (especially after a reverse in a skirmish at Newnham Bridge) to deter the Yorkist lords from invading Kent with garrison forces in July 1460.[53]

After the Yorkist triumph in England, Somerset surrendered Guines Castle to Warwick, but for much of 1461 another castle in the March, at Hammes, was in Lancastrian hands, and was held against garrison forces from Calais and Guines between April and October, when its captain capitulated on lucrative terms. Back in England, Somerset and Trollope were to be among the architects of the revival of Lancastrian fortunes. Trollope was prominent in the victories at Wakefield in December and at St Albans in 1461, winning a great reputation for his courage. He was killed at Towton.[54] So the early conflicts were heavily sustained by the involvement of the Crown's main group of professional soldiers, and successes on both sides were in some cases based on their participation. The conflicts of 1459–61 in which these professionals were involved raised their profiles, and doubtless their expectations and self-esteem. Expelled from picking over the bones of France, they were tempted to raise weapons against fellow countrymen by the prospect of English morsels. It was hardly conducive to the peace and stability of the realm for Calais soldiers to acquire a taste for soldiering in England, and a sense that they should have a say in ordering the affairs of the realm.

As lieutenant in the March under Edward IV from 1461 onwards, Warwick and his energetic deputies nourished the loyalty of the garrisons to him. The financial arrangements made with the Staplers ensured their wages. All this paid off for Warwick and Clarence when they went there in 1469 to raise rebellion against Edward. At Calais they issued a manifesto denouncing the King's councillors, and, in a re-run of the 1460 rebellion, sailed to Kent with a force with which they seized London, sealing the success of their supporters in England. However when, beaten men, they fled back to Calais the following year, though Warwick's deputy, Lord Wenlock, sympathised, the soldiers would not admit them on land.[55]

In the campaigns of 1471, soldiers from Calais only intervened after Edward's armies had killed Warwick at the battle of Barnet and destroyed the Lancastrian cause at the battle of Tewkesbury. Warwick's deputy at Calais, Sir George Broke, sent 300 soldiers from the garrison to support Fauconberg in his assault on London; the rankers may have anticipated opportunities to plunder in the city, or, at least, in its suburbs. After the failure of Fauconberg's attacks on the city, and retreat into Kent, Edward dispatched a force to Calais under his new lieutenant there, his trusted chamberlain, William Lord Hastings, and another of his leading supporters, John Lord Howard. The rebel captains at Calais submitted and received pardons. They (and earlier recalcitrant soldiers in garrison there) may have from the start of their venture across the Channel calculated that opponents would be anxious to negotiate with them, rather than risk undermining the defence of the King's precious French fortresses. Castles in France were priceless strategic and symbolic possessions for English kings. As Sir Thomas More said to his son-in-law, 'son Roper... if my head could win him [Henry VIII] a castle in France... it should not fail to go'.[56]

Yorkist and Tudor kings especially needed to maintain the garrisons in good order in the March, in view of the resurgence of French monarchical power and, once more, the recurrence of wars with the French Crown – but they also needed to take them out of domestic politics. They were generally successful in achieving these objectives. Pay was secure. The lieutenancy was no longer put in the hands of magnates, but of lords and knights closely associated with the King's chamber, courtiers who gave close personal loyalty and service to the King. Henry VII, copying Edward IV, put his chamberlain, Lord Daubeney, in as lieutenant. Edward and his successors kept other appointments there in their own hands, giving them to officers of the royal household. Any rumour of subversive talk among officers at Calais is likely to have alarmed Henry VII – such as the allegation that Sir Nicholas Vaux, lieutenant of Guines, and Sir Anthony Browne, lieutenant of Calais Castle, when there was speculation about the succession, had said that 'they had two good holds to resort unto, the which they said should be sure to make their peace, howsoever the world turn'.[57]

Indeed, in the winter of 1484–5, the exiled Henry had himself been privy to an attempt to subvert loyalties to Richard III

there. His supporter John de Vere, Earl of Oxford, imprisoned in
Hammes Castle, won over its captain, Sir James Blount, to Henry's
cause. They went into France, leaving behind a garrison whose
allegiance they had turned. Despite a siege by garrison troops
from Calais, Oxford was able to slip reinforcements into the castle;
safe-conducts for the garrison were eventually negotiated.[58]
Maybe the soldiers at Hammes had been won over to the
unknown Tudor by promises that, backed by the French Crown,
he could provide higher wages. We do not know what happened
to the Hammes company. A good deal has been heard about
Henry's foreign mercenaries at Bosworth. Could it be that he
had a company of tried and tested English professionals too? The
conflict in the March in 1484–5 is in some ways reminiscent of
events there in 1459–61, but the failure of Oxford to subvert
Richard's other commanders and main body of garrison troops
reflects the changed relationship of military personnel in the
March to the Crown. Henry Tudor, after the failure of his supporters to get a grip on the March, tried Warwick's alternative
invasion strategy of 1470, basing his force on Normandy, with
backing from the French Crown. The main standing forces of
the English Crown, a factor in provoking and sustaining the civil
wars, were no longer of such crucial account in doing so.

NEW OPPORTUNITIES ABROAD:
THE BURGUNDIAN OPTION

The conflicts of 1459–61 were probably the last military fling
for many veterans of the French wars. They may have given
some participants of a new generation a taste for soldiering, as
later episodes in the Wars of the Roses may have done – the
fighting in 1469–71 and the campaigns of 1483, 1485 and 1487.
There were unemployed soldiers around: John Paston hired
some to defend Caister Castle against the Duke of Norfolk's
siege in 1469, as we have seen, and towns probably contracted
companies to meet the demands placed on them in this period
of internecine conflict.[59] Yet after 1471 there was no sustained

domestic warfare to give continued employment to soldiers. Opportunities arose because the Crown once more occasionally raised forces to support allies abroad or allowed them to recruit soldiers in England. Besides, there were Edward IV's invasion of France in 1475, Richard, Duke of Gloucester's invasion of Scotland in 1482, and Henry VII's of France in 1492. None of these expeditions led to lengthy campaigns and continuing warfare. However, the recapture of Berwick on the expedition of 1482 necessitated the reconstitution of powerful garrisons in the town and castle, especially in view of James III's and James IV's ambitions to recover it.[60] Moreover, Edward's ally the Duke of Albany, James III's rebellious younger brother, handed over his castle at Dunbar to an English garrison in about April 1483. It was to be occasionally besieged, and fell before the end of June 1486, after an investment which had lasted from 6 December 1485. Henry VII did not value this far-forward possession; he made no attempt to have the castle relieved.[61]

Nevertheless, many Englishmen remained keen to seek fame and fortune on military service abroad, in the footsteps of their forbears, if necessary under foreign princes. The awe with which some foreign observers reported the amount of blood shed in some of the battles of 1460–1 and 1469–71 suggests that the Wars may have served as a good advertisement for the courage, tenacity and skills of the English and Welsh in combat. The Flemish noble Philippe de Commynes, speaking from personal experience, emphasised the desirability of having large numbers of longbowmen if they were to be effective. As he says, Burgundian military tactics were heavily influenced by those of the English. His generally high opinion of the potential of English soldiers (doubtless encompassing the Welsh, too) continued to be a common one on the continent. The renewal of large-scale warfare in north-west Europe provided them with a steady, long-term market for their skills.[62] From the late 1460s until the 1490s, the service of the Dukes of Burgundy, rulers of much of the Low Countries, was the best nursery of war available for English and Welsh soldiers. A leading Norfolk landowner, Sir John Howard, sent his young son and heir Thomas to go with other English gentlemen, possibly in 1465, to serve his military apprenticeship with the future Duke of Burgundy, Charles, at war with Louis XI of France. Apparently young Thomas won golden opinions, and on his return to England was made esquire of the body by Edward IV.[63]

Duke Philip the Good (d. 1467) employed individual English archers, but his son Charles the Bold from the start of his reign recruited them to form companies, some retained on a long-term basis and others on contracts of up to six months. Archduke Maximilian of Habsburg (the future emperor), who governed the Low Countries in right of his wife, Charles's daughter and heir Mary, and after her death in 1481 on behalf of their infant son Philip, favoured short contracts.[64] Mounted archers were particularly in demand, but foot archers and a few men-at-arms (the latter more expensive to employ) were also needed. The pro-Lancastrian Charles's rapprochement with Edward IV had facilitated organised, large-scale recruitment in England. In 1467 Edward licensed contracts for his campaign against Liège: up to 500 Englishmen, mainly archers, served on it.[65] Charles's marriage the following year to Edward's sister Margaret (d. 1503) established an Anglo-Burgundian link which was an encouragement for Englishmen to seek their fortunes by military service in the Low Countries. Margaret of York was to make a habit of employing them in her guard.[66]

In 1473 500 English archers took part in Charles's invasion of the duchy of Guelders; later that year, Sir John Par and John Sturgeon esquire planned a muster of thirteen men-at-arms and 1,000 archers for the ducal service at Southwark.[67] In Charles's report on his confrontation with the army of the Emperor Frederick III at Neuss in Lorraine in 1475 (which did not result in a battle), he mentioned the joint dispositions of the English archers of his household guard and of a separate company of them commanded by Sir John Middleton.[68] When, that year, Edward IV made a truce with Louis XI, and returned with his army from Calais to England, over 2,000 of his soldiers opted to join Charles's service. In the last two years of Charles's reign (1476–77), his English mercenaries were in the thick of the fighting to conquer Lorraine and defend ducal lands against French attack. Up to his death in battle at Nancy, he maintained ten English companies (each with a nominal strength of 100), including four composed of mounted archers, 'the companies of the guard'.[69] In 1476, in the camp at Lausanne, the *trésorier des guerres* accounted for 1,277 English troops among the 9,748 on his books.

According to Commynes, 300 English formed part of the garrison at Nancy. Its defence against the forces of the Duke of Lorraine was commanded by a member of the influential Croy family, Jean de Rubempré, Lord of Bièvres. The English were captained by Colpin, 'a valiant man although from humble stock whom he [Rubempré] had brought with others from the garrison at Guines into the duke's service'. After Colpin was killed by a cannon-shot, the morale of the English plummeted, with no hope of speedy relief. It was Commynes' opinion that their agitation was one of the reasons why Rubempré negotiated the surrender of Nancy – the historian's verdict was that 'they did not understand siege warfare very well'.[70] If he was right, the point suggests that campaigning in the Wars of the Roses had failed to provide soldiers to garrison Guines – one of the king of England's most vulnerable frontier fortresses – with the potential expertise and stomach to defend it effectively.

In Charles's final battle, English soldiers redeemed any blots on their reputation from this episode and from recent outbreaks of disorder in some of their companies. Charles, encamped outside Nancy, and determined to recover it, was surprised and overwhelmed by a devastating Swiss attack. A defensive line of cannons and archers had been hastily formed to hold their advance, which it did briefly until the positions were outflanked. The English took heavy casualties. John Turneboulle, captain (*centenier*), afterwards mustered only thirty-four of his company of ninety-six.[71]

English mercenaries continued to play important roles in the service of Charles's heirs in the crisis after his death and for long afterwards. In 1478 Thomas Everingham of Stainborough (Yorkshire) was in command of eighty archers garrisoning Oudenaarde in Flanders. They were part of a force which defeated the French at Izegen.[72] When Archduke Maximilian fought the invading French at Guinegate next year, Everingham commanded about 500 foot archers.[73] In 1480 agreement was reached between Edward IV and his sister the Duchess Margaret, as part of an anti-French alliance, for the supply of thirty men-at-arms and 1,500 archers. They were to be organised in retinues of equal size captained by Middleton and Everingham, with Sir John Ditchfield commanding a section of Middleton's retinue. Sailing from Hull, this army joined up with 'the old English' who had been garrisoning Cassel. Soldiers directly under Middleton's command were licensed to return home from mid-March 1481 onwards, but the other companies took part in the campaign against rebels in Holland. Maximilian authorised their discharge by May.[74] He continued to employ English soldiers. They fought for him at Dixmude in Flanders in 1489 against rebels and their French allies, where young Henry Lovel, Lord Morley, was killed, and they were to garrison Sluis, a move co-ordinated with Henry VII's invasion of France.[75]

Though employment in Burgundian service might be erratic and brief, and the payment of wages a problem, the service had considerable attractions for Englishmen who aspired to be soldiers. They were needed intermittently over a long period; the rates of pay were reasonable.[76] There continued to be high hopes of honour and gain from serving Charles and Maximilian, who projected themselves as the foremost exponents of chivalry of their day. Charles knighted Ditchfield in 1475, and Maximilian knighted Everingham before the battle of Guinegate.[77] The services of those who had distinguished themselves in the wars of Burgundy were eagerly snapped up at home. Middleton was a knight of the king's body in 1480; he and Everingham were active in 1482 in the defence of the northern Marches, where Gloucester was lieutenant-general.[78] Everingham appears to have taken part in the suppression of the revolt against King

Richard in 1483, since he was well rewarded with forfeited estates afterwards.[79] The following year, in close co-operation with the King, he was in command of a naval force based in Scarborough, which was hotly engaged in a seafight with the Scots.[80]

One factor which established the option of Burgundian service as attractive was the high regard in which Charles held English archers. This was reflected in the remarkable tolerance the mettlesome prince displayed towards the indiscipline of some of them in the difficult campaigning conditions of his last years. A crisis arose at the siege of Neuss; 300 Englishmen threatened to desert unless they received their pay. Charles responded by threatening to attack them, and they calmed down. Two captains were arrested. The same day, after supper, a quarrel arose among the English over a girl. The Duke set out to appease them in person; they failed to recognise him, and bows were loosed in his direction. A rumour spread round the camp that the English had wounded the Duke and they were attacked; some were killed, some robbed. However, next day Charles had it proclaimed that their goods were to be returned and 'that there was to be no debate or argument with them, for he recognized them as his friends and subjects, and he pardoned them for having offended him'.[81] Next year, in camp at Lausanne, English mercenaries clashed bloodily with Italian ones. The following month many of the English left their posts and made for Charles's quarters, brandishing bows and demanding pay. Appearing at a window, the Duke addressed them in English: he persuaded them to lay down their arms and kneel to beg his pardon.[82] There are parallels between the mutinous behaviour of his English troops and that exhibited on occasion in the past by garrisons in the March of Calais, incensed over arrears of pay.

On contract in the Burgundian army, English soldiers had good opportunities to learn their trade according to the most up-to-date European methods and doctrines, especially as developed by Charles, who avidly promoted professional organisation. In his report on the field dispositions adopted by his army at Neuss in 1475, he describes how his archers were grouped together so that they co-operated with the other arms.[83] As we have seen, Burgundian rulers used the English to garrison towns as well as in the field. They were also selected as shock troops to attack urban fortifications. At the siege of Nijmegen in 1473, the English seized the Nieuwstadgate, but, lacking support, they were forced to withdraw. At the siege of Neuss they assaulted a gate, but had to withdraw with heavy losses.[84] In 1480 Everingham, with 120 men under his command, captured a gate at Dordrecht, a prelude to the fall of the town.[85]

Maybe inexperience in siege warfare was a factor in the English failures at Nijmegen and Neuss. The one notable if brief assault on urban fortifications in the Wars was the Bastard of Fauconberg's on London in 1471 – in which, as we have seen, elements of the Calais garrison were involved. Considerable professionalism was shown by both the besieged and besiegers.[86] However, on his invasion of France in 1475, Edward IV eschewed siege warfare. In 1482, during Gloucester's invasion of Scotland, the Earl of Northumberland invested Berwick Castle, whose captain, lacking hope of relief, eventually surrendered.[87] Maybe there was a leavening of English soldiers available by the 1480s who had valuable continental experience of siege warfare. Spaniards were complimentary about the actions of the English crusading company who took part in the siege of Loja in Granada in 1486.[88] In 1492 Henry VII showed more boldness than the battle-hardened Edward IV by investing a French town, Boulogne – but only for a fortnight.

It is, indeed, unclear whether English soldiers with experience of Burgundian service influenced tactics in the battles of the Wars of the Roses, bringing to bear the doubtless formidable skills in manoeuvring in formation, in conjunction with pikemen, hand-gunners and cannoneers, which they had learnt in some of the principal theatres of Western European warfare in the period. The pick of their formations are likely to have been unavailable, under contract to the Burgundian rulers, unless released by them for service in England. In 1471 Duke Charles

gave limited financial and material help to Edward for his invasion of England. It may be that the force of a few hundred with
which he landed, and which supported him staunchly through
difficult circumstances, included some English archers from the
Low Countries, and so may the company under the Spanish
captain Salaçar, probably released from Maximilian's service,
which is likely to have been a reliable component of Richard
III's army in 1485.[89]

If English veterans of the wars of Burgundy served on occasion in the Wars, either as individuals or in companies, they may
have had an influence in training and steadying inexperienced
and hastily raised recruits. Yet the forty French captains who
tried to teach Scottish recruits pike drill before James IV's invasion of England in 1513 seem to have had little success.[90] English
veterans, however, would have had the advantage that they spoke
dialects of the same tongue as indigeneous levies, and were
expert in handling weapons familiar to them. One can imagine
captains of repute such as Middleton and Everingham, and their
old soldiers of Burgundy, having their skills studied on the 1482
campaign with the awe with which those of Chandos, Calveley
and Knolles were regarded in the fourteenth century. High
professional standards were apparently shown by Henry Tudor's
archers in his vanguard at Bosworth. They were commanded
by John de Vere, Earl of Oxford, a thoughtful and experienced
soldier. Polydore Vergil describes how the Earl disengaged and
regrouped his troops, then relaunched them into attack in a
tighter formation – tricky and demanding manoeuvres once
battle was joined. The Duke of Norfolk, commanding the royal
vanguard (probably composed in part of his retinue and other
arrayed men from East Anglia) does not seem to have been able
to get it to respond with the same level of coolness and expertise. If Vergil's description is accurate, Oxford's archers helped
to execute a model advance which would have earned praise
from leading exponents of fifteenth-century continental warfare.
However, we cannot be certain that they were Welsh or English
archers – they may have been French.[91]

Native veterans and aspirants in the 1470s and 80s may have hoped that an English prince or lord would emerge in what at times augured to be the piping times of peace, who would provide large-scale employment abroad. Gloucester, who led a retinue on the invasion of France in 1475, was disappointed by the premature curtailment of the campaign, and in the early 1480s gave active employment to military men as lieutenant general of the Marches. He even set up a new, if small, garrison, in the fort at Bewcastle in the West March, in 1478. This was a forward frontier post in desolate Bewcastle Waste, likely to provide plenty of action against reivers from Liddesdale who filtered through the Waste in order to raid farms in the Eden valley.[92] However, when king, he had to curb his ambitions to intervene in France, concentrating on shoring up his shaky basis of domestic support.

Another possible leader of professionals achieved military prominence in 1483, at the start of Edward V's brief reign. This was the King's uncle (and Edward IV's brother-in-law), Sir Edward Wydeville. He had become conspicuous as (in Sir Thomas More's phrase) one of the 'promoters and companions' of Edward IV's vices.[93] An indication that he was something of a stylish dandy may have been his depression at Loja in Granada in 1486 at having lost two or three teeth from a blow to the mouth, dealt to him when scaling the walls of the town. King Ferdinand of Aragon and Castile did his best to console him.[94] Wydeville had already gained military standing in Edward's reign. In 1472 he was in the force of 1,000 archers commanded by his brother Earl Rivers which helped Duke Francis of Brittany to repel a French invasion.[95] Gloucester respected his military talents, appointing him in 1482 as one of the knights banneret in the army for the invasion of Scotland.[96]

Soon after Edward IV's death, the regency council appointed Wydeville to the command of ships based at Southampton, with the aim of intercepting a French fleet threatening English commerce in the Channel. When Gloucester seized Edward V and arrested Rivers, he was anxious to get control of the fleet and to destroy Wydeville – who was inclined to defiance – offering rewards to anyone who took him dead or alive. In obedience to royal orders, most ships were taken back to port. The Italian observer Dominic Mancini recounts the dilemma of the captains of two requisitioned Genoese ships in terms which suggest Wydeville's high standing among professional soldiers. They had on board 'a most select group of British [*sic*] soldiers, and ones that by every kind of tie were most devoted to the commander Edward'. One of the ship's captains laid on a lavish dinner for the soldiers; 'they now lay upon the decks sodden with the wine of the previous night, or wandered about overcome with drowsiness'. A favourable wind had enabled the captain to get under way, and he succeeded in getting the sleepy, biddable soldiers below decks, ostensibly so that the Genoese sailors could work the ship more easily. 'Shortly afterwards they [the soldiers] were called up one by one from below the hatches and trussed up with ropes and chains by the Genoese'. Wydeville managed to retain the loyalty of the two ships' companies that he commanded in person, and escaped with them to Brittany, to join Henry Tudor.[97]

At this stage Richard seems to have been more fearful of Wydeville than Tudor. Within weeks of his accession, the envoy he dispatched to Duke Francis was instructed to sound out 'the mind and disposition of the duke against Sir Edward Wydeville and his retinue, practising… to ensearch and know if there be any intended enterprise out of land upon any part of this realm'.[98] Wydeville was, indeed, implacable towards the usurper. He may have been a principal source of the Spanish version of the 'black legend' about Richard III, since he visited the court in Spain in 1486 and came to be on friendly terms with King Ferdinand. The historian Alonso de Palencia (d. 1490) wrote that he had taken flight from the cruelty of Richard, usurper and murderer of princes.[99] The well-informed Continuator of the Crowland Chronicle, who singles him out as 'a most valiant knight', says that he fought for Henry at Bosworth. He was one of those rewarded soon afterwards by Henry for his services overseas and in the battle.[100] With such glittering prospects opening up for Wydeville, after his years of exile, it is the more curious that he soon left England, as if he had been one of Henry's foreign mercenaries. It may be that he was a swaggering courtier-soldier, and realised that he was temperamentally unlikely ever to be one of the King's intimates. Perhaps he was the sort who might have hit it off as a courtier with Henry VIII. Andrés Bernáldez, in his *Memorias*, gave a detailed description of his extravagant appearance at the Spanish court, in armour and finery which was 'very pompous [*ponposo*] and foreign in fashion'. Maybe in 1486 he wanted to seek out adventures as an acclaimed leader in the world of professional soldiers. More like English lords and captains in lulls in the later-fourteenth-century phase of the Hundred Years War, he seems to have taken a crusading vow, and he led a company off to join the Catholic Monarchs of Spain, Ferdinand and Isabella, in their current campaign of the war against the Muslim kingdom of Granada. He landed at Sanlucar with a company which Spanish commentators variously estimated as between 100- and 300-strong, and whose appearance and accoutrements made an excellent impression.[101] At the siege of Loja, according to Bernáldez, Wydeville said that he wished to fight according to the custom of his country. He dismounted; clad in plate armour (*blanco*), carrying his sword and axe, he advanced with a troop of his soldiers, similarly harnessed, and armed with axes. He threw himself into the midst of the Moors with great courage, dealing lethal blows. The Castilians followed the English lead, and the Moors were pushed back into the suburbs.[102]

However, Wydeville's commitment to crusading turned out to be only a temporary one. The Catholic Monarchs of Spain probably considered that, however welcome his contribution had been, they had no need to retain his services with further costly grants. Wydeville left Spain, returning home through Portugal, and visiting Lisbon. He was well received by King John II. He had hopes that Henry's deteriorating relations with the French Crown would open up a more rewarding field of activity – Brittany, where he had campaigned and resided. English nobles who read histories such as Froissart's *Chronicles* and continuations of *The Brut* must have been well aware how, under Edward III, the support of an Anglophile duke there had repeatedly brought honour and profit for the Crown and its captains. Edward IV had made alliances with Duke Francis in 1468, 1472 and 1473 which stipulated that English troops would go there, either to invade France with Breton support or help to defend the duchy against Louis XI's forces. However, Edward was wary about providing props for the Duke's ambitions to act like a sovereign ruler, without any sure prospect of tangible returns. The Duke backed down from confronting Louis' superior forces, concluding truces with him.[103] In 1488 Duke Francis faced invasion from the Regency government of the young Charles VIII, intent on thwarting his intention to marry his daughter and heir Anne to Maximilian. According to William Paston, it was rumoured that plans were afoot to send military aid to the Duke:

Also, where as it was said that my Lord Woddevyle and other should have gone over in to Brittany, to have aided the Duke of Brittany I cannot tell of none such aid. But upon that saying there came many men to Southampton, where it was said that he [Wydeville] should have taken shipping, to have waited upon him over; and so when he was countermanded, those that resorted thither, to have gone over with him tarried there still in hope that they should have been licensed to have gone over; and when they saw no likelihood that they should have had licence, there was 200 of them that got them in a Breton ship, the which was late come over with salt, and bade the master set them on land in Brittany. And they had not sailed not past six leagues but they aspied a Frenchman, and the Frenchman made over to them; and they feared as though they would not have meddled with them, and all the Englishmen went under the hatches, so that they showed no more but those that came to Southampton with the ship, to cause the Frenchman to be the more gladder to meddle with them; and so the Frenchmen boarded them, and then they

that were under the hatches came up, and so took the Frenchman,
and carried the men, ship and all into Brittany.[104]

Wydeville's reputation seems to have been a magnet for military
men. He put himself at the head of the English mercenaries who
sailed to Brittany. Apparently, he went without royal licence – a
grave offence, which suggests a restless and unbiddable character.
He and many other English soldiers were killed in the crushing
defeat of Duke Francis by the French at St Aubin-du-Cormier.
His death was noted by Castilian historians. Francis capitulated,
and died soon afterwards. This increased the threat of French
domination. Besides strenuous efforts to shore up the Duchess
Anne's independent role, in 1489 Henry dispatched an army
of 6,000 to Brittany, commanded by Robert, Lord Willoughby,
which occupied Morlaix and Concarneau. However, as Breton
resistance crumbled, the soldiers had to be withdrawn.[105] No
charismatic commander like Wydeville appears to have replaced
him as the leader of English professional soldiers, though Lords
Willoughby and Daubeney were to carry on worthily the tradition of nobles serving the Crown as commanders in war.
However, the Crown only re-established itself as a formidable
military presence on the continent, deploying large numbers of
professionals, with Henry VIII's invasion of France in 1513.

FOREIGN MERCENARIES IN ENGLAND

The pool of experienced English soldiers, and those who might
be termed professional, was small from the 1470s onwards. They
were not always easily accessible or available for domestic conflict, but those who took part are likely to have had an impact
disproportionate to their numbers. In the later stages of the Wars,
exiles plotting invasion who could not recruit sufficient numbers of
them, and were unsure of stirring up renewed support for rebellion
in England, recruited foreign mercenaries. Their use sometimes
flowed from the deals made with foreign princes eager to keep the
dynastic conflict alive as a way of muzzling hostile English kings.

The employment of foreign mercenaries by English kings was as old as English kingship itself. Edward I had used them notably in his Welsh and Scottish wars, and Edward III in the Hundred Years War. In the muster roll for the Earl of Arundel's expedition against Charles VI of France and his uncle Philip the Bold, Duke of Burgundy, in 1388 we find listed 'Herre Nikel Rebintz' and several other men-at-arms whose names sound Dutch or German.[106] For his expedition of 1415 to France, Henry V hired ships (and probably their crews) from Dutch ports, and there were many individuals with Germanic names in Lancastrian armies in France, particularly specialists such as artillerymen.[107] There were, however, drawbacks about employing foreign mercenaries in domestic conflict. They were expensive. It was often not feasible to raise them as speedily and secretly as native levies. Their military skills might be difficult to integrate with those of the latter. Their presence was likely to arouse misgivings among English folk: the original version of Magna Carta had stipulated that King John's mercenary captains should be expelled from the realm. In the 1450s and 60s it would, indeed, have added to Henry VI's and Edward IV's security and provided them with a stable nucleus for an army, if they had had foreign companies of the guard on the scale that Charles VII and Charles the Bold did. However, that would have imposed an unwelcome financial burden on English monarchs strapped for cash.

The earliest mention of the use of foreign mercenaries in the Wars of the Roses seems to be the contemptuous dismissal in *Gregory's Chronicle* of the skills of a company of gunners who fought on the Yorkist side at St Albans in 1461, deployed ineffectively.[108] In 1462–3 Margaret of Anjou's attempt to revive Henry VI's cause in Northumberland depended on Brézé's force of *c*.2,000 mercenaries, subsidised by Louis XI. They did well in difficult terrain and unfamiliar circumstances, showing their abilities in defending castles, but they could not sustain their control in the face of the overwhelming force deployed by Edward IV and his lieutenants.[109] This campaign was the first in which foreigners had a high profile in the Wars. When Edward

landed in Yorkshire in 1471, part of his force consisted of a company of 300 Flemish handgunners.[110] When Margaret of Anjou
landed in the West Country to oppose him later that year, she
probably had French soldiers in her force: the 'Forey of France'
executed after Edward's victory at Tewkesbury may have been
one of them.[111] Richard III seems to have been maintaining a
foreign company in England from at least 6 March 1484 under
the Spanish captain Salaçar – an exceptional measure, an index
of his sense of insecurity. It is to be presumed that they stood
by him at Bosworth until the position appeared hopeless, when
Salaçar vainly urged Richard to flee.[112] As recent accounts of
Henry's invasion have emphasised, it was financed by the French
Crown, and mercenary companies, both French and Scottish,
were an important constituent of Henry's army. His grant of an
earldom (of Bath) to Philibert de Chandée, captain general of
his French soldiers, suggests that they played an important part
in his victory at Bosworth. Henry was to be sparing in creating
new titles of nobility.[113]

Thereafter foreign mercenaries (and probably some English
ones too) were to be a main prop for further dynastic broils.
Margaret of York, dowager duchess of Burgundy, supported the
impostures and invasions of Lambert Simnel and Perkin Warbeck
(the latter masquerading as Edward IV's younger son Richard,
Duke of York) in Henry VII's reign. The backbone of the force
with which her nephew the Earl of Lincoln invaded England
(with Simnel in tow) in 1487 was composed of German and
Swiss mercenaries, commanded by a leading German captain,
Martin Schwarz of Augsburg. When they and their Irish allies
were routed at Stoke, they were, according to one source, allowed
no quarter.[114] Nevertheless, with the Duchess Margaret's aid,
Warbeck was able to recruit mercenaries in the Low Countries
in the 1490s. Rodigue de Lalaing and Pedro and Fulano de
Guevara were well-reputed captains in a force of over 1,300 with
which Warbeck hove to off the coast of Kent in 1495. After a
reverse near Deal, he moved on to try his luck in Ireland, then
Scotland. Not all his mercenaries went on his further voyages;

some were lost in the skirmish, and Lalaing turned up separately in Scotland, with a force of sixty Germans, to serve James IV on the intended invasion of England. Lalaing refused to have anything to do with Warbeck, whom he blamed for abandoning the companies which had landed in Kent. Lalaing, an illegitimate member of a notable family from the Low Countries, was to be appointed captain of the archers of Maximilian's son Philip, Duke of Burgundy. Perhaps on the continent, hazarding one's military skills among the touchy and changeable English was regarded as an especially brave, chivalrous venture. Henry VII responded to James IV's belligerence by hiring mercenaries who had fought in Alsace for René, Duke of Lorraine – but the projected English invasion of Scotland in 1497 was cancelled.[115]

It is unlikely that the foreign mercenaries who got inland in significantly large numbers in England between the 1460s and the 1490s made any impact, except, sometimes, a notable military one. Their presence is only occasionally noted in English sources; their English employers wanted to dispense with their services as soon as possible. The presence even of aliens who came with peaceful intent, such as Italian and German merchants and Flemish artificers, might arouse hostility and cause riots.[116] Maybe the mercenaries had more of an effect than one can prove. Their formidable fighting skills, outlandish behaviour, camaraderie, and the gains they either flaunted or boasted about, may have spurred young men to try their fortunes abroad as soldiers; there may even have been chances for likely lads to fill empty places in the ranks of swaggering companies briefly in their midst. We may conclude that, although professional soldiers, both native and foreign, were often crucial elements in the various phases of the Wars, they rarely made up the bulk of the rank and file of the forces which fought in them.

ARRAYED MEN

Most soldiers who served in the Wars of the Roses were raised in England and Wales through organisational methods derived from the systems which had habitually been used to raise forces during the Hundred Years War, either to constitute companies for service abroad or for regional defence of the homelands. These systems, as they had evolved in the fourteenth century, were still in use in their traditional forms for waging war against the king's enemies abroad and at home well into Henry VIII's reign. Companies of men-at-arms and archers were raised by lords, knights and esquires, who contracted with the Crown for service with them on foreign expeditions. For defence against invasion, heavy reliance was placed on companies raised by local communities and generally recruited from among them; these companies often co-operated with or worked alongside the retinues of king and lords.

In domestic conflicts, servants and tenants of nobles and gentlefolk induced to serve in their companies may well have felt that it was an honour to ride beneath the banner of the lord, wearing his badge or colours, and have been eager to profit by receiving his wages for war. There was doubtless anticipation of his future goodwill and patronage as a consequence of faithful military service – and that of the Crown. However, there may often have been elements of compulsion in the summons. Many probably answered it with heavy heart, feeling that they were fulfilling inescapable obligations. During the Lincolnshire rebellion of 1536, two royal commanders accused Sir John Thrimbleby of assembling all his tenants as if he intended to join the King's forces, threatening to burn the houses of those who refused to go with him, and taking his whole company over to the rebels.[117]

The bulk of the companies in the field in most of the major campaigns of the Wars of the Roses are likely to have been composed of communal levies. In England, for generations kings had maintained, and redefined by statute, the ancient general obligations of adult males to take up arms in defence of king and realm. As we have seen, this sometimes included clergy.[118] Laymen were expected to maintain arms appropriate to their station, practise with them, and attend musters to have them inspected. A statute of 1388, which was re-enacted in 1410, prescribed that artisans and labourers were to possess bows and practise shooting on Sundays and feast days. In the fifteenth century, the obligatory period for active service was thirty days. The community from which the recruits were drawn had to provide them with wages for this period.[119]

The Crown appointed commissions of array charged with raising levies in a shire for inspection or service. These commissions were sometimes headed by a magnate with estates there, and they customarily comprised the sheriff, local knights and other militarily minded gentlefolk. In Edward IV's commission for Westmorland of 2 June 1463, the arrayers were empowered to summon and muster all lieges, for them to array according to their degree, and to attend on the King or others for the defence of the realm. The arrayers were to conduct the levies and were empowered to rule them. All sheriffs, mayors, bailiffs and constables in and out of liberties (areas of private jurisdiction) were to assist and obey them.[120]

In arraying, the role of the sheriff (or his deputy) was pivotal, since he and his officers, through having proclamations made, and royal writs delivered, were the principal customary channels of communication from the king to the mass of lieges. On 11 May 1464, Edward ordered the sheriffs of sixteen shires to have proclamations made that every man between the ages of sixteen and sixty was to be well armed, and ready to assist the King at a day's notice 'in Resistance of his Enemies and Rebels, and the Defence of his Realm, under the Pain that shall fall thereupon'.[121] The texts of proclamations, besides being read out at market crosses, were probably posted in public places, or passed around – for rebels during the Wars nailed up and distributed their 'bills', attempting to justify their resort to arms and to incite people to join them.[122] During the Pilgrimage of Grace, bills were sometimes set up on church doors. The church door was often a meeting-place and a marketing locality for villagers; the parish priest might be the only person in the community able to read. In 1536 a bill set up on the church door at Leeds in Yorkshire ran enigmatically: 'Commons, keep well your harness. Trust you no gentlemen. Rise all at once. God shall be your governor and I shall be your captain'. Bills which were set up shortly before this one, at four churches in Yorkshire, demonstrate one way in which summonses to arms were communicated at ground level. In the bills, the parish priest was ordered to tell the village constable to assemble the parishioners: a time and place were given.[123] At other times it may have been more usual for the constable to receive his orders by messenger from an arrayer or from the sheriff's office. During the 1536 revolt, men were sometimes summoned by the pealing of the parish church's bells – presumably a traditional call to arms. A device to inform neighbouring parishes that the men of a community were in arms was to peal them backwards. Levies might also be summoned by lighting beacons: in pastoral and woodland regions, dwellings might be too scattered for ease of communication by bells.[124]

The administrative units into which the rural parts of shires were divided (the hundreds and their equivalent in some northern shires, called wapentakes), each had their customary camping and mustering ground. There the arrayers had the task of inspecting the levies and organising them as companies. Edward's commission of 3 July 1468, appointing a commission for Cornwall, ordered them to array men-at-arms and other fencibles (*Homines Defensibiles*), light horsemen ('Hobelars') and archers in readiness to meet the threat of invasion. There were fears that Louis XI would back Lancastrian exiles and plotters. The Cornish arrayers were told to divide the levies by thousands, hundreds and twenties, or as they thought best. Beacons and watches were to be set.[125]

The organisation of the levies by arrayers was customarily facilitated by the fact that they were raised from townships and hundreds. Arrayers are likely to have preferred to keep them in their native groups or amalgamate them with levies from their neighbourhood. It was best to combine men who were used to working together and spoke similar dialects. At the muster of Lincolnshire rebels at Louth in 1536, the levies were drawn up by wapentake, and at the general muster of the Pilgrims outside

York, the men of each wapentake formed a separate company, with as its ensign a cross from one of its parish churches.[126]

Probably at some stage in the successive musters, men who were physically disabled or inadequately armed and equipped – the latter termed 'naked men' – were sometimes dismissed. There was a preference for 'tall' men, who would make an impressive show; height was needed the better to wield longbow, bill or poleaxe. The assembled arrayed men sometimes appeared woefully inadequate in the eyes of commanders. In 1486 Henry VII, going on progress to make his first solemn entry into York, received news of risings against him among the northerners. He summoned inadequately equipped arrays: 'he collected and brought up from the county of Lincoln a great multitude of men without arms, seemingly rather to pacify than exasperate a hostile population'. Presumably he calculated (rightly) that a large demonstration of support, rather than the threat of dire punishment, would deter the rebelliously inclined, and that the way to keep the – presumably lukewarm – Lincolnshire commons on side was not to insist that they buy arms, or to denigrate and dismiss them, but to make them feel that they constituted an honourable 'army royal', who would persuade their Yorkshire neighbours to stay loyal in a peaceable way. When Charles Brandon, Duke of Suffolk, arrived at Huntingdon to rally forces against the Lincolnshire rebels in 1536, he found that 'such men as are gathered there have neither harness nor weapons'.[127] It may be that some of the failures to engage forces in the Wars of the Roses were caused by commanders' doubts as to the morale and equipment of hastily raised levies. For instance, the East Anglian levies signally failed to oppose the advance of Edward's smaller force into southern England in 1471.[128]

At the general muster at latest, companies had to make the crucial choice of their 'petty captain', or have it made for them. At Louth in 1536, the commissioner of array who lived in each wapentake was chosen as the captain of its company.[129] In 1461, John Paston the youngest reported on the disorganised state of Norfolk levies: 'most people of this country have taken wages, saying they will go up to London; but they have no captain, nor ruler assigned by the commissioners to await upon, and so they straggle about by themselves, and by likeliness are not like to come to London half of them'.[130] Thus it was essential for good discipline to establish firmly the chain of command. Problems in doing so occurred particularly in rebel forces. In 1536 the commons of Beverley, mustered on West Wood Green, grew unruly. They rushed towards members of a local gentry family, the Stapletons, crying 'with terrible shouts "Captains! Captains!"'. In view of their unruly demeanour, William Stapleton undertook to be their captain, but relations between him and his men were to be for some time uneasy.[131]

A parallel system of array had been developed in Wales. In February 1460, Jasper Tudor, Earl of Pembroke, was commissioned to call out the lieges in Wales to counter the threat of invasion (from the Yorkists in exile). He was to muster men-at-arms and archers and depute his servants to hold musters.[132] In January 1471 Henry VI's government issued a commission of array, covering the Principality and Marches in South Wales, to guard against the threat of a Yorkist revival; the sheriffs were to assist the arrayers.[133]

How effective was the arraying system in the later Middle Ages, and how well did it function in general in the Wars? There is reason to believe that statutory injunctions to practise with the bow were widely observed, not necessarily out of zeal to fight in the king's wars or in rebellions, but because skill in archery was profitable and prestigious. A 'bowshot' was a common measure of distance. Frequent petitions of grievance to the Crown testify that, especially in a century when many great landowners were emparking waste agricultural land, in order to nurture and protect their game, trespassing in private chaces (as well as in the king's forest preserves), in order to shoot and poach, was something of a national sport. Illegal hunts were often carried out by mixed companies of gentlefolk and commoners. Popular ballad heroes – Robin Hood and Adam Bel – were described as living with their companies in the king's forests, killing and consuming his deer. Nevertheless, Adam and two of his fellows win the king's archery competition. In *A Geste of Robyne Hode*, the sheriff of Nottingham provides, as a prize for a competition, an arrow with a silver shaft and a head and feathers of gold, which, it is implied, is a uniquely valuable prize.[134] The supreme skill of one of Adam Bel's companions, William of Cloudesle, wins him an office with a fee of eighteen pence a day from the king, and from the queen the office of gentleman of the chamber with 12d a day. His companions become yeomen of her chamber, his young son a servant of her cellar, and his wife her gentlewoman and governess of her nursery.[135] The ballad of Adam Bel is one of day-dreaming wish-fulfilment, in which skill in archery transforms these outlaws from Cumberland, a remote and rough place in the eyes of most English people, into holders of coveted offices in the royal household, stepping stones to gentility and wealth! In this and other episodes, these ballads emphasise the importance for safety and achievement of teamwork, mutual dependence and good comradeship – qualities which were a necessary complement to technical skill on campaign as well as the competitive sports of village companies.

As we have seen, the bow was not the only weapon in whose use common folk were expert. In everyday living they needed to be skilled in fighting at close quarters with knife, dagger and whatever lay to hand, in order to defend themselves in brawls and assaults. At Agincourt, when the archers had used up all their arrows, 'seizing axes, stakes and swords and spearheads that were lying about, they struck, hacked and stabbed the enemy'.[136] Adam Bel and his company were mean sword and buckler men. In the ballad about them, the mayor of Carlisle wields a pole-axe against them.[137] At Loja in 1486, Wydeville's crusaders did terrible execution with their axes.[138] Many common soldiers fought with the bill – which was to be used by them with deadly effect against the unwieldly and inexpertly handled pikes of the Scots at Flodden. The bill was an even cheaper weapon than the bow and arrow. Like the poleaxe, it could be cobbled together from farm equipment – a pole with a scythe fixed to

its head. Communal farming skills such as mowing and threshing
– as well as the common sport of fighting with staves – made
the bill a potentially formidable weapon in the hands of farm
labourers.

So group farming activities, some perhaps performed in
unison rhythmically by males of all ages, were helpful in instill-
ing disciplines which could be adapted for military purposes.
We do not have evidence that arrayed men practised together
regularly in large bodies, like the later trained bands; they were
ad hoc forces gathered on a big scale occasionally for emergencies. The fact that the shire arrays were made up of units of
neighbours may have given them some coherence and *esprit
de corps*. The men of a parish or even of a hundred, drawn up
beneath their parochial crosses and banners, are likely to have
wanted to outshine their neighbours, with whom they may have
been accustomed to having competitions in archery, football and
stave-fighting. Communal disgrace had to be avoided.

The arraying system remained basically unchanged over a long
period – but, in the majority of shires, it was never put to the
test to resist a major foreign invasion. When arrays were called
out to resist foreign incursions, a heavy responsibility rested on
the king (if present) and leading nobles, with their well-equipped
and well-motivated retinues, to instil discipline and put heart
into these scratch (and sometimes ragged) soldiers. The chronicler Walsingham blamed the difficulties of the levies in Sussex
in combating French raids on the coast in the 1370s on the
failure of the leading local landowners, John of Gaunt, Duke of
Lancaster, and the Earl of Arundel, to reside with their retinues
and defend the land.[139] However, the men of Dartmouth were
widely praised for the stoutness with which they repelled a
French incursion in 1404. They did not need noble leadership:
their seamen had a long history of privateering and piracy, and
in recent years had been heavily engaged in breaking the truces
with France and its allies. As a result of Henry V's conquests,
the need of southern English communities within easy striking
distance of the coasts to maintain their defences was greatly

diminished. Until 1435, the continental littoral from Holland to Finisterre was in the control of the English and their allies.

However, by 1451, apart from Calais, this control had evaporated; southern English coastal communities had experienced French raids anew. This changed situation is likely to have revived the array system. There were the widespread commissions for the assignment and funding of archers in 1457. In the second half of the fifteenth century, the arraying system in numerous shires probably remained in much better shape for exploitation in civil war.[140] Indeed, there were occasions when scratch levies performed well in the Wars. In 1471, Jasper Tudor and his nephew Henry (aged fourteen) were besieged in Pembroke Castle. The siege was broken by Daffyd Thomas; according to later tradition,

> he had suddenly gathered together a rude rabble to the number of
> eight thousand within the compass of eight days and so attended
> by his ragged regiment, with hooks, prongs, glaives and other
> rustic weapons, he sets upon the besiegers, forceth his brother
> [commander of the besiegers] from the siege, rescueth the two
> Earls, and so conveys them to Tenbie... and ther safelie enshipped
> them for Brittany.[141]

If that was how it was, Henry Tudor, then at an impressionable age, may have optimistically recalled it when he relied on the Lincolnshiremen in 1486. The commons, when fired up, could give a good account of themselves, even when scruffy and indifferently equipped. Kings and nobles, however, preferred not to rely on a ragged regiment of rustics, whom they considered to be ill armed and accoutred. In the illuminations of manuscripts, they had themselves and their sort portrayed as leading men to war turned out, to do their commander credit, with identical and uniformly fine weapons, shiny helmets and harness, and colourful tunics. The reality could be very different! A later London chronicle was to recall sneeringly the reactions of countryfolk to the arrival of the Bastard of Fauconberg's rebellious army and navy to invest London in 1471:

Whereof the fame being blown into Essex, the faint husbands
cast from them their sharp scythes and armed themselves with
their wives' smocks, cheese cloths and old sheets and weaponed
them with great and heavy clubs and long pitchforks and ashen
staves, and so in all haste sped them toward London, making their
avaunt that they would be revenged upon the mayor for setting so
easy pennyworths of their butter, cheese, eggs, pigs and all other
victual, and so joined them unto the Kentishmen.[142]

It may be that womenfolk in Essex agitated for their men to
join in the rebellion, for peasant women in London's hinterlands took leading roles in processing and marketing foodstuffs
for the capital. The men's donning of smocks, cheesecloths and
sheets, items associated with females and their domestic labours,
if it occurred, may have been intended to promote the wives'
complaints about civic price-fixing. The outlandish attire could,
too, have been intended as a means of identification, perhaps
agreed with boisterous humour – it was the merry month of
May. One wonders whether some of the women came along
too, having exchanged clothes with their menfolk. 'Women',
Professor Manning has written, 'played a significant role in Tudor
and Stuart social protest'. They were prominent in food and
anti-enclosure riots. The Elizabethan scholar William Lambarde
noted that 'sundry women were punished in the Star Chamber,
and that worthily: because putting off that fastnesse which besee-
meth their sexe they arrayed themselves in the attire of men,
and (assembling in great number) they most riotously pulled
down a lawfull enclosure'. Presumably the Essex arrays joined
the Kentishmen and Calais soldiers in their assaults on Aldgate
and Bishopsgate, which were repulsed in hard fighting.[143]

There were some parts of England, besides the seaside, which
were generally considered to produce arrayed men who were formidable soldiers. England's land frontiers were either ill-defined
in rugged terrain, or easily penetrable in flat estuary lands. They
were under threat from the denizens of Welsh and Scottish hill
country, and in the North had the formidable military potential

of the Scottish Crown and magnates near their doorsteps. In these frontier regions of England, the need to organise for defence was deeply embedded in communal history, and gave their levies a specially hard cutting edge, eagerly sought in civil conflicts. As we have seen, the shires near Scotland were lands where society was permanently organised for war. There, the steward and receiver of estates needed to know swordplay as well as law and accountancy. In Northumberland, castles besides the bishop of Durham's on the frontier line at Norham were sometimes garrisoned in time of truce, not only to safeguard against Scottish reivers, but also against English ones from the disordered lordships of Tynedale and Redesdale. In 1438 Walter Tailboys, Lord of Redesdale, appointed Roger Widdrington, scion of a local knightly family, as constable of Harbottle Castle, to hold it in time of peace, as well as war, 'abiding and dwelling in his proper person with his meinie [retinue] and household in the dungeon [keep] of the castle'.[144] In time of war, the royal lieutenant or one of the regional wardens of the Marches might have under his command in the field urban and clerical as well as rural levies, some of them from a variety of northern shires, not just the Border ones. At the battle of Otterburn (Redesdale) in 1388, the levies from Newcastle were badly cut up, and at Humbleton Hill (Glendale) in 1402 the levies inflicted a devastating defeat on another Scottish army of invasion. If the ballads composed about the valour of the men of Northumberland in these battles were being sung in the taverns of southern England by the 1450s, that must have caused apprehensions about their intervention in civil war. Moreover, the northern arraying system had been generally tested in recent decades, by war with Scotland in 1436 and 1448–49.

4

Campaigning

...while the face of war may alter, some things have not changed since Joshua stood before Jericho and Xenophon marched to the sea.

George MacDonald Fraser, *Quartered Safe Out Here: A Recollection of the War in Burma*, 1993

We almost entirely lack the authentic voice of the English and the Welsh common soldier recollecting the experience of riding or marching on campaign in their countries, bivouacing, and fighting there, or, indeed, abroad in the later Middle Ages. The camp followers are invisible as well as silent, and civilian memories of encounters with soldiers are, for the most part, generalised and stereotyped. Chroniclers were often eager to provide information about warfare, but many of them in the period were monks and canons, whose lives generally centred on the performance of the liturgical offices in their communities. They were reliant on accounts of battles found in the often official newsletters which circulated widely, and on the oral testimony of visiting laymen who had taken part in campaigns. So they often had access to, and decanted a good deal of information on the subject, but they lacked the personal insights and emotional reactions which Henry V's biographer, the anonymous chaplain who was with his army in 1415, revealed in abundance. Even Froissart, the chronicler of chivalry who haunted princely courts, avid for information about battles, seems never to have been present at one. He eagerly sought out and interrogated participants, but his vivid reconstructions are bereft of precise topographical knowledge. John Whethamstede, abbot of St Albans, gave accounts of the battles fought in the vicinity of the abbey in 1455 and 1461, and he was certainly staying there during the first battle, which was fought in the streets aligned along the abbey's boundary walls with the town. Whethamstede conveys to us horrified reactions to the harsh mindset of soldiers in and after combat, and to the sight of stripped corpses in the streets after the first battle, but his accounts are clouded by his tendency to seek refuge in rhetorical verbiage.[1]

The chief interest of clerical – and other – chroniclers regarding warfare was in battles and their outcomes, since these were the judgements of God. They were rarely concerned with the humdrum circumstances and experiences of the common soldiery. Since monks and canons were usually scions of genteel families from country or town, and sometimes writing with noble patrons in mind, they focussed on the exploits of nobles – they, and gently born members of their retinues, were among the principal informants. St Albans Abbey, with its famous shrines and splendid guest accommodation, was a magnet for such visitors. However, chroniclers often ascribed collective experiences and feelings to the mass of combatants. The chaplain's account of them on the 1415 campaign carries particular conviction. On the journey from Harfleur towards Calais, he says, 'we thought of nothing else' but the likelihood that the enemy would deny them victuals and overwhelm them, 'so very few of us as we were and made faint by great weariness and weak from lack of food'. They were to spend a cheerful night after succeeding in crossing the River Somme; they speculated as to how far this had shortened their route. So the common desire seems to have been to run away from the French as fast as possible. When they found the tracks of a large army ahead, 'the rest of us in the army (for I will say nothing of those in command), fearing battle to be imminent', prayed loudly for God to show mercy 'and turn away the violence of the French'. On the eve of battle, most of the army bivouaced in gardens and orchards, in heavy rain the whole night through.[2] The chaplain, because of the magnitude of the victory the next day, and his desire to demonstrate the extent of God's favour to the English, felt it appropriate to reveal (unusually among chroniclers) the previous dire straits and faltering morale of the soldiers.

The monk-chronicler of St Albans, writing in the early fifteenth century, had a particular appreciation of the achievements of common soldiers. According to him, it was, surprisingly, the archers who routed the Scots in 1402 at the battle of Humbleton Hill: 'victory [was] not by the hand of nobles and lords, but by means of poor men and servants!' No lord, knight or esquire took a step until the archers had defeated the enemy.[3] He gave a detailed and enthusiastic account (perhaps based on a newsletter) of how in 1404 'common folk or country folk' ('plebani sive rustici') had bravely fought and worsted a force led by Guillaume de Chastel and a galaxy of Breton lords, which had attacked Dartmouth. Henry IV, he asserted, was deeply impressed, and duly rewarded the commons.[4] To the chronicler, this was an example of how God's beneficence might on occasion lead to a reversal of the natural order.

BOYS AT WAR

Because chroniclers generally tended to concentrate on the role of nobles in warfare and ignore the mass of soldiers and their behaviour on campaign, we lack information about what must have been features of army life too obvious to be commented on, such as the presence of camp followers, including boys and women. We have some information about the military education of princely and noble boys. They were taught to handle weapons from an early age: Henry VI was provided with eight swords of various lengths at the age of nine, to help in teaching him swordplay.[5] Some of these boys went on campaign at a young age. Edward III's son, John of Gaunt (the future Duke of Lancaster), at the age of ten was on his father's ship when it was heavily engaged in a bloody battle off Winchelsea in 1350. He was six years younger than his elder brother, the Black Prince, had been at the battle of Crécy, when their father had refused to send him aid against the French cavalry, with the terse command that he was to be allowed to win his spurs. The future Henry V was aged eleven when he went on Richard II's campaign in Ireland in 1399; the late Duke of Gloucester's son Humphrey went too, ripe at eighteen.[6] The Earl of Westmorland in 1536 approved the participation of his son, aged about thirteen, in the Pilgrimage of Grace.[7] Chaucer was being realistic in delineating his Knight, supposedly on pilgrimage in the 1380s or 90s, as having been on campaign from at least 1343–44 onwards. One real knight, Matthew Gournay, who took part then in the siege of Algeciras, died only in 1404.[8] He was probably 'first armed' in boyhood.

'Plebeian' and 'rustic' lads were doubtless taught how to defend themselves, and equip themselves for combat, from an early age, especially by practising archery alongside their peers and elders – not only to win plaudits and prizes for their developing skills, but to improve their chances when poaching. Christine de Pisan (1365–1430?), a remarkable Italian authoress, widow of a French noble, wrote that 'young Englishmen are still instructed from early youth [in archery], and for this reason they commonly surpass other archers. They can hit a target from a distance of six hundred feet'.[9] A statute of 1512 enjoined every man to provide the boys in his house between the ages of seven and seventeen with a bow and two shafts, 'to induce and learn them and bring them up in shooting'.[10] At the age of about five, Hugh Latimer knew how to buckle on his yeoman father's harness when he left home to go on campaign in 1497.[11]

Reminiscences of the skirmish at Nibley Green in 1470 were to be handed down from 'such as carried victuals and weapons to some of these companies… and after climbed up into the trees (being then boys of twelve and sixteen years) to see the battle'.[12] However, references to boys on campaign, especially

those not likely to have been sprigs of nobility, are sparse. When
Robert de Vere was defeated in the skirmish at Radcot Bridge
in 1387, a boy was one of the few killed.[13] In January 1400, after
the 'Epiphany rising', in favour of restoring King Richard II, had
been crushed, eighty prisoners were brought before the court of
the steward and marshal of the household, convened at Oxford
in the presence of Henry IV. The cases against seventeen of the
defendants were immediately dismissed, since they were 'only
servants and grooms of the others, and are of no reputation or
valour nor discretion, and for the most part are under age as it
is clearly obvious to the eye'. These were remitted to prison in
Oxford Castle to await the King's grace.[14] A London chronicler,
describing the battle of Blore Heath (1459), uses a phrase which
implies that the presence of boys in or near a battlefield might
be expected. Henry VI's forces, advancing to the battleground
the day afterwards, 'found neither man nor child'. Henry VIII
thought he could plausibly persuade foreign courts in 1536 that
the rebels in Lincolnshire were, for the most part, boys and
beggars deceived by the false rumours of traitors.[15]

Henry V's Ordinance of War (1417) for camapaigning in
France forbade the presence of 'children' in armies and garrisons under the age of fourteen, except for the sons of gentlefolk
– setting out on the path to chivalry at a tender age. Soldiers
were ordered to bring a child to their captain, and the captain
to bring him to the king or constable – presumably so that the
boy's fitness to serve could be examined, and his obligations
awesomely dinned into him. Boys and pages, with foot archers,
were liable to lose the right ear, if they cried 'To horseback'
(perhaps precipitating unauthorised withdrawals from the camp
or field). They were apparently subject to the general prescriptions in the ordinance.[16]

On more extended campaigns, boys doubtless had to earn
their keep by playing sometimes hazardous roles. One of them is
indicated by Fluellen's remark, apropos the French attack on the
baggage train during the battle of Agincourt, 'Kill the poys and
the luggage! 'tis expressly against the law of arms' (*King Henry*

V, Act IV, Scene VII). Besides acting as servants and grooms, they helped to guard the impedimenta during engagements. A Spanish account of dispositions made in preparation for a fight with the English defenders on the Dorset coast in 1404 suggests that boys might on occasion need to be integrated into battle formations. The commander, Pero Niño, positioned 'the soldiers' boys and those who were ill armed' with his archers and cross-bowmen.[17] The English practice of dismounting for combat made the safeguard of horses (often the most valuable moveable possessed by a commoner), and their tethering in a position convenient for escape, priorities which boys probably helped to fulfil. They – and other camp followers – are likely to have tended too to the needs of their masters up close to the battle lines as well as in the rear, when they were in action. Commynes described the archers in Burgundian service drawn up for combat before the battle of Montlhéry (in the Ile-de-France) in 1465: 'We found all the archers with their boots off and with a stake driven into the ground before them, and there were many barrels of wine broached for them to drink'.[18] The Burgundian chronicler Enguerrand de Monstrelet gave a description of the archers at Agincourt: 'for the most part, without any armour, and in jackets with their hose loose, and hatchets or swords hanging from their girdles; some indeed were barefooted and without hats'.[19] Presumably, they removed headgear because it might be an impediment when firing, and took their boots off to steady their grip and to alter their stance nimbly. When they discarded apparel in order to work more at ease, they must have been anxious to have their gear, especially boots (and spurs, in the case of mounted men-at-arms and archers), safely stowed. Doubtless they appreciated auxiliary help in fashioning, carrying and hammering in their stake, and in safeguarding mallets. When they were engaged, the intensity of physical labour and concentration made it highly desirable that others should refresh them from the barrels, topping up their bottles and jugs. The high rate of fire, especially in the opening volleys, made it necessary to bring up reserve stocks of arrows or retrieve spent ones – for which agile lads, dodging like ballboys at a tennis match, would have been ideal. So they would have been as well, if they took on a role rather like that of a caddy, passing up arrows to the archer, when he was heavily engaged, so that he did not have either to stoop for them or pause to select ones with a different type of head. Perhaps, too, the boys shouted advice about varying the range and angle of deflection. When archers entered into close combat, using knives, axes and mallets, as they did after the lines were engaged at Agincourt and at Verneuil in 1424, they needed to have their prized main weapon, their bow, besides their other accoutrements, gripped by reliable hands.

WOMEN AT WAR

Women, like boys, are an almost invisible component of medieval armies. Joan of Arc seems to have been an exceptional example of a woman who both commanded and fought in the field. A potent taboo against participation was the need to assume male attire, in order either to avoid detection or to deter men's sexual predatoriness. As Scripture laid down, 'The woman shall not wear that which pertaineth unto a man' (*Deuteromony*, Chapter 22, verse 5). Such blatant sartorial role-reversal seemed to threaten the natural order, offending God, presenting temptation, encouraging other extravagances, undermining male authority, and stirring up popular discontent. In Knighton's *Chronicle*, the story was told of how in 1343

> a rumour arose and great excitement among the people because, when tournaments were held, at almost every place a troop of ladies would appear, as though they were a company of players, dressed in men's clothes of striking richness and variety to the number of forty and sometimes fifty such damsels, all very eye-catching and beautiful, though hardly of the kingdom's better sort... And thus they paraded themselves at tournaments on fine chargers and other well arrayed horses, and consumed and spent their substance, and wantonly and with disgraceful lubricity

displayed their bodies, as the rumour ran. And thus, neither fearing God nor abashed by the voice of popular outrage, they slipped the traces of matrimonial restraint... But God in this as in all things had a marvellous remedy to dispel their wantonness, for at the times and places appointed for those vanities, He visited cloudbursts and thunder and flashing lightning and tempests of astonishing violence upon them.[20]

Yet there were precedents to be found in the classics for such 'unnatural' behaviour in war. Giovanni Boccaccio, in his *De mulieribus claribus* ('Famous Women'), compiled in the 1360s, has, among heroic examples of them, warlike Amazon queens. Chaucer, at the start of *The Knight's Tale*, alludes to the Amazons, and how they were tamed by Duke Theseus of Athens, and feminised through his marriage to their queen, Hipolita. Chaucer assumed his courtly audience's familiarity with the subject:

And certes, if it were not too long to hear,
I would have told you fully the manner
How there was won the realm of Femenye [land of the Amazons]
And of the great battle for the nonce
Between Athenians and Amazons,
And how besieged was Hipolita,
The fair, the hardy queen of Scythia,
And of the feast that was at their wedding.[21]

Readers of romances may have got a guilty sexual frisson from examples of warlike role-reversal such as that of the Amazons. Marina Warner has cited a fourteenth-century romance written in France, *La Fille d'un Roy*, in which Ysabel, a princess, in order to evade an unwanted marriage, escapes disguised as a man. She takes up soldiering, entering the service of the emperor of Constantinople in his wars against infidels. In one battle, she captures five kings, and binds them together 'like dogs in harness'.[22] In France, Dr Warner points out, warrior heroines found in classical literature, such as Virgil's Camilla, were cited to explain and justify Joan of Arc's behaviour.[23] However, in England it was associated with witchcraft. According to a London chronicler, 'there was a woman taken armed in the field the which was called la pucelle de Dieu, a false witch, for through her power the dauphin and all our adversaries trusted wholly to have conquered again all France, and never to have had the worse in places that she had been in, for they held her among themselves as for a prophetess and a worthy godess'. Yet, when there was no nobleman to maintain family honour and interest, allowances were made for women who stepped into the breach, temporarily assuming a masculine role. Froissart greatly admired the leonine qualities displayed by Joan of Flanders, wife of John de Montfort, claimant to the duchy of Brittany, after he was captured in 1341 by the French. Besieged in Hennebont, 'the countess, who had clothed herself in armour, was mounted on a warhorse, and galloped up and down the streets of the town, entreating and encouraging the inhabitants to defend themselves honourably. She ordered the ladies and other women to unpave the streets, carry the stones to the ramparts, and throw them on their enemies. She had pots of quicklime brought to her for the purpose'. The countess headed a sally against the enemy's camp; later, 'equal to a man', she is described as defending herself on shipboard with a sharp, rusty sword. In Wales, a story about a lady who supposedly donned male attire, and displayed lethal skill at archery, to avenge family honour, seems to have been told with a certain relish. The lady was Elen Gethin ('the terrible'); she married Sir Thomas Vaughan of Hergest, who was killed at Edgcote in 1469, fighting for his half-brother, William Herbert, Earl of Pembroke. Elen was the daughter of Daffyd Fychan ap Daffyd ap Cadwgan ap Philip Dorddu, of Llynwent. Her father and his kinsman, John Hir ('the tall') fell out at a drinking bout at the former's house, and fought till Daffyd was killed. Elen disguised herself as a man and went to John Hir's house at Llandavi, where she accepted a challenge to an archery contest. She shot him through the heart.[24] For the countess of Montfort and Elen

Gethin, male attire gave an empowerment which could be toler-ated only because it was donned in exceptional circumstances, for a specific and limited purpose.

There were semi–combatant roles sometimes assumed by women which were accepted as necessary or even laudable. These were cases of convenience or necessity, in which women were not depicted as flouting or deceiving male authority, or arrogating permanent masculine roles. They might not in these instances need to don men's clothes, for common women were used to performing heavy labouring and menial tasks in their skirts, though if they needed to help man battlements or to move agilely in the field, some modification of dress would have been practical and protective of modesty.

When places were under assault or siege, the distinction between the status of the inhabitants and soldiers became blurred, as at Hennebont. A chronicler at St Albans abbey noted approvingly that, when the Bretons were attempting to land at Dartmouth in 1404, the assault on them by the commons was notably assisted by the stone-throwing of their womenfolk. Women living on another vulnerable frontier, the border with Scotland, might be credited with the ability to handle weapons. In the ballad *Adam Bel*, Wyllyam of Cloudesle prepared to defend himself from arrest by the authorities in the strongest chamber of his house in Carlisle. He took his sword and buckler, his bow and 'hys chyldren thre... Fayre Alice [his wife] followed him as a louver true / With a pollaxe in her hande'. In this society, the ideal of love seems to have been pugnacious rather than courtly.[25]

During sieges, encouragement and material assistance by women could be vital in sustaining the effectiveness as well as the morale of soldiers in combat. When Charles the Bold unsuc-cessfully besieged Beauvais in 1472, the defence of the city was materially aided by its womenfolk. As marks of recognition of their contribution, Louis XI granted them the privileges that they could wear whatever clothes they wished and precede the men in civic processions.[26] John Knox, in his *History of the*

Reformation in Scotland, recounted how the forces favouring the Protestant cause and their English allies were in 1560 heavily repulsed by the French garrison which the Queen Regent, Mary of Guise, had placed in Leith. He turned his invective on some female Leithers, doubtless sturdy lasses used to heaving fish creels: 'The French men's harlots, of whom the most part were Scots whores, did no less cruelty than did the soldiers; for besides that they charged their pieces, and ministered unto them other weapons, some continually cast stones, some carried chimneys of burning fire, some brought timber and other impediments of weight, which with great violence they threw back over the wall upon our men, but especially when they began to turn their backs'. Note the ease he attributes to the lasses in priming handguns![27]

Women could play useful auxiliary roles in besieging towns, too. Charles the Bold showed great practicality (but without a successful conclusion) in organising his female camp followers into a pioneer corps at the siege of Neuss in 1474. Hoping to blockade a branch of the Rhine by sinking earth-filled barges, he had some of the 4,000 women in his camp marshalled for the work: 'These women were given a banner by the duke with a woman painted on it, and in going to and from their work, they went with the banner, preceded by trumpets and pipes'.[28]

The Duke seems to have set out to recognise the military contribution female camp followers might make and to rouse a martial spirit in them. One wonders whether other women besides St Joan longed to be soldiers, observing the empowerment they might gain, and freedom from the inhibitions of skirts – and whether some resorted to disguising themselves as men in order to enlist. There are well-known examples from more recent centuries of soldiers who were eventually discovered, after injury or death, to have been female. One alleged instance was celebrated in a ballad of around 1690: it concerned a young wife who lived in London and enlisted for service in Ireland. The crew of the ship which transported her there gained a healthy respect for her ability to defend herself, and the captain thought that her delicacy indicated a gentlemanly background. At the siege of James II's supporters in Cork in 1690, undertaken under the command of John Churchill, Earl of Marlborough, she was said to have fought bravely in the assault led by the Duke of Grafton. Badly wounded in it (she lost two toes), she was repatriated; discovered to be a woman, she died on the way back to London. The ballad concludes with an injunction to women to take heed − but it is laudatory.[29] Kate Adie has recently outlined the military careers of some of these disguised women. Daniel Defoe imaginatively reconstructed the career of Kit Ross, who fought in Marlborough's campaigns on the continent. She had enlisted as a soldier in order to find her press-ganged husband. Discovered as a result of being wounded at the battle of Ramillies in 1705, she was reunited with her husband, but her martial spirit and accomplishments were so admired that she was appointed as an army victualler (sutler), with the dangerous task of foraging ahead of the main forces.[30] Could it be that, among the lads arrayed to follow great captains like York and Warwick, there was the occasional servant girl who donned hose and jack? Perhaps we shall never know!

There is considerable evidence for the presence of female camp followers in continental armies of the later medieval and Renaissance periods. Military brothels were common in Italy. In 1386, when the army of Verona was defeated by the Paduans, 211 prostitutes were captured and escorted with great honour to Padua, where they were entertained in its lord's household.[31] One is reminded of how the British in 1941, during the defeat of Marshal Graziani's army in Cyrenaica, captured a motorised brothel. Charles the Bold, in his Ordinance of War of 1473, decreed that no one henceforth was to appropriate a female camp follower for himself, but each company (100 strong) was to have no more than thirty women in common.[32] Besides prostitutes, soldiers often had perfectly respectable women in their train, wives and servants doing domestic chores. However, a common assumption may have been that none of them was respectable. At her trial, Joan of Arc said that her mother had told her that her father had dreamt of her leaving home with men-at-arms, and had said to her brothers, 'Indeed, if I thought that it would come to pass as I fear concerning my daughter, I should like you to drown her, and if you did not do so, I would drown her myself'.[33] A variety of women appear in the woodcuts depicting the lives of professional soldiers, for which there was a vogue in Germany in the early sixteenth century. These were companies of *Landsknechte*, who had copied and adapted the tactical units and fighting methods of the Swiss. One example of such illustrations is Albrecht Altdorfer's series on 'Baggage Train and Camp Followers' (1517–18). This shows soldiers and women bearing baskets, tools and cradles. In this cosily domestic scene there are children, dogs, a goat and a pet pig. In Niklaus Manuel's sketchbooks showing scenes of camp life, women are prominent. They appear in embraces and carnal activity; also, a couple converse, a woman cooks, another eats by herself in the entrance of a temporary hut.[34]

The delineation of the soldier's life and that of his womenfolk reflected not only changes in representational techniques, but also change to a taste which might be characterised as bourgeois. The medieval illuminator, catering for his noble patron, might well depict common soldiers drawn up for combat or engaged in a siege, but eschewed humdrum, unwarlike scenes. In doing so, and in airbrushing womankind, he was reflecting a focus on warfare as judgement by bloodshed, the domain of masculine, not feminine humours and attributes. Can we infer from continental evidence that women were present, giving a variety of 'support services', in later medieval English and Welsh armies abroad and at home? There is not much evidence to support the proposition. There are no regulations about women in Richard II's Ordinances of War for his campaign in Scotland in 1385 or in Henry V's (closely modelled on Richard's) for France in 1417. However, in 1383 Henry Despenser, bishop of Norwich, published ordinances for the preaching of the crusade which he was to lead to Flanders, ostensibly to attack supporters of the schismatic pope at Avignon, but basically aimed to undermine the predominance of French influence in Flanders. One of his ordinances laid down that 'confessors publish in their sermons that no woman should be so bold as to pass over on the said expedition unless by special licence of the bishop of Norwich written over his seal'.[35] Maybe, especially since this was a holy undertaking, he wanted to be able to license worthy women, wives and domestically useful camp followers, and reject those whom he considered to be of loose morals. A prelate who prided himself on his understanding of soldiering, he had probably had to accept that on an expedition captained by hardened professionals (therefore containing a high proportion of old soldiers in the ranks, who valued their comforts on campaign), women could not be banned.

The presence of women among soldiers is noted by English chroniclers only when they wanted to emphasise exceptional circumstances. An episode in 1379 which scandalised monastic chroniclers suggests that some English soldiers about to embark on overseas service were determined to commandeer women and exploit them sexually. An expedition under the command of Sir John Arundel and other knights, intended for service in Brittany, mustered at Southampton. Some of the retinues were stationed outside the port, and these, according to the chroniclers, got out of hand. They raped married women and virgins, and dragged them off to the ships – in one version, as many as sixty women, notably nuns, novices and other ladies from a convent (probably Romsey Abbey). When the expedition embarked, storms blew the fleet right round into the Irish Sea. They did not abate after the women were superstitiously thrown overboard. The fleet was wrecked on the Irish coast and the men drowned.[36] What was particularly reprehensible to the chroniclers was that the women were respectable. Soldiers' normal female victims and servants were, presumably, of humble status, the indigent, desperate, and malcontent, with little material to lose. Maybe the unruly retinues encamped outside Southampton were annoyed and frustrated because they did not have easy access to the town's prostitutes. In the fifteenth century there is evidence of their brisk trade, catering, among others, for mariners; by the 1480s there were brothels in East Street and at West Quay.[37]

An atrocity story involving women, probably circulating in England when there was intense anti-Welsh feeling during Owain Glyn Dŵr's revolt, was picked up by a chronicler at St Albans. He says that when, in 1402, Glyn Dŵr decisively defeated the levies of Herefordshire near Pilleth in Maelienydd, the 'Welshmen's womenfolk' ('foeminae Wallencium') vilely mutilated English corpses.[38] It can be strongly presumed that these women were camp followers.

A few later English Ordinances of War suggest that prostitutes might be expected to congregate around expeditionary forces. The Earl of Salisbury, in his ordinance 'at his sieges in Maine and other places' (1425?) made a decree 'For Women that use Bordell [brothel] the which lodge in the Host':

> Also that no manner of man have, nor hold, a common woman [prostitute] within his lodging, upon pain of losing a month's wages; and if any man find or may find any common woman lodging, my said lord giveth him leave to take from her or them all the money that may be found upon her or them, and to take a staff and drive her out of the host and break her arm.[39]

Henry VIII's ordinance for his invasion of France in 1513 attempted to solve the problem of prostitution in his army by banning women altogether, in his decree 'For bordel keeping in the host':

> Also that no man bring with him any manner of woman over the sea, upon pain of forfeiture of their goods to the marshal and their bodies to be imprisoned, then to remain at the king's will. And that no man hold no woman within his lodgings beyond the sea [i.e. in France], upon pain of imprisonment and loss of a month's wages. And that no common woman presume to come within the king's host, nor nigh the same by the space of 3 miles of the same, upon pain if any be so taken to be burned upon

the right cheek at the first time. And if any be taken within the host or within 3 miles of the same, after she or they have been so banned, then she or they to be put into ward of the provost marshal, there to remain in prison so long as shall please the marshal and to have further punition as by him shall be thought convenient.[40]

If the enforcement of the ordinances was successful, it was a remarkable tribute to the efficiency of English military organisation. The large number of *Landsknechte* hired by Henry to rendez-vous with him and his English army at Calais would, it is to be assumed, have brought their customary womenfolk along. If they were well supplied with female support, that may have been one of the causes of the tensions which emerged on the expedition between the Germans and English – though there is no evidence that that was so. Pious and puritanical behaviour was attributed to the army sent against the Scots that year by a Venetian envoy, Nicolo di Favri of Treviso, writing from London: 'They did not take wenches with them, and they are not profane swearers, like our soldiers; indeed, there were few who failed daily to recite the office and our Lady's rosary'. It may be that their experienced commander, Thomas Howard, then Earl of Surrey, well versed in the potential disorderliness of the English civil wars, was keen to enforce the expulsion of women. Faced with the savagery of Border warfare, in a terrain where victuals were scarce, the soldiers may have been more concerned to have the Blessed Virgin and St Cuthbert on side than bonny lasses, and the latter less eager to congregate as camp followers than had been the case in the douce Midlands a quarter of a century before.[41]

Women are practically invisible in the armies of the Wars of the Roses. Margaret Beaufort (d. 1509), the mother of Henry VII, is alleged to have remarked that she would willingly go with crusaders against the Turks and 'wash their clothes, for the sake of Jesus'.[42] Since the contemporary warfare with which she was best acquainted was that in England, this remark might be taken to imply that laundresses were familiar figures in the armies of the Wars. The companies of foreign mercenaries on which reliance was placed particularly in the later stages of the Wars – most notably, the *Landsknechte* captained by Martin Schwarz in 1487 – are likely to have been accompanied by wives, children and other women. Kings and nobles who contracted for their service probably encouraged this, to deter the soldiers from alienating English folk by paying attentions to their women, whose customary greeting of strangers with a kiss set the pulses of some foreign male visitors racing.

The one set of ordinances surviving from the Wars of the Roses (and probably typical of earlier ones issued during them), is that promulgated by Henry VII for the 1487 campaign. One clause has the aim common to some other ordinances we have discussed – to exclude the presence of prostitutes: 'And that no common woman follow the King's host, upon pain of imprisonment and open to be punished in example of all other'.[43] A herald's account of the campaign valuably comments on its implementation. At Leicester, he says, the ordinances were put into execution: 'And in especial voiding Common Women, and Vagabonds, for there were imprisoned a great number of both. Wherefore there was more Rest in the King's Host, and the better Rule'. At Loughborough 'the Stocks and Prisons were reasonably filled with Harlots and Vagabonds. And after that there were but few in the Host, unto the Time the field [the battle of Stoke] was done'.[44] One wonders whether suchlike flocked back after the victory at Stoke, to profit from the eagerness of soldiers, laden with its spoils, to block out its terrors and celebrate their survival. The herald's remarks highlight the concern of kings and other commanders that the presence of prostitutes would result in disorders.

The herald's remarks also lead to the impression that prostitution was a problem in the armies of the Wars: as in this case, they generally moved along main roads, passing through and by towns in some of the most heavily populated parts of England, where poor women tempted to turn a quick profit abounded.

Moreover, access was easy for the women, since many of the soldiers were slow-moving footmen. When retinues came to town, big money was in the offing. Cecilia, a single woman living in Lichfield, said in 1466 that, when the Duke of Clarence had visited recently, she had made the equivalent of £3, and had been known fourteen times day and night by members of the Duke's household.[45]

Poor women for whom prostitution was a by-employment, as well as professional prostitutes, may have had field days when these motley armies encamped near their townships, especially since it is unlikely that common soldiers took their wives or sweethearts with them; the majority were not full-time mercenaries or in any sense professional soldiers, who might be accustomed to do so. Long campaigns were not generally antici- pated. Artisans needed their wives to stay at home to carry on labouring during their absence, and husbandmen needed theirs to carry on the round of agrarian and pastoral tasks, though commanders avoided launching campaigns during August, the time of harvest, when labour was most needed in the fields. Some campaigns took place or commenced in the autumn – in September/October 1459, from late October 1462, in September/October 1470 and October/ November 1483. That was a difficult time for women to take time off in many places: from September onwards, they were involved in harvesting and treating cannabis, principally women's work.[46] Men setting off for war in September and October might be particularly con- cerned that the women should take more than their usual share in seasonal agricultural tasks. October was the time for the last ploughing before the planting of wheat, for the manuring and marling of fallow fields, and the threshing of corn. When, during the Lincolnshire revolt of 1536, arrayed bands gathered early in that month at Hambleton Hill, general opinion was that they should march on London. However, one of the leaders, Thomas Moigne, reminded the people that it was time to sow wheat and till the fields for next year, and advised them to send only a small number forward. His advice was rejected.[47] Since honest

women were often needed to maintain the momentum of hus-
bandry and craft production, and to oversee the household in
their menfolk's absence, it is hardly surprising that women with
the armies were suspected of being harlots and ne'er-do-wells.

IMPEDIMENTA AND LODGINGS

What sort of material objects is the typical English or Welsh
common soldier setting out on campaign in the civil wars likely
to have taken, besides weapons and 'harness'? The many marching
infantrymen must have needed stout pairs of boots, especially
since they often went along unyielding and potholed Roman
roads. The Roman writer Vegetius, whose *Epitoma Rei Militaris*
was accorded great authority in the Middle Ages, had written that
fully drilled infantry should cover twenty miles in five hours in
the summer, and, in winter at the faster rate, twenty-four miles.
Commanders are likely to have been anxious to maintain a good
pace, even if they did not have such armchair learning.[48] Warm
clothing and cloaks were often needed, especially for sleeping
out at night. Besides the autumn campaigns, there were notable
ones which commenced in January, February and March 1461,
and in March in 1470 and 1471, sometimes obliging soldiers
to be content with Lenten fare, notably salted fish. This was a
convenient time of year for the husbandman to leave his plough,
before the first ploughing of fallow land in April – but a raw
time for the fasting soldier. Towton was fought on 29 March in a
snowstorm. Unusually, a campaign took place over the winter in
1462–3, in Northumberland – one which centred on the control
of castles. It may be that adverse weather conditions (as well as
inhospitable and unproductive terrain) accounted for the dismal
performance of Edward IV's forces. He had a major problem over
desertion. On Twelfth Night (6 January 1463), when his soldiers
who were besieging Alnwick Castle may have been carousing, a
Scottish force carried out the remarkable feat of both penetrating
their lines to enter the castle, sortieing out with the garrison and
returning across the Border, without significant loss.[49]

1 Philip the Good, Duke of Burgundy (d. 1467), on left, and his son and successor as Duke, Charles the Bold (d. 1477).

2 Philippe de Commynes (d. 1511). Historian of Flemish noble origins who served Charles the Bold, and abandoned his service, becoming the councillor of his arch-enemy, Louis XI of France.

3 Dunstanburgh Castle, Northumberland. Warwick 'the Kingmaker' on Edward IV's behalf oversaw the siege of Henry VI's supporters in 1462, and took the surrender of another Lancastrian garrison in 1464.

4 Bamburgh Castle, Northumberland. Warwick and his brother John Neville, Lord Montague, were involved in the sieges of Lancastrian garrisons in 1462 and 1464.

5 Alnwick Castle, Northumberland. Edward IV's soldiers were lax in besieging the French garrisoning the castle on behalf of Henry VI in the winter of 1463–1464.

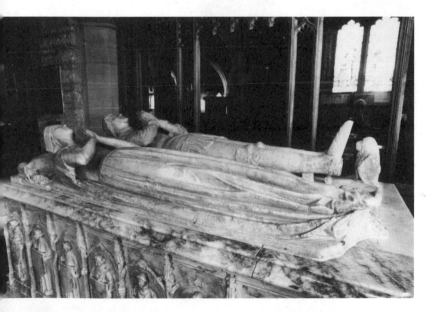

6 Sir Thomas Vaughan and his wife Elen Gethin ('the Terrible'). Tomb and effigies, Kington Church, Herefordshire. She allegedly disguised herself as an archer to avenge the death of her father. Thomas, probably in his late sixties, fought for Edward IV at Edgcote against rebels supporting Warwick in 1469 (as did his half-brother William Herbert, Earl of Pembroke) and was killed in the battle.

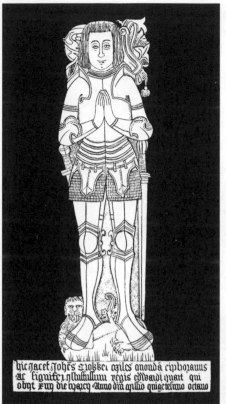

Left: 7 Sir John Crokker (d.1508). Monumental brass, Yealmpton Church, Devon. Its inscription records that he was cupbearer and standard-bearer to Edward IV.

Below: 8 Sir Robert Whittingham. Tomb effigy, Aldbury Church, Hertfordshire. Whittingham was a high-ranking official of Henry VI's son Edward, Prince of Wales, who, like his master, was killed in the battle of Tewkesbury in 1471. He is depicted wearing the Lancastrian livery collar of SS.

Above: 9 Pembroke Castle, Dyfed. Henry VI's half-brother, Jasper Tudor, Earl of Pembroke, and Jasper's nephew Henry Tudor (aged fourteen) were besieged here by Edward IV's supporters in 1471. The siege was relieved by a 'rude rabble'.

Right: 10 William Catesby esquire. Monumental brass, Ashby St Ledgers Church, Northamptonshire. An influential councillor of Richard III, he was one of the few soldiers executed after Bosworth on Henry VII's orders.

11 Thomas Howard, Duke of
Norfolk (d. 1524). Monumental
brass, now destroyed, on his tomb in
Thetford Priory, Norfolk. The text
of his biography, which was affixed
to the tomb, survives.

12 Warkworth Castle, Northumberland.
The Lion Tower, erected by Henry Percy,
fourth Earl of Northumberland. Restored
to the earldom by Edward IV in 1470,
he refrained from supporting Henry VI's
cause when Edward invaded England
in 1471, and failed to engage his forces
on Richard III's side at Bosworth. He
became a stalwart supporter of Henry VII,
and was killed in 1489 trying to stem a
popular uprising in Yorkshire.

Right: 13 John Sacheverell esquire and his wife Joan. Monumental brass, Morley Church, Derbyshire. The inscription records that he died in the battle of Richard III at Bosworth – i.e. fighting on the king's side.

Below: 14 Sir John (later Lord) Cheney, K.G. (d.1499). Tomb effigy, Salisbury Cathedral, Wiltshire. Richard III exchanged blows with this man of exceptional stature at Bosworth. He fought for Henry at Stoke; and is depicted wearing the Lancastrian livery collar of SS, with a pendant of devices used by Henry, a portcullis, and the red and white rose.

15 Sir Humphrey Stanley (d.1505). Monumental brass, Westminster Abbey. The inscription describes him as Knight of the Body to Henry VII. He fought for the king at Bosworth and Stoke.

16 Swiss or German cavalry. *Mittelalterliches Hausbuch*, c.1480.

CURIONS DUE

Left: 17 Richard, Duke of York. Stained-glass window, Trinity College, Cambridge.

Below: 18 St Albans Abbey (now Cathedral), Hertfordshire. Abbot Thomas Whethamstede recorded eyewitness testimony to the savagery of the soldiers who fought in the battles of St Albans in 1455 and 1461.

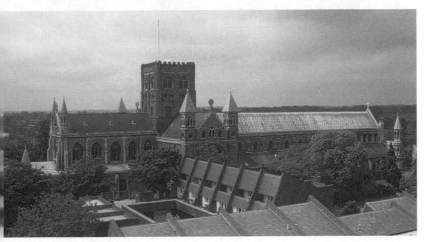

19 Sandal Castle, West Riding, Yorkshire. The Duke of York was staying here in 1460 when his soldiers, bivouacking and foraging in the neighbourhood, were attacked by the army rallied by Henry VI's queen, Margaret of Anjou. He sallied out and was killed in the battle of Wakefield.

20 Chantry chapel on Wakefield Bridge. Near here, the Duke of York's teenage son Edmund, Earl of Rutland, was slain by Lord Clifford, after surrendering, in the rout of the Yorkists at Wakefield.

Above: 21 The Cock Beck, near Towton, West Riding, Yorkshire. Many Lancastrian soldiers were said to have drowned in this stream, when fleeing after defeat by Edward IV's army at Towton in 1461.

Left: 22 Saxton Church and (foreground) the tomb of Ralph Lord Dacre. The battle of Towton was fought in the parish of Saxton, and Dacre was killed fighting for Henry VI.

23 Lionel Lord Welles, K.G. Tomb effigy, Methley Church, West Riding, Yorkshire. He was a courtier-lord who had been the lieutenant's deputy at Calais, and was killed in his mid-fifties, fighting for Henry VI at Towton.

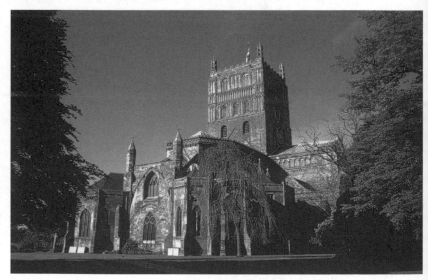

24 Tewkesbury Abbey, Gloucestershire. After Edward IV's victory here over the forces of Margaret of Anjou and her son Edward, Prince of Wales, some of their soldiers who had sought refuge in the church and churchyard were killed on consecrated ground.

Left: 25 Tewkesbury Abbey. A circle of gilded suns, the device of Edward IV, in the vault over the sanctuary, proclaims his triumph. Not far off in the choir lie the remains of Edward, Prince of Wales, son of the last Lancastrian king.

Below: 26 Sir John Crosby (d. 1475). Tomb effigy in St Helen's Church Bishopsgate, London. As a sheriff of London in 1471, he helped to organise the defence of London Bridge against the assaults of Kentishmen and soldiers and sailors from Calais opposing the restoration of Edward IV.

27 Sir John Savage (d.1495). Tomb effigy, Macclesfield Church, Cheshire. Raised to knighthood by Edward IV after the battle of Tewkesbury, in 1485 he defected from Richard III to Henry Tudor, and was one of Henry's captains at Bosworth, and in 1487 at the battle of Stoke.

28 Sir Robert Wingfield (d.1481). Stained-glass window, East Harling Church, Norfolk. Knight of the Body and Comtroller of the Household to Edward IV. He is depicted wearing the king's livery collar of suns and white roses.

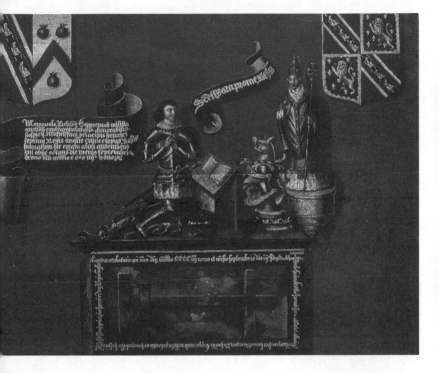

29 Sir Richard Edgecombe (d.1489). Panel in the chapel of Cotehele Manor, Calstock, Cornwall, depicting his and his wife Joan's tomb at St Morlaix, Brittany. He made a dramatic escape from Richard III's officers in 1484, fought for Henry Tudor at Bosworth, and was to be appointed by him Controller of the Household.

30 Sir Robert (later Lord) Willoughby de Broke, K.G. (d.1502). Tomb effigy, Callington Church, Cornwall. He took part in the 1483 rebellion against Richard III, fought for Henry Tudor in 1485, and became one of his principal captains in foreign and domestic campaigns.

31 The battle of Bosworth. Stone frieze, Stowe School, Buckinghamshire. It was possibly originally erected in Castle Hedingham, Essex, by a descendant of John de Vere, earl of Oxford, one of Henry Tudor's principal captains.

We can gain an idea of what some esquires carried about their person from the circumstances of Robert Goushill's death at the battle of Shrewsbury in 1403. He had been an esquire of Thomas Mowbray, Duke of Norfolk, highly regarded by his master. Within two years of the Duke's death in 1399, he married the dowager duchess, Elizabeth. In 1403 they had two little girls, aged three and two. The chronicler of St Albans tells the tragic story of how Goushill, newly knighted before the battle, lay wounded, and was killed and robbed by his own servant. Goushill had gasped out to him, 'I am almost suffocated by my arms, so remove my gauntlets and arms, to allow my spirits to revive strongly'. He asked the servant to take care of his wedding ring, and £40 he carried in a purse. The servant robbed him as well of collars, jewels and rings. Goushill's effigy, in armour, lies on his tomb in Hoveringham church (Nottinghamshire), next to that of his coroneted duchess.[50] Others too took a small fortune into battle, some of it doubtless on their person. Nicholas Leveson, esquire in the retinue of Lord Dudley at the battle of Blore Heath (1459), was 'wounded and maimed and left on the field for dead, and spoiled of horses, goods and harness', for which Henry VI granted him £20 in compensation.[51] Gentlefolk needed to dress and arm according to their status, and to wear appropriately valuable rings and reliquaries. They needed to conceal valuables and coin in their apparel, in order to pay for good victuals for themselves and their servants, for fair lodgings, physicians' fees, and bribes – in hope that, if they had to yield, a captor could be tempted to release them rather than hand them over to higher authority for probable execution.

Common soldiers needed to conceal their wages about their person – and their loot. They stripped the dead and the moribund, searching for small valuables kept next to the skin. Looters spirited them away in their own apparel, like the soldier in Henry V's army in 1415 who had a stolen pyx up his sleeve.[52] The successful looter was himself vulnerable to thieving fellow soldiers. The chaplain's account of the 1415 expedition referred to 'the thieves among us who are given more to pillage than to pity and care nothing for the tears of the innocent as long as they can lay their hands on plunder'.[53] How easy it must have been for thieves and vagabonds to tag along in the hastily constituted armies of the civil wars, where they could exercise their predatory talents more speedily on often newly hailed companions! When prohibitions on looting civilians were well enforced, unnatural bulges in colleagues' sleeves, jackets and hose were presumably supremely interesting to the covetous.

We may guess at other objects the common soldier carried – devotional trinkets, keepsakes, written charms, ointments, medicine, tinderbox – and dice. Commynes mentions the archers of Charles the Bold's night watch on one occasion playing dice. His ordinances of 1473 forbade playing the game, and so did Henry VIII's of 1513, which also forbade all other soldiers' games 'whereby they shall waste their money or cause debates to arise'. The games specified were playing at cards, tables (board games), closh (possibly ninepins) and 'handout'.[54] For some of their belongings, such as basic rations and utensils, soldiers doubtless had knapsacks. In 1327 Scottish horsemen invading England each had a bakestone and bag of oatmeal stowed on horseback, with which to make oatcakes; English and Welsh soldiers in the Wars may have had equivalents.[55] Christine de Pisan lists utensils necessary in war – earthen pots, goblets, and leather buckets to hold water, and, for winter campaigning, large earthen pots for making soup and for cooking meat, large cauldrons, large, medium and small pans, wooden spoons, bowls and trenchers, goblets and cups, empty barrels and sets of bellows.[56] It is unlikely that the footmen of the Wars had the elaborate utensils which a ladylike Italian housewife considered essential to store, prepare and serve food, especially as most campaigning did not take place in the depth of winter. Grindstones and hearthstones were necessary for baking bread, and so was a kettle to seethe stockfish (dried cod) and drain off the salt from it. Perhaps men from the same village brought with them suchlike gear for communal use.

For the transport of their bulkier arms and impedimenta, kings and nobles probably used the great carts and barrels with which

their households customarily itinerated. How did common soldiers convey any bulkier goods they may have had? Possibly
some companies had their own farm cart with storage barrels,
though lacking the sophistication of the dedicated, enclosed
military waggons which some illustrations show following each
company of *Landsknechte*.[57] The better-off English and Welsh
commons may have hired a man, woman or boy to act as
carriers of arms and impedimenta, perhaps clubbing together to
do so; or brought their own packhorses or hired them for bulkier objects. They may have contracted with the likes of Patryk,
tenant farmer of Melton Mowbray (Leicestershire), who in 1417
hired himself and his horse to accompany the pilgrim Margery
Kempe on her travels in England.[58]

BIVOUACS

In royal armies, and doubtless in other well-constituted ones, it
was the task of the harbinger to select and assign lodgings and
campsites: Henry VII's ordinance of 1487 presumably echoed
earlier ones in the Wars in its threat of imprisonment and punishment at the king's discretion for those who disobeyed this
official.[59] Touchy questions of status were involved in the allo-
cation of quarters. When Edward IV encamped his army near
Chipping Sodbury (Gloucestershire) in 1471, it was right that he
and the main 'battle' (including the knights and esquires of the
body) should have their tents pitched at the highest point, on
Sodbury Hill.[60] In 1385 Richard II's army, on the way to invade
Scotland, was encamped in fields near Beverley (Yorkshire); all
the lords wanted to lodge as near the King as possible. Some
of the soldiers of the King's half-brother Sir John Holand and
Sir Ralph Stafford became involved in a dispute over where
lords should lodge. A favourite esquire of Holand was killed;
furious, he traded insults with Stafford and killed him with a
single blow from his sword. Richard managed to calm down
the explosive situation, so that the issue did not interrupt
his campaign.[61] However, variance over lodgings could have

serious consequences in sapping military coherence. It produced discontent in the army commanded on Edward IV's behalf by William Herbert, Earl of Pembroke, shortly before its defeat at Edgcote by Warwick's supporters in 1469.[62]

In the more prosperous parts of England (such as Kent and the East Midlands), comfortable billets might be available in the much improved housing built by well-to-do peasants, including the big barns and byres they used in the larger-scale farming which they now practised. In towns and on the roads, especially along main routes, inns had sprung up to cater for better-off travellers. Margery Kempe and her fellow pilgrims had no difficulty in finding decent lodging in an inn in Leicester in 1417.[63] However, on campaigns, good roofed accommodation was occupied by magnates and gentlefolk. If it was necessary to sleep in the open, they and their domestic servants were most likely to have tents. Common soldiers, if they could not find farm buildings to lie in, improvised shelter under the stars. Except in abominable weather, this was not a hardship for countrymen, who were probably often out in the fields at night in August, to make an early start with harvesting, or, if they were pastoralists from hill country, lodged in scanty shelters at the summer shielings. We have an account of the sleeping arrangements of some of the Lincolnshire rebels one night early in October 1536, the day after they had set out from the mustering ground, Hambleton Hill. Some slept in the fields around Market Rasen. On the way there, a group led by Edmund, old Lady Tailboys' chaplain, met the abbot of Barlings, and compelled him to give them hospitality for the night. They entered the monastery and were served beef and bread and 'the meat that was on the spit for the brethren's supper'. Some slept in chambers and others on the 'hay mows' in the barns. They were so menacing to the abbot that when he turned to the altar for Mass, 'he could scarcely say his service'. He offered them a crown (a coin worth 5 shillings) apiece to buy horses.[64]

The leaders of the subsequent Pilgrimage of Grace, centred in Yorkshire, tried hard to prevent such intimidating and extortionate treatment of civilians (though they were not so nice in the case of potential opponents) – and such are likely to have been common attitudes among the commanders and captains of the Wars of the Roses.[65] They often shared with the governing elites of towns a reluctance to admit the soldiery within their walls – most notably so in the case of London after the Lancastrian victory at St Albans in 1461.[66] Snugly lodged in towns, the soldiery might carouse, commit outrages, and become indisciplined and tempted to desert. The way in which discipline could quickly deteriorate is reflected in Commynes' description of his experience with the English soldiers who crowded into Amiens to be freely entertained after Edward IV had ceased hostilities with Louis XI in 1475: 'we entered a tavern where a hundred and eleven bills had been run up although it was not nine in the morning. The house was full, some were singing, some were sleeping and were just plain drunk'.[67]

Let us take some examples of billeting and bivouacing. The rebels who wished to restore Richard II in January 1400, when they had retreated to Cirencester (Gloucestershire), encamped in a field, whereas the lords lodged in an inn, where the townsmen barricaded them. The lords' soldiers presumably melted away in these adverse circumstances.[68] The separate billeting of commanders and soldiers, when circumstances were at a difficult juncture, tested the morale of armies. In 1403 the rebellious Earl of Northumberland, retreating northwards, had his request for his army to lodge in Newcastle refused by the citizens, who closed the gates and manned the walls. They allowed him to stay in the city with members of his household for the night. However, his suspicious soldiery mounted an attack on the walls, which was repulsed by the townsmen's archery. The earl, disheartened by news of his son Hotspur's death, disbanded his army, and made what was doubtless a mournful journey northwards with his household to his castle at Warkworth.[69]

When the Yorkist lords invaded England from Calais in 1460, and reached London with 500 horsemen and a large number of footmen and commons from Kent, Sussex and Surrey, the civic

governors were divided as to whether they should be admitted – especially as Lord Scales commanded a garrison loyal to
Henry VI's cause in the Tower of London. A compromise was
reached. The Yorkist lords lodged in the city at Greyfriars within
Newgate, and their army was allowed to pass through – probably
over London Bridge, along Bridge Street and Lombard Street,
through Cheapside and West Cheap and out through Newgate.
The soldiers encamped just outside the city bounds, north of the
walls and Smithfield, in a field adjacent to the Priory of St John
of Jerusalem at Clerkenwell.[70] This well and other wells nearby
provided a necessary resource for an army. In 1470 Edward IV,
isolated by revolts in favour of Warwick, fled south from York to
the port of King's Lynn in Norfolk. A minute in the Hall Book
of a meeting of Congregation on Monday, 1 October records the
provision made for night watches, and guards on the town walls
and South Gate. There was also entered under this date a memorandum of the arrival the previous day of Edward IV, late king
of England, at ten o'clock at night. In his company were Earl
Rivers, Lord Cromwell (Humphrey Bourchier), Lord Hastings,
Lord Say and 3,000 knights, esquires, valets and others. This is a
surprising number – perhaps exaggerated to excuse the reception
of Edward to supporters of Henry VI. The memorandum goes
on to say that they stayed till Tuesday, 2 October, and that Edward
embarked with these lords at about eight o'clock in the port of
Lynn, with the exception of Cromwell (perhaps left behind in
order to be a 'sleeper' for Edward's cause).[71] Commynes' version
of the King's flight (if he was refering to the same stage in his
itinerary) differs: 'Edward was quartered in a fortified village,
or at least a building which could only be entered by a bridge.
This was very useful to him, as he told me himself. The rest of
his men were camped in nearby villages... by divine providence
the king was camped close to the sea and some ships were following him, bringing victuals'.[72] The fortified structure which
Edward described does not correspond to any known to have
been within the capacious walls of Lynn. However, a few miles
south-east of the town is Middleton Tower, a moated house

rebuilt earlier in the century, whose main remaining feature is an imposing brick gatehouse, which had fine accommodation. The house was owned by Rivers.[73] Safe in the knowledge that he could not be easily surprised in this snug billet, did Edward stop off and sleep here too?

In the campaign of 1485, the burgesses of Shrewsbury had to admit Henry Tudor's army, and Richard III's apparently occupied Leicester. Henry is traditionally said to have stayed in a house in Wyle Cop, Shrewsbury, and 'King Richard's Chamber' was traditionally pointed out as the King's room in the Blue Boar Inn, Leicester.[74] Leading cities were better placed to bargain over admissions, as York did with a weakly supported Edward IV in 1471. In 1536 the leaders of the Pilgrimage agreed that the footmen in their large regional army should not be allowed to enter York, as they were poorer and less easy to control than the horsemen.[75]

We have snippets of information about kings and other commanders camping out in England and Wales on campaign. In 1402 an expedition led by Henry IV against Owain Glyn Dŵr in Wales pitched tents in pleasant meadowland. They feared attack in the night, and must have bedded down prepared to fight, for the King slept in his armour, with his lance handy. That night a violent storm arose; Henry was lucky to escape injury when his tent collapsed on him. His less well-housed soldiers must have had similar experiences, and would have been in a sorry state the following morning, especially if bivouacing in the open. The campaign was then terminated.[76] In 1460 Henry VI seems to have shared some of the hazards and inconveniences of his army encamped outside Northampton, for in the brief fight that ensued some of his leading peers were slain outside his tent: presumably he had slept there rather than in more comfortable accommodation in the neighbouring convent or town.[77]

When, in 1471, Edward IV arrived in Barnet to confront the Earl of Warwick, he ordered his men in the village out of it to encamp with him in the field, since the enemy was nearby. Later on that year, in anticipation of a battle with Margaret of Anjou's army, he ordered his soldiers to leave Bath and encamp with him three miles out of town. At Barnet he had gained a tactical advantage over his opponents, causing them to fire their guns at too long range to hit his camp, since he 'and his host, kept passing great silence all night, and made, as who saith, no noise, whereby they [the enemy] might not know the very place where they lay'.[78] This was a tribute to discipline which any continental commander of professional soldiers might have envied. Perhaps Edward was consciously emulating Henry V's order the night before Agincourt. There, when, like the French nearby, men began to call out in the dark for their fellow, servant or comrade, he 'ordered silence throughout the army under pain of forfeiture of horse and harness on the part of a gentleman should he offend, and of loss of his right ear by a yeoman and anyone else of lower rank who presumed to infringe the royal order, without hope of obtaining a pardon. And he at once moved off in silence to a hamlet nearby... And when our adversaries noted how still and silent we were, thinking that, being so few, we were smitten with fear and perhaps intended to make off during the night, they had fires lit and set heavily manned watches across the fields and roadways. And, it was said, they thought themselves so sure of us that that night they cast dice for our king and his nobles'.[79] It is not beyond the bounds of possibility that Edward had campaigned alongside veterans of Agincourt.

In 1487, when Henry VII set out from Leicester to confront the invaders in the North, his army camped one night in a wood, and the next night his vanguard was on a hill, and the main 'battle' nearby in a village and adjacent field where beans were being cultivated. The King slept in a gentleman's house in the village; quite apart from questions of status, it was especially important for commanders to get some peaceful sleep – which, apparently, Richard had failed to do the night before Bosworth. In 1487 Henry VII's army was encamped at Radcliffe on Trent, near Nottingham, before the advance on Newark to confront the Earl of Lincoln's army. A herald present recalled: 'That evening there was a great scry [alarm], which caused many cowards to flee...

And in this scry I heard of no Man of worship that fled but rascals'. One can imagine that there was often much restlessness among 'green' soldiers the night before combat was anticipated, and that experienced commanders like Edward were concerned to select campsites which were reassuringly secure, and arranged so that they provided a good environment in which to cook and take rest, with the range of facilities which Vegetius had specified.[80]

VICTUALS AND FODDER

Light is thrown on how soldiers were victualled by Henry VII's 1487 ordinance of war. He ordered victuallers to provide sufficient bread, ale, other victuals and fodder on his army's approach, for which they would be paid a reasonable cash price, fixed by the clerk of the market or another royal officer. Disobedient soldiers were liable to be executed.[81] Presumably these were traditional arrangements, generally favoured too by rebel leaders, though they may not always have had sufficient authority over their followers to impose severe penalties. Detailed market prices might be announced. When the armed Pilgrims were about to enter York in 1536, it was proclaimed that there was to be no spoiling, and everything was to be paid for honestly. Soldiers were to pay 2d for a meal, and prices for food and horsemeat were fixed.[82] Such correct exchanges were hard to enforce, especially on scattered forces. The moral stature and personality of captains and the morale of their soldiers were important factors in keeping them in line. William Stapleton, captain of rebels mustered at Beverley in 1536, impressed on the commons that he would never have the name of a 'captain of thieves'. They became restless and suspicious when he left them on the business of the rebels' high command. On his return, he thanked them for choosing him as their captain, though he was a stranger, and said that he had worked harder than any of them, but that, if they wanted to choose another captain, he would obey them willingly. The commons cried,

'We will have none other captain and whosoever after speak against the captain, the rest will strike him down'. Stapleton resumed his authority and ordered that 'every man pay honestly' for what he took. However, when his companies were taking part in the investment of Hull (with whose citizens the men of Beverley had historic economic enmities), he seems to have done little at first to discourage their seizures, and he and his kinsmen made free with other people's property. When he was billeted in the mayor of Hull's house at Sculcoates, his men used the hay and grass there as horsefeed, and commandeered the mayor's crane, peacock and pigs. They seized a herd of seventy-five oxen belonging to Archbishop Lee of York's brother, and Stapleton had ten or eleven wethers intercepted which were being driven to victual the besieged. Some 'honest men' complained to Stapleton that his orders were being disobeyed, and that, if the offenders were not punished, ' they should be robbed themselves'. A watch was set, and two men were caught thieving, one of whom was in charge of the company's victuals, the other 'a naughty fellow, a sanctuary man of Beverley and a common picker. Whereupon the whole company made exclamation.' Stapleton condemned the men to death, a friar was sent for to hear their last confessions, and the company was assembled at the waterside to witness their drowning. 'The sanctuary man was tied by the middle with a rope to the end of the boat and so hauled over the water, and several times put down with an oar over his head.' The friends of the quartermaster, a householder, interceded for him not to receive similar treatment. Both were reprieved and discharged; after that, 'privy pickings' ended.[83] The tensions over supply within Stapleton's company are likely to have replicated characteristic ones in previous armies campaigning in English civil wars. One admires the way in which he resolved them by targeting the fugitive from justice, but calculating that an actual execution would be bad for morale.

In this case, problems arose where there was abundance, after harvesting, in a region of the East Riding of Yorkshire with a mixture of prosperous agriculture and pastoralism. Discipline was harder to maintain when continuous and sufficient supply broke down, in barren country and areas where crops had failed. 'On any expedition', the classical authority Vegetius had written, 'the single most effective weapon is that food should be sufficient for you while dearth should break the enemy.'[84] Echoing his prescriptions, Christine de Pisan had written that 'the wise commander… will not wait for foragers, who all too often cannot find anything to take, but will have provided for everything before his departure, not only all the supplies needed for war, but all sorts of victuals that he will have sent before him in carts and bundles: wheat, wines, salted meat, dried beans, salt, vinegar, which is quite refreshing with water when wine is lacking in summertime, as well as all other useful things that he will distribute wisely'.[85] This was often a counsel of perfection in the hurly-burly of civil war. In 1471 Edward IV faced serious supply problems in the course of the campaign against the Lancastrians who had landed in the West Country. So soon after the campaign which had culminated in the victory of Barnet, his purveyors did not have much time to stockpile victuals, but were able to exploit London's unrivalled markets. In the Cotswolds, according to the official account of the campaign, his foragers were unable to secure 'in all the way, horse meat, nor man's meat'. Apparently he was urging his forces forward, to catch up with the retreating Lancastrians, at too fast a pace for foragers to scour or for markets to be held. At Cheltenham (Gloucestershire), he 'comforted himself, and his people, with such meat and drink as he had done to be carried with him, for the victualling of his host'.[86]

It was often necessary to resort to the lottery of foraging. In 1399, Henry of Bolingbroke's forces, advancing south from Doncaster to challenge Richard II's supporters, 'by the advice of the lords divided themselves into companies, some advancing on the right and others on the left, in order to gather and preserve the corn and other provisions they needed.' Their enforced and premature harvesting is unlikely to have been appreciated by the farmers, but the fact that they moved swiftly through England was some alleviation. They were so well supplied that they could afford to let their horses trample the corn when they reached hostile Cheshire.[87] The division made into foraging companies suggests that groups (presumably existing military formations, or ones amalgamated for the purpose) were responsible for victualling themselves and had their individual commissariat, as seems to have been the case with Stapleton's company in 1536. Such arrangements were practical, but may have produced friction and mayhem between companies, when one had been more successful in the search for foodstuffs and fodder. This sort of tension is likely to have occured in armies of the Wars of the Roses, when large numbers of footmen were trudging along, unable to compete as foragers with horsemen. A London chronicler remarked glumly that 'spearmen they be good to ride before the footmen and eat and drink up their victual'.[88]

Foraging could be a difficult and dangerous business for those engaged in it and, if it went badly, a threat to the morale of the army. Commynes describes how, when Charles the Bold's army was outside Paris in 1465, confronting Louis XI in the city, in order to avoid heavy skirmishing, his foragers 'were forced to go long distances to forage and many men were necessary to guard them'. However, he says that, with the abundant supplies of the Ile-de-France and Paris available, it proved feasible for the opposing armies to sustain themselves: 'nothing became dearer except for bread, which rose a penny in price'.[89] In English domestic conflict, securing leading market centres and ports was vital. For the most part, commanders could not risk the hazards involved in manoeuvring in leisurely manner, allowing thorough foraging along the way: they needed to move fast on the principal regional centres or the capital. In 1403 the rebel 'Hotspur' (Sir Henry Percy) aimed to supply his army at Shrewsbury, and, in face of the burgesses' defiance, threw a cordon round the town. His hesitation about assaulting it enabled Henry, arriving unexpectedly, to rush soldiers in for its defence. Percy, likely to have been strapped for supplies, was forced to hazard battle.[90]

Commanders in the Wars aimed to control the more fertile parts of the realm, mainly in central and eastern parts. In 1459 the Duke of York, forced out of the grain-producing Midlands by Henry VI's army, had to fall back on Ludlow, which probably lacked such an abundance of victuals to sustain his army for long. On 29 December 1460, when York and his brother-in-law Salisbury were celebrating Christmas at Sandal Castle (Yorkshire), and the Duke's men 'were roaming through the countryside for victuals', they were attacked below the castle on the fields sloping down to Wakefield.[91] Margaret of Anjou's subsequent Lenten campaign may have failed to capitalise on this victory and the one at St Albans because, though her army was advancing through some of the most fertile regions of England, foodstuffs were seasonally scarce. Her soldiers' foraging may have built up the reputation which they gained for destructiveness, undermining her military success.[92] The Lancastrians' campaigns in the northern Border shires in 1462–4 failed because they were not strong enough to win control of the leading market centres there. They could not hope to assault the formidable and well-manned defences of Newcastle and their siege of Carlisle failed. For a time they managed to hold Hexham; when they lost this, in a fight nearby, their cause in the Borders faded. Natural circumstances conspired against them: there were bad harvests generally of wheat and barley in England in 1461 and 1462.[93] With an economically bleak basis for their operations, the effects of dearth probably hit them harder than it did their opponents.

SOLDIERS AND CIVILIANS

Armies' constant search for food and fodder was probably the most general source of friction with civilians . Even when soldiers' markets functioned successfully in the ways envisaged in the 1487 ordinance, urban and rural traders are likely to have resented having prices fixed by a military official rather than the accustomed market officials. Moreover, soldiers' need for grain or bread may have had the effect of driving up prices, increasing the hardships of the poor. Yet it was probably foraging that caused the most resentment. This gave ample opportunities for seizures without payment, and for the theft of valuables and goods of all kinds by inveterate thieves. Relations between soldiers and civilians are likely to have been tense in times of dearth – campaigning was probably more tolerable in the years 1469–71 because this was a period of good harvests.[94] Relations are likely to have been fraught too in regions where agrarian resources were poor – such as in much of the Marches towards Scotland and in Wales. In 1384 an English army returning from an invasion of Scotland (probably typically) depleted the meagre stocks available in Northumberland, to the misery of the inhabitants. The far larger army with which Richard II invaded Scotland the following year seems also to have inflicted misery in Northumberland. In November 1385 the payment of royal compensation was recorded to the abbot and convent of Newminster, for damages done by the King's lieges in the last expedition, as well as damage inflicted by the Scots.[95]

The Lancastrians doubtless gathered support for their incursions in the English Borders in 1461–4 from reivers recruited in the lordships of Tynedale, Redesdale and Hexham, and in the neighbouring parts of the Scottish Marches. The reivers' habitual objectives were either to take preys or ransoms, and they welcomed having sanctions to do so, and were often eager to hire their swords to local lords. Despite the proximity of Henry VI, or even his presence on raids, these made little headway.[96] It is curious that a statue, which appears to celebrate his posthumous cult, is in Alnwick parish church, since local inhabitants are likely to have suffered from the presence of Lancastrian garrisons in Alnwick Castle in 1461 and 1462, and the appearance of the Scottish relief force in 1463. However, the encampment of Edward IV's large besieging army over the winter of 1462–3 may have then been their main source of misery.[97]

Much of that army was composed of contingents from south of the River Trent – then considered the frontier between northern and southern England. However, southern soldiers were probably familiar to Border folk, since they had customarily travelled up to serve in the garrison at Berwick and on expeditions against the Scots, as did soldiers from other parts of northern England and from Wales. Owain Glyn Dŵr had served his military apprenticeship in 1384 and 1385 on English service in Scotland.[98] For many northerners, the occasional passage of soldiers from other parts of the realm was probably a traditional evil, less to be feared than the cruelly ravaging incursions of Scots and neighbouring English reivers.

Northern companies of soldiers had often travelled through southern England on their way to embarkation ports for expeditions abroad in the Hundred Years War. For northern society was heavily involved in the campaigns, as reflected in the agitation among former soldiers in Cheshire and Lancashire in 1393 at the prospect of the permanent cessation of the wars in France.[99] It is probable that apprehensions in the South about the depredations of soldiers were traditionally high when they were from the North: they spoke incomprehensible dialects of English, and there were long-held views (based on the experience of immigration) that northerners were poor, and avid to acquire southern silver. In 1386 a large army encamped in the shires around London for defence against the expected French invasion. Pay seems to have run out, at least for some of the northern contingents; southern chroniclers echo complaints of plundering by men from Wales, Cheshire and Lancashire. Henry Knighton, canon of Leicester Abbey, had local knowledge about this:

> One of them came to the fields of Sapcote in Leicestershire and took a mare from the plough and its owner and the neighbours chased him, and recovered the mare, and gave the thief a good beating. And the thief immediately returned with 140 of his companions who were archers from Cheshire, intending to kill the farmer and burn the village, whereupon the villagers had to make fine with them, and promise to pay them £10 by a certain day, which they did.[100]

Thus East Midlands folk had the bitter novelty of experiencing the sort of terror and extortion familiar to Borderers who paid blackmail, Irish families who paid for *slainte*, and French peasants who paid *appatis*. Folk memories in the South may have caused particular tension whenever northern forces appeared there during the Wars of the Roses, and it may be that memories among northerners of past hostile receptions were a deterrent to the Pilgrims of Grace from leaving their own 'country' to march on London. Indeed, people disliked companies of soldiers who were 'strangers' from anywhere else invading their 'country', and are likely to have been especially antagonistic if they spoke a foreign tongue, like the Welsh.

Civilians had other reasons for discontent at the progress of armies through their midst, besides foraging. The owner or owners of the beanfield on which the commons in Henry VII's army encamped in 1487 can scarcely have been pleased with the state the field was left in – nor can others in like case. Tension over liaisons with soldiers may have threatened the mores of village society like the presence of GIs could do in rural England during the Second World War. Civilians could get caught up in disputes over the spoils of war. William Blakwell and his son of the same name petitioned the Archbishop of York, the Chancellor (George Neville, who demitted office on 8 June 25 1467). They said that after the battle of St Albans (in 1461) 'divers misdoers and common robbers' in the (Lancastrian) Duke of Exeter's company – Robert Borton, John ap Res (clearly, a Welshman) and others to the number of sixteen – came to William the elder's house at Totteridge and left there a jack, two salets and a horse which they had robbed from the Earl of Warwick's men in the battle. They charged William to keep the items safe for them. However, after the 'field of York' (the defeat of the Lancastrians at Towton), Warwick's deprived men came to William and requested their possessions, which he gave them, he alleged, with a clear conscience. That was not the end of the affair. John ap Res, who was a refugee in sanctuary in London, at St Martin's church, took out an action for detinue of goods against Blakwell. This apparently failed. His former companion in the field, Borton, had become a good Yorkist with an influential patron, the Lord Treasurer. The last had William the younger arrested and detained in the Fleet prison. Father and son besought the Chancellor for a writ of 'corpus cum causa', enabling the latter to be brought from prison before him in Chancery.[101] Presumably Exeter's men in 1461 knew that they would soon have to retreat, and considered that their spoils would be safest if left behind. Here perhaps we have a case of collusion in theft between soldiers from the regions and local inhabitants who saw in Queen Margaret's invasion an opportunity for gain. There were surely many other combatants who tenaciously spirited away goods taken in the Wars, or pursued claims to them, and other civilians whom they involved in their schemes, and who sometimes consequently experienced unwelcome hassles.

It is not clear whether, in the Wars, there were fears among civilians that soldiers would spread disease among them. Henry VIII and his commanders for his invasion of France in 1513 showed concern that epidemics should not break out in the army. The King may have been reiterating traditional preventive measures, especially for the benefit of the many English soldiers camapigning for the first time. This was what was laid down in the Ordinances issued in London beforehand:

> Also the king straightly chargeth and commandeth that if it happen that his host tarry by the space of 3 days or above in one place or ground, be it at siege or otherwise, that then every man keep clean his lodging, not suffering any carrion, filth, or any other unwholesome or infective stinking air to be in or near the same his lodging, but forthwith to bury the same deep in the earth upon pain to be punished after the discretion of the marshal.[102]

Particular concern was shown when the army undertook a siege. When Thérouanne was invested, these orders were once more proclaimed, with an addition: 'And if any person will ease himself, to go out of the compass and precinct of the field, or else bury it in the earth, upon pain of imprisonment after the discretion of the marshal'.[103] In Henry V's army besieging Harfleur in 1415, dysentery had become rampant, carrying off far more men, the Chaplain remarks, than the sword.[104] An afflicted army could wreak havoc through infection among civilians, too: fears of such outcomes were a universal deterrent from all but the briefest investment of towns in the Wars. Maybe the soldiers involved and the civilians who came in touch with them had less to fear from the spread of infection because the former often did not work for long together, and they tended to pass quickly through villages and, as we have seen, were sometimes kept out of towns and cities by their commanders.

Some civilians got good pickings from soldiers – for instance, entertainers who are likely to have hovered round their bivouacs and in the alehouses along the ways. We know that companies were sometimes given a good send-off on their departure from cities.[105] Among the familiar denizens of the highways were minstrels and other musicians, jugglers, dancers and acrobats, jesters and players, and bear-baiters. Some entertainers formed companies – they were such a common phenomenon that the nobles who plotted the downfall of Henry IV thought they would gain easy access to Windsor Castle on Twelfth Night disguised as a company of 'mummers', as we have seen, presumably with their faces fantastically masked.[106] Soldiers in all ages have delighted in momentarily being transported into a fantasy world of music, laughter and longing. Some minstrels and players had respectable credentials, being retained by lords, and were on the roads either money-making on vacation, or having been dispatched to entertain the household of the lord's friend. However, generally itinerant entertainers were often regarded by the authorities as 'vagabonds'. Such may have been among the vagabonds expelled from the royal army in 1487.[107] Other vagabonds may have been peddlars and pardoners, and, as well, the very poor, the crippled and the *déracinés* who lived by begging. They were the sorts who flocked to receive the customary almsgiving dispensed from the households of the rich, and to show their histrionic skill as bedesmen, in return for handouts at distinguished funerals. For both the sturdy and the disabled beggar, the seller of false relics and the quack, and for the cripple willing to fetch and carry, the scraps and doles provided by the company of soldiers may have been alluring. Soldiers who feared they might soon die or be themselves reduced to beggary by disabling wounds and the loss of their weapons may have been specially keen for the boon of prayers from the poor, whom Christ had declared blessed.

The Wars did produce benefits for many civilians. We can infer that they generated a market in the spoils of war, the more conspicuous of which soldiers may have often been anxious to offload, in case they were reclaimed – especially if they were expensive and luxurious objects inappropriate to their own status, and bore heraldic or other marks of provenance. No common soldier, it seems, wanted to be found concealing the crown of England at Bosworth. Campaigns might provide a bonanza for purveyors and producers of foodstuffs, cloth and various sorts of goods and services, for ale brewers, shoemakers and cobblers, and blacksmiths, bowyers, weavers and metalworkers, and for the carrying trade. When, after the threat of invasion receded in 1386, the armour of the especially lanky monk at Westminster was put up for sale, no one bought it – presumably there was a glut of harness on the market. When, in 1462, Beverley prepared a contingent for Edward IV's muster at Newcastle-upon-Tyne, the burgesses paid out for the embroidering of a new banner and its fitting to a staff, and for lengths of red cloth to make the soldiers' jackets. John Loryman was paid for hiring a horse and pack to carry his harness and victuals to Newcastle.[108] Moreover, some of the war-related demands were ongoing over the thirty years or so of intermittent and, in some periods, occasional campaigns. For able-bodied men were obliged by law to have their weapons, harness and other equipment at the ready. Fears that civil war might unexpectedly break out again must have been common, a normal mindset for several decades, when tensions between magnates remained high, and pretenders to the throne lurked abroad. Besides, for the militarily ambitious, there was sometimes the chance that war abroad might take off as in the old glory days. That, too, required readiness in case of urgent enrolment and departure.

Let us conclude with animals universally prized – not least for the status their possession conferred, especially in war. The Wars are likely to have helped to stimulate horse-breeding and rearing, and the trade of farriers and saddlers, partly to provide packhorses, but above all mounts, both essential components of the armies. Some of the Midlands horsefairs, such as those at Penkridge (Staffordshire) and Northampton, were to achieve a national significance. Many horses and ponies bred and reared throughout the realm ended up working in the south-east – a benefit to commanders who could recruit there. Woodland and pasture regions specialised in breeding and rearing horses, such as ponies for use as packhorses. It is probable that the equine economy of some less prosperous and more marginal regions benefited especially from the need for horses in the Wars of the Roses, regions such as the hills on either side of the frontier with Wales, the Staffordshire moorlands and forests, the Peak District and the Borders with Scotland. Recruits with mounts from some of these regions were probably prized for the skills they had developed in scouting, foraging and raiding. Such skills were characteristic of the reivers of the Anglo-Scottish Borders. Henry VIII was to be keen to employ Border horsemen in his French wars.[109]

5

Hopes and Fears

Falstaff [Plain near Shrewsbury]. Though I could 'scape shot-free at London, I fear the shot here: there's no scoring but upon the pate... I am as hot as molten lead, and as heavy too: God keep lead out of me! I need no more weight than my own bowels. – I have led my raggamuffins where they were peppered: there's not three of my hundred and fifty left alive; and they are for the town's end, to beg during life

King Henry IV, First Part, Act V, Scene III

What may have been the mindset and expectations of soldiers on setting off on campaign in the Wars – their aspirations and their apprehensions? Typically, they could have looked forward to an encouraging Godspeed from kinsfolk and neighbours who saw them as surrogates fulfilling common obligations to king or lord. Sometimes they may have been cheered on and buoyed up because they were seen as defenders of their shire or region against invasion. This is likely to have been the case for contingents from south-eastern shires who mustered to oppose Margaret of Anjou's army in 1461, and for the men of the East Riding of Yorkshire who flocked to the Lancastrian colours later in the year to oppose Edward IV. In 1470 the commons of Lincolnshire set off to war convinced that they had to fight to save their communities from punishment

by Edward.[1] Cities sometimes gave wine to companies they had
hired, and it is probable that both civic rulers and captains were
keen that they should make a brave sight when they set off in
fulfilment of the community's public obligations, their high wages
having been paid for by the inhabitants. The company was sometimes provided with showy uniforms to maintain civic honour.[2]
It was important for men of standing to assemble soldiers whose
appearance did them credit. In January 1461, when the southward
advance of Margaret of Anjou's army was expected soon, Clement
Paston wrote to his brother John in Norfolk, advising him to
come with armed men 'cleanlier arrayed than another man of
your country would, for it lies thee more upon your worship,
and toucheth you more near than other men of that country,
and also ye be more had in favour with my Lords here'. In 1536
the captain of Thomas Cromwell's company, Richard Cotton,
reported to him on his presentation of the men to the Duke of
Norfolk, royal commander against rebels. He wrote that 'to the
advancement of your honour… I have returned back 40 of your
company of such as were worst horsed, so that we are now 160
of as well horsed men as any are in the company… There were
divers of Essex men which are tall men of person and good
archers to the number of 12 which had no saddles but rode upon
panels after their country fashion which I thought was not to your
honour. So I have bought them saddles with other apparel for
their horses according as in my own conceit was meet for your
honour'.[3] These sort of sentiments may not have been confined
just to gentlefolk. The self-esteem of the ill mounted archers may
have soared when they were more fittingly provided for.

For experienced and well-equipped soldiers, there was often
the inducement of high wage rates. In January 1400, to oppose
the rebels who wished to restore Richard II, a proclamation was
made in London that those willing to serve Henry IV and the
city would receive 18d a day as lances and 9d as archers, sixpence
and threepence up respectively on the standard rate. By eight
o'clock the next day, thousands were said to have enrolled. A rate
of 12d a day for a soldier was offered for service in the Wars by

the city of Coventry in 1470, Earl Rivers in 1471, and the city of York in 1485.[4] Thomas Cromwell's captain was to report to him that 'Great murmur and grudging there was among your lordship's company because they thought the wages of 8d by the day was too little to find them and their horses. So as well as my poor wit shall serve me I have pacified them with fair words so that there is little said thereof now among any of us'. In particular, he was concerned that those of Cromwell's household servants among them who were younger brothers of slight means would 'mar their horses for lack of meat or else make such shifts for money that shall not stand well with your lordship's honour' [i.e. presumably, thieve]. Maybe some of Cromwell's company had been comparing notes with others whose employers were less thrifty.[5]

Many of the common folk who saw service in the Wars probably did so when obliged to guard the gates and walls of their cities and towns, like the watches set at King's Lynn during and after Edward IV's flight abroad from there in 1470.[6] Large numbers of men from London and York were needed to guard the long circuits of these most highly prized urban objectives – one reason, perhaps, why chronicles produced by and for Londoners show a keen awareness of campaigns. Though London experienced a short but sharp siege in 1471, the Wars (characteristically of later medieval English civil conflict) saw few sieges of towns. The harshest memories for many participants are likely to have been the tedium and cold of night watches. As for campaigning in England, soldiers could generally anticipate strenuous riding or marching for a few weeks, in easy outdoor living conditions – though the writer of the official account of Edward's campaigns in 1471 appears to echo the grumbles of soldiers about forced marches in hot weather, and shortages of food and water. Edward's opponents, when they reached Tewkesbury, 'had so travailled their host that night and day that they were right weary for travailling; for by that time they had travailled thirty-six long miles, in a foul country, all in lanes and stony ways, betwixt woods, without any good refreshing'. The majority of the Lancastrian army, who were footmen, were exhausted and needed to rest; also, 'horsemen were right weary of that journey, as so were their horses'.[7] Campaigning in rugged terrain north of the River Tees and in Wales could be miserable all the year round. Besides the prospect of hard toil, short commons and poor shelter, there were the dangers of guerilla attacks and ambushes for which much of the country was often suited, and in which local fighters were adept. In Northumberland, even the high road threading through the coastal plain, often distant from the rim of the Cheviots, was unsafe. In 1464 the Lancastrians set traps for Warwick's brother, John Neville, Lord Montague, travelling with a military retinue from Newcastle to Norham-upon-Tweed in order to escort Scots envoys. He evaded a trap laid by Sir Humphrey Neville, lying in wait with over eighty spearmen and bowmen in a wood near Newcastle. When he was about nine miles past the safe haven of Alnwick, he was ambushed while crossing Hedgeley Moor by the Duke of Somerset and other Lancastrian lords, whom his force managed to beat off.[8] However, the numbers of Englishmen involved in campaigning in these more challenging kinds of country were, for most of the Wars, small.

For many of those setting off on the mostly short campaigns in more douce regions of England, there were enjoyable prospects as well as forebodings. There was the camaraderie; there were the physical challenges, and there was the excitement of visiting unknown places. There might be combat, with its rush of adrenalin – and its exhilaration in stabbing and beating, to which the skeletons in the gravepit found at Towton Hall bear sad witness.[9] Indeed, as companies moved away from their own country, the dialects became harder to understand, and the inhabitants maybe less welcoming, though shared political allegiances might form a bond. Moreover, throughout England, there were unitary attitudes in popular culture which may have helped in bonding with strangers. There was strong general devotion to the conjoined cults of the Blessed Virgin Mary and St George as, respectively, England's proprietor and protector, and to St Thomas of Canterbury as its principal martyr and upholder of the rights of the Church against royal tyranny.[10] Archery was a universal sport (as was football, frowned on by the authorities); the presence of strangers may have led to impromptu contests. Travelling minstrels had created common mythical heroes; a chaplain who headed bandits operating in Sussex and Surrey in the early fifteenth century went under the name of 'Friar Tuck'.[11]

On campaign, one might sample a variety of ales and meet flirtatious girls, the virtue of some of whom was easily purchased. One might relax in alehouses in a more unbuttoned and swaggering way than on home ground. Though there were not profits to be made from nobles' ransoms, or from sacking or 'ransoming' villages, in ways fondly recalled by veterans of the French wars, there were likely to be plenty of opportunities to seize clothes, harness, weapons, purses and horses in the aftermath of battle. There were fine trophies for the picking, for which common soldiers, if they had to hand them over to their captains, could at least hope for some remuneration. At Radcot Bridge in 1387, as Robert de Vere spurred his horse in flight, he threw away his sword and gauntlets. The chronicler at Westminster Abbey had heard that his Franciscan confessor, drowned in a marsh there, had had a knapsack which contained £800 in gold coins, and that a horse of de Vere's was carrying £4,000 in gold. The victorious noble rebels were said to have secured the horsepack, and a baggage cart (presumably de Vere's), laden with gold and silver plate, clothing, bedding, tableware and other utensils.[12] At the battle of Shrewsbury, Henry Parker made off with a pair of knives and seven spoons of gold and silver, belonging to the King.[13] Proclamations sometimes made by commanders before battle that only the commons were to be spared were an incitement for soldiers to swarm round the distinctively armed and apparelled nobles, and perhaps win a small fortune in chattels by killing them. Charles the Bold's body was discovered stripped. Bishop Ruthal wrote after Flodden that 'The English did not trouble themselves to make prisoners, but slew and stripped the King, bishops, lords and nobles, and left them naked on the field... my folks under

St Cuthbert's banner brought home his [James IV's] banner, his sword and his qwysschys, that is to say the harness for his thighs'. When Henry Tudor ordered that Richard III's body should be 'covered from the waist downwards with a black cloth of poor quality', it was presumably a gesture, if a somewhat minimal one, of decency because eager plunderers had made a thorough job of looting the harness and raiment of the fallen King.[14]

The returning soldier who had survived a notable fight intact and had material gains to display would win prestige in his community. Teenage boys may have been fired by such examples to enrol. As minors under strict rule of their elders, and as labourers, servants, apprentices and undergraduates, they were low in status. Typically, they lived narrowly constricted lives on short commons in meagre and cold lodgings, their morals as well as their work controlled by a master, if not a father. There were, indeed, brief periods of the year when they were licensed to behave in less inhibited ways, within traditional bounds – enjoying revels, sometimes in role reversal with their superiors, notably during the Christmas and Prelenten festivities. Then there were the celebrations of May Day and Midsummer's Eve out-of-doors in uninhibited and lascivious junketings. However, boys sought more haphazard, dangerous and disapproved ways of letting off steam, by staging or joining in riots. The Welsh chronicler Adam Usk recalled how, when he was studying canon law at Oxford in his youth in the late 1380s, southern and Welsh students were embroiled with the northerners for two years, resulting in loss of life. He stated with a certain pride how he was among those indicted and tried for felonious riot, 'as the chief leader and abettor of the Welsh, and perhaps not unrighteously'. He was acquitted, but said that his brush with the law taught him a lesson.[15] Apprentices were to the fore when there were urban riots against aliens – most notably on 'Evil May Day' in London in 1517. This rising was preceded by rumours that all aliens in the city would be slain, and was triggered when an alderman tried to arrest a young man. A crowd of them were watching two play at 'Bucklers' in Cheapside, contrary to the hastily imposed curfew. Young men resisted the alderman's attempt, crying 'prentyses and clubbes', which signalled the start of the riots. Afterwards, those arrested were brought in through the streets tied in ropes, some men, some lads, some children of thirteen years. 'Poor younglings' were among those convicted of treason and executed – harsher treatment than Henry IV had meted out to rebel lads at Oxford in 1400.[16] Maybe the Wars of the Roses offered more honourable and socially acceptable opportunities for mayhem to restless young men who chafed at the restrictions in their lives and craved excitement and danger.

Even though companies may sometimes have set out for war in a holiday mood, memories of previous civil conflicts must have suggested that there was a high chance of the campaign ending in a battle. Indeed, in some campaigns most of those in arms never fired a shot or raised a bill in combat. The Duke of York's assault on Henry VI in St Albans in 1455 was over so quickly that major forces on both sides could not come up in time. Most of the forces in the 1459 campaign did not engage – the confrontation at Ludford Bridge did not lead to the anticipated battle. The forces led by Warwick and Clarence in the North in 1469 never engaged with Edward IV's, fresh from their easy victory at Losecoat Field, and the forces led by these two lords in 1470 did not need to fight Edward, as Lord Montague's desertion from his cause undermined his attempts to resist. At Bosworth, notoriously, many of the companies were engaged briefly or not at all.

There were particular reasons to fear combat in the battles of the Wars of the Roses, as well as for optimism about survival unscathed. Young men setting forth on their first campaign may have been buoyed up by stories of the extraordinarily few English casualties at Agincourt (their small numbers further diminished by hearsay), but there must have been a growing awareness, especially after the battles of 1459 and 1461, that major engagements in civil wars could be different. For those companies which clashed in battle, the chances of being killed or maimed were high, because of the large numbers of archers deployed on both sides, and the common soldiers' lack of complete sets of plate armour, which by this period offered good protection against arrows. In medieval warfare, flesh wounds alone could easily result in death through infection.

As we have seen, medieval surgeons and physicians had some remarkable successes in treating wounds. Theodoric of Bologna, bishop of Cervia, in his treatise on *Surgery* (1267), demonstrated the feasibility of curing intestinal as well as scalp and chest wounds, emphasising the need to deal with infection particularly in the first kind. He devoted chapters to the extraction of arrows and the treatment of the sort of wounds which they caused.[17] The Englishman John Arderne, who practised at Newark (Nottinghamshire) from 1349 to 1370, wrote a treatise expounding his procedures for treating anal fistulae. Their occurrence may have become more prevalent as a consequence of Edward III's wars, especially as a result of chevauchées. Arderne's editor, Sir D'Arcy Power, wrote that, 'Wet, cold, long hours in the saddle weighed down by the heavy armour of the time, would readily lead to this condition in the knightly class'. Arderne says that he first cured it in the case of Sir Adam Everingham of Laxton. Adam, born *c.*1306, first went to war ('was armed') at the age of nineteen, and participated in Edward III's early campaigns – the siege of Berwick and battle of Halidon Hill (1333), the naval battle of Sluis and the siege of Tournai (1340). When he was serving Henry of Grosmont (future Duke of Lancaster) in Gascony in the 1340s, he suffered from a fistula. Arderne says that he consulted leeches and surgeons widely (for instance, from Bordeaux, Bergerac, Toulouse, Narbonne, and Poitiers), who all pronounced him incurable. He hastened back home, where 'he did off all his knightly clothings and clad mourning clothes, in purpose of abiding dissolving or losing of his body being nigh to him'. However, Arderne took six months to cure him, 'and afterwards whole and sound, he led a glad life by 30 years and more, for which cure I got much honour and loving through all England.' Indeed, Sir Adam may have followed Edward III to war again, to Scotland in 1356 and to France in 1359.[18]

For his specialist operation, Arderne charged on a sliding scale, according to status (and concomitant wealth). He never accepted less than £5. If his fees were typical, it is unlikely that any but the wealthiest commoners could afford to pay for serious surgery and treatment after a battle – most would have to depend on the charity of patrons or the pious. The primary concern of the physicians and surgeons at the scene of battles, who were contracted to serve nobles, was for the welfare of their patron and his close friends.[19] With valuable medicines and instruments in their bags, physicians may have been cautious about wandering around the menacing environment of a battlefield in the immediate aftermath, just at the time when the chances of saving the incapacitated wounded were highest. That was when large numbers succumbed. Many were doubtless finished off by pillagers like Goushill's esquire at Shrewsbury. Some may have survived by feigning death, others because they were concussed or in a coma. A combination of nakedness and falling temperatures at night would have provided the *coup de grâce* for many, but may have saved some, as the chill brought them round. The removal of soiled clothing by looters took away a strong source of infection. There was the hope for the immobile of rescue by their servants and friends, scouring the field. There were some remarkable survival stories. At Barnet in 1471, the Duke of Exeter was 'greatly despoiled and wounded and left naked for dead in the field, and so lay there from 7 of clock till 4 after noon, which was taken up and brought to a house by a man of his own, and a leech brought to him, and so afterwards brought in to sanctuary at Westminster'.[20]

The rapid development of gunpowder technology and the greater availability of improved cannons and firearms in the second half of the fifteenth century increased the hazards of potentially lethal wounds, especially for the lightly harnessed common soldier. One casualty was Henry Walter of Guildford (Surrey), who in 1484 was serving in a fleet which set out from Scarborough (Yorkshire), under the command of Sir Thomas Everingham. In an engagement round about 6 June, Walter received a terrible stomach wound from a cannonball. He was not expected to live. After the battle, he was put overboard in a small boat, 'in case his wound proved dangerous or noisome to his companions'. There he lay, in agony and delirious, for eleven days. He experienced visions of Henry VI, and of a favourite saint of his, Erasmus, lying 'just as he is often represented in churches as being tortured by his executioners'. St Erasmus was said to have been disembowelled by having his intestines wound round a windlass. Only when the ship put into port did Walter receive medical treatment. He was taken to a hospital – hospitals which gave succour to indigent wayfarers may have afforded respite to some injured soldiers after the battles of the Wars. Robert Copland, in *The Highway to the Spitalhouse* (London, *c.*1530) refers to relief being given to 'maimed soldiers'. In hospital (presumably at Scarborough), Henry Walter certainly received professional medical attention. Yet physicians (*medici*) did not dare take on the case; they said that he would die soon. However,

> He found a surgeon who contrived to cut away the gangrened flesh on both sides as far as he might, and to bind the wound at last and soothe it with ointments; so giving him, not health, but the hope of health. For so it was that whenever they took off the bandages and tore away the plasters, and were ready to cleanse the wound, whatever food he had taken that day showed itself there all undigested.

Walter decided to go home – an ordeal for an invalid, especially if he lived as far away as Guildford. This was at about the time (August) when Richard III had Henry VI's remains translated from Chertsey Abbey to St George's Chapel, Windsor Castle. The King had taken a keen interest in Everingham's expeditions and had recently made frequent visits to Scarborough. The invalid sent his sister with an image of himself in wax on pilgrimage to Henry's new shrine; afterwards he started to recover slowly, and was able to make the pilgrimage and testify at the shrine himself.[21]

As we have seen, if an English soldier of the rank and file was captured on campaign, there was a good chance that he might be spared and released, though relieved of anything of value. This may have been a normal convention of civil war in England, as Commynes was to allege.[22] In 1387 the Duke of Ireland's soldiers from Cheshire who had surrendered to the army of the Lords Appellant at Radcot Bridge were allowed to go home, deprived of their weapons and horses. Some, however, drowned in the Thames, and large numbers were ridden down in the adjacent marshes by those in pursuit of the Duke.[23]

When the Yorkist lords had arrayed their soldiers to attack the King's encampment at Northampton in 1460, they had it proclaimed that 'no man should lay hand upon the king nor on the common people, but only on the lords, knights and squires'.[24] Edward IV, according to Commynes, was to strive to enforce this rule.[25] However, it is likely that, in the heat of battle, men whose blood was up preferred to kill. At Northampton, panic may have ensued in the main 'battle' of the King's army after Edmund, Lord Grey of Ruthin, led its vanguard over to the Yorkist side; fleeing men were likely to arouse merciless pursuit. 'Many were slain, and many were fled, and were drowned in the river [Nene]'.[26] The multiple wounds inflicted on the victims from the grave-pit at Towton Hall indicate that they were either not allowed to surrender or that they were savagely beaten to death after surrender. Abnormal developments in left arm-bones suggest that some or all of them were archers, common soldiers, not gentlefolk.[27] Contemporaries considered the battle at Towton to have been exceptionally long and hard-fought. These killings may have been the work of men utterly keyed up by the intensity of combat, in an exhausted frenzy compounded by hunger and thirst and cold. Rather than face pursuers such as these, many Lancastrian soldiers waded into the River Wharfe at Tadcaster, and were drowned.[28]

In 1471 Edward IV, attempting to conquer the realm for a second time, seems to have wearied of trying to save the commons arrayed against him. At the battle of Barnet, according to

Commynes, 'the slaughter was exceedingly heavy' because King Edward decided, when he left Flanders, that he would no longer adhere to his custom of shouting that the common soldiers should be saved, and that the nobles should be killed, as he had done in his earlier battles. He had conceived a deep hatred against the people of England for the great favour which he saw the people bore towards the Earl of Warwick, and also for other reasons. So they were not spared this time'.[29] At Tewkesbury, where Edward defeated the remaining Lancastrians, a harsh policy probably contributed to the deaths of 'a very large number of the common soldiers'.[30] However, at Bosworth, according to Polydore Vergil, when Richard was killed, 'all men threw down their weapons, and freely submitted themselves to Henry's obedience'. If so, Henry must at some point have given an order to spare those who surrendered; indeed, the casualties appear to have been light. The second continuator of the Crowland Chronicle wrote that only three of those who surrendered were executed – William Catesby, Richard's leading councillor, was beheaded, and a father and son named Brecher were hanged. The chronicler says that Henry was praised by everyone for his clemency, 'as if he was an angel from heaven'. As Henry had former knights of Edward's body in his company, he must have known about the slaughters perpetrated in his name in the battles of 1471, and set out to distance himself from such harshness.[31]

Accumulating folklore about the slaughter in the conflicts of the Wars (such as that so long remembered at Towton) may have induced, by the 1480s, if not before, a widespread desire not to be enlisted, or, if enlisted, to avoid full-scale combat. There were the deterrents of the devastating firepower of archers, the possibility, if captured, of not being allowed quarter, the likelihood, if badly wounded, of having one's throat slit, or being left to die. The ways in which many of the armies of the Wars were constituted and composed posed particular risks that they would give way to panic and disintegrate. Then flight posed the dangers of death by misadventure, or from the instincts of the hunters, or at least the loss of a trail of discarded and abandoned possessions. Many of the armies were fragile coalitions of royal and noble retinues and levies from different shires, cobbled together at short notice, and often unused to working together, if at all, in the field. These were unlike the experienced retinues under well-trusted leaders which in 1424, commanded by John, Duke of Bedford, the infant Henry VI's uncle and Regent of France, against the odds won the battle with Charles VII's formidable army at Verneuil in Normandy. There the English front was broken by a cavalry charge, but the soldiers doggedly regrouped and advanced rather than disintegrating.[32]

In the Wars, kings and magnates did not have the luxury of commencing their campaigns with prolonged if debilitating sieges (as Henry V had done at Harfleur in 1415), where they could harden their troops and develop their working relationships. One chronicler from London recounted sorrowfully how the day before Margaret of Anjou's army triumphed at St Albans in 1461, it had had a success at Dunstable – probably over levies from Bedfordshire: 'the king's company lacked good guiding, for some were but new men of war, for the chiefest captain was a butcher of the same town; and there were the king's company overthrown only by the Northern men. And soon after the butcher, for shame of his simple guiding and loss of the men, the number of 800, for very sorrow as it is said, hung himself; and some men said that it was for loss of his goods, but dead he is – God knows the truth'.[33] Noble leaders and their captains, even when expert at war, may often have been mistrusted by the rank and file from the start, especially in the light of the crucial treachery of Trollope at Ludford Bridge and Lord Grey at Northampton. In the thick of the battle of Barnet, the soldiers of the Lancastrian Earl of Oxford only too readily believed that Warwick and his men had gone over to Edward. Crying 'treason', 800 of them withdrew, facilitating Edward's victory.[34]

The need to inspire confidence in the soldiers reinforced the decisions of some nobles to fight on foot, as the main body of English soldiers were accustomed to do, and as Henry V and his nobles had done with them at Agincourt. Edward, over six feet tall, was a figure easily recognised in the lines. The high toll of nobles killed or captured in battle in the Wars reflects the fact that they were in some respects more at risk than the humblest and most naked soldier, since their opponents were frequently urged not to spare the gentlefolk, and their armours, however flexibly tailor-made, hobbled nimbleness in flight, as well as making them conspicuous. According to Commynes, Warwick was concerned about this; he 'was not used to dismounting to fight for after bringing his men into battle he used to mount his horse. If the battle was going well for him he would throw himself into the fray but if it was going badly he would make an early escape. This time however [at Barnet] he was constrained by his brother, the Marquis of Montague, who was a very courageous knight, to dismount and send away his horses. So it happened that the earl was killed this day with the marquis of Montague and a very large number of men of noble birth.'[35]

It is not clear whether Richard III and Henry Tudor were mounted throughout the battle of Bosworth. Certainly Henry must have been tempted to prepare for a speedy exit, considering his inexperience in warfare, the greater size of the royal army, and the failure of Lord Stanley to come in on his side in the early stage of the battle. For Richard, being mounted had the advantage of making him conspicuous to his troops; if Niclas von Popplau is to be believed, he did not cut a striking figure (unlike Edward).[36] His cavalry charge, presumably with knights and esquires of his household concentrated in his main 'battle', may have alarmed the soldiers of his 'forward' battle, engaged on foot under the Duke of Norfolk's command with Henry's forward, and also the remaining soldiers on foot in his own battle. Frustrated by Norfolk's lack of success, and alarmed by Stanley's passivity, Richard was presumably anxious to avoid the fate of Warwick and Montague, apparently trapped with the footmen at Barnet – where he had fought on the victorious side. Yet, for his lines engaged on foot, or expecting to be imminently engaged, with their attention riveted on the immediate dangers around or ahead of them, the King's famous charge at Henry's company,

on the periphery of their vision, or known only from confus-
ing shouts in the hubbub, may have demoralised them from the
moment he broke out of the lines. What must have been clear to
them was that the King and his picked spearmen, on horseback,
were distancing themselves from the mass of the army, on foot.
The integrity of armies in battle in the Wars depended on the
close co-operation of the experienced and the novices, the well
armoured and the lightly protected, the horse and foot. In the one
battle in which Richard had the supreme command, he made a
fatal decision, widening rather than diminishing the fault lines
which characteristically ran through the armies of the Wars. He
did so because of his sickened recognition of the appearance of
another typical sympton of their fragility: the leaders of his army
had varying political agendas. His action suggests his distrust, too,
of the mass of arrayed men who were still loyal in dispositions,
a distrust likely to have been borne of experience, and likely to
have been shared by other commanders in the Wars.

For soldiers who set out light-heartedly or unwillingly, but
who soon had forebodings that they were being led to disaster,
there was the option of desertion, either as a company, or singly
– though, for many, especially those serving in fellowship with
men from their own community, the latter course would have
been inhibited by the pressure for group-loyalty. The sources are
unenlightening on the subject; they do not give the impression
that armies haemorrhaged on the line of march, but that they
might collapse speedily in battle. The miserable circumstances of
besieging armies were always inducements to desertion, and this
may have been true of the relatively few sieges in the Wars. In
1462 young John Paston was in the army which Edward IV had
led north to recapture the three great castles in Northumberland
garrisoned by the Lancastrians, at Alnwick, Dunstanburgh and
Bamburgh. On 11 December Paston wrote to his elder brother
John from Newcastle: 'In case we abide here, I pray you purvey
that I may have here more money by Christmas Eve at the
furthest, for I may get leave for to send none of my waged men
home again; no man can get no leave for to go home but if

they steal away, and if they might be known [found out], they should be sharply punished. Make as merry as ye can, for there is no jeopardy [hazard] toward not yet.'[37] Young John's reference to merriment reflects rueful anticipation of missing the Paston household's Christmas festivities, snug in Norfolk, and of spending the holidays amidst the barely comprehensible strangers of Newcastle – incentives for other southerners to desert, especially arrayed men required to serve beyond the statutory period.

There are hints that there was a willingness to desert in Richard III's army in 1485 – though these may have stemmed from the eagerness of his soldiers afterwards to disssociate themselves from his rule, and from Tudor propaganda. Polydore Vergil says that the King's army advanced to Leicester flanked by horsemen. Perhaps this was a well-tried expedient, not just to protect the less well equipped and experienced men, and the baggage, but to prevent them from slipping away. According to Vergil, Richard's soldiers were deserting from the outset of the battle, and the majority would have gone over to Henry but for the King's mounted scouts preventing them by 'rushing back and forth'.[38] If the sluggishness which Vergil attributed to the rank and file in Richard's army was not an inventive gloss, it may have been caused not by their alleged hatred of the King's supposed crimes, but by resentment at the timing of his summonses to array, in time of harvest. We know that the corn was standing in Leicestershire when the battle was fought (22 August), for Henry swiftly granted compensation for his soldiers' destruction of it in the vicinity.[39] Many rural communities must have been infuriated at labour being diverted to war in a crucial period in the agricultural year, and many labourers upset that opportunities to make good wages safely were thwarted by orders to gain them dangerously. No previous commander in the Wars had dared to launch a campaign in August. If Henry Tudor did so deliberately, it was a shrewd move, fitting in with the composition of the opposed armies. For he relied to some extent on mercenaries, and on recruitment of domiciled supporters, in the first instance, in Wales, in most of which grain production was marginal – whereas the King needed to recruit heavily in prime

English wheat-growing regions. Henry's strategy may have been worked out by the veteran commanders whom he had with him. As the Crowland Continuator remarked, they were 'notable for their military standing before this disturbance as well as in the conflict just begun'.[40] On Henry's side there were distinguished knights who had fought alongside Richard. Perhaps they predicted that the King (who had experienced how his brother had been taken by surprise by his enemies in 1469 and 1470) would overact to news of the invasion, hastily dragging husbandmen on a large scale away from the harvest.

Despite the hazards faced in battle by shakily constituted armies, they often, as has been seen, performed tenaciously and with great bravery in the field. Indeed, on occasion it may have been lords, knights and esquires, and veterans and professional soldiers, who were principally behaving like this: participating gentlefolk had their lives, honour and family fortunes at stake in the conflicts. The London chronicler who gave a vivid account of the battle of St Albans in 1461 (and perhaps was a participant on the losing Yorkist side) asserted that 'The substance that gate [won] that field were household men and fee'd men. I ween there were not 5,000 men that fought in the queen's party, for the most part of Northern men fled away, and some were taken and spoiled out of their harness by the way as they fled. And some of them robbed ever as they went, a pitiful thing it is to hear it'.[41] He was saying that it was the officers and servants of the queen's and lords' households, and the recipients of her annuities and of the latter's who actually won the battle. The chronicler probably had his own agenda in emphasising this: the defeat of the men of his 'country' and its neighbouring 'countries' by suchlike was honourable, whereas defeat by what they regarded as a northern rabble was not. Other contemporary accounts of the battles focussed on the engagement and losses of nobles and gentlefolk. However, as regards some hard-fought fights, it was probably not balanced of the writers to concentrate on their contributions alone, while ignoring that of the commons. Contemporary corrrespondence about Towton doubtless gives inflated figures for the dead, but the extraordinary totals given (a reflection of shocked reactions at the scale of the slaughter) suggests that they were to be counted in thousands – and these must have included many besides household men and fee'd men.[42]

Mainly mundane motives have been suggested above for participation by the commons – the necessity of responding to demands by Crown or lord (or both), the excitement of being briefly freed from the customary bonds and burdens of society to seek out adventure, the hopes of gain. Were common soldiers sometimes motivated by political and other more abstract considerations? As we have seen, rebellious lords on occasion broadcast manifestos asserting that they intended to enforce reform of the conduct of government through the traditional panacea of expelling from office and punishing the King's 'evil' counsellors. In this period their intended constituency included rich and respectable commoners, some of whom were capable of appreciating and, indeed, themselves articulating broad political concepts about the relationship of kingship to the common weal of the realm.[43]

Moreover, as has been suggested, some commons who put on their harness when potentially hostile forces from other parts of the realm were approaching may have been animated by patriotic determination to protect their 'country', as well as their own families, tenements, chattels and livelihoods. The concept of honour was not entirely alien to societies of peasants and artisans, at least in their higher reaches. The earliest surviving ballad of Robin Hood, *A Gest of Robyn Hode*, dating from the later fifteenth century, describes him as a yeoman, a status accorded customarily to certain sorts of superior servants, but by this period a well-established self-description used by many farmers with aspiring lifestyles. In the ballad, Robin is depicted as an embodiment of the courtly and chivalrous virtues – a sort of popular equivalent of Sir Gawain, knight of King Arthur's Round Table.[44] Tenants serving in their landlords' retinues, and recipients of such patrons' minor offices and favours may sometimes have been fired up by pride and zeal in serving a particular noble house, especially if their forefathers had done so too. Hotspur's men at the battle of Shrewsbury had shouted (absurdly) 'Henry Percy King'.[45] Maybe displays of adulation by troops helped to turn the heads of some magnates during the Wars towards usurping the Crown or, at least, towards kingmaking. St David's day (1 March) was a red-letter holiday in 1461 for the Earl of March (fresh from his victory over Welsh opponents) and Warwick. Outside the walls of London, to the north of Aldersgate:

> The host mustered in St John's field and there was read among them certain articles and points that king harry the vi had offended in against the realm. And then it was demanded of the people whether the said harry were worthy to reign still and the people cried nay; and then was asked if they would have the Earl of March to their king and they cried yea.

Then 'certain captains' went to his residence in the city, Baynard's Castle, 'and much people with them and told him that the people had chosen him for king'; he thanked them, and accepted.[46] This was heady stuff for the commons, too: formally, it was a crowd of them who first *en masse* withdrew their allegiances from Henry and gave them to Edward. Who composed much or most of this crowd? The account provides pointers. St John's Fields had been used before as a camping ground for armies. It was a 'host' (army) which was 'mustered', and 'captains' who went as its main delegates to Edward. So a little-known, youthful noble was acclaimed king by his army, like some antique Roman emperor raised on a shield. We must not omit the possibility that some of these common soldiers, who were all taking on an awesome responsibility in the eyes of God, and other soldiers in the Wars, were pledging their allegiances and fighting out of dynastic conviction.

BOOSTING MORALE

Those about to take part in a battle were conscious of its deep religious significance. Even though they had confessed beforehand, their souls might be condemned to suffer if they shed blood in an unrighteous cause. There were soldiers' ceremonies marked by words of intercession and gestures of humility, which reflect this consciousness, possibly heightened by the vivid concepts of Purgatory current in the period. Before the English fought the invading army of David II at Neville's Cross near Durham in 1346, they knelt and prayed.[47] At Agincourt they also put earth in their mouths, and Charles the Bold, reporting on their preparations for battle at Neuss in 1475, describes them as 'according to their custom, making the sign of the cross on the ground and kissing it'.[48] Commanders' concerns about licentious and quarrelsome behaviour may have stemmed not only from the threats this posed to good order, but to the bestowal of God's goodwill on their cause. In his Ordinances of War of 1473, Charles the Bold forbade blasphemy; the Venetian observer of the Earl of Surrey's army in 1513 described the soldiers as eschewing it in favour of prayerfulness.[49] By contrast, one recalls Joan of Arc's references to English soldiers as 'Goddams', because of their habitual oath.

Kings and would-be kings needed to reassure their troops of their faith in God's favour, by appearing in majesty on the battlefield, though Christine de Pisan, weighing the pros and cons of such royal involvement, had been dubious: 'no one can foresee to which side God will give the good fortune of victory'. She cited the cases of Charles V of France and Giangaleazzo Visconti, Duke of Milan, successful warleaders who never left their palaces. However, she argued that it was preferable for a king to go in person against rebellious subjects, in order to instil fear in them at their defiance of majesty.[50] The English favoured regal display in the midst of any dangers. At the battle of Shrewsbury in 1403, to confuse the enemy as well as to reassure his men, Henry IV had three 'false Henries' in the field, wearing 'royal coronets on top of their helmets'.[51] The Burgundian chronicler Monstrelet says that at Agincourt, 'the Duke of Alencon gave him [Henry V] a blow on his basinet that struck off part of his crown.'[52] Henry VI, when he was trying to rally support in

Northumberland in 1464, had a crown with him, which had a double circlet, to reflect his coronation in France as well as England. After his supporters were defeated at Hexham, among the spoils he had to abandon was his 'bycokete [Old French *bicoquet*, ornamental cap], richly garnished with 2 crowns'.[53] Richard III was probably following well-established precedents in wearing a crown at Bosworth. His soldiers would have been even more disheartened than they apparently were if he had hidden rather than projected his majesty.

So when the king was present on the battlefield, the secureness of the crown glinting on his helmet was a focus of anxious attention. The transfer of Richard's crown on the spot to Henry's head was an unmistakeable sign of God's will. In every conflict, soldiers nervously scanned their surroundings for signs of numinous activity. Gutierre Diaz de Gamez uniquely provides us with the observations of a medieval standard-bearer. He emphasises the weight of responsibility he bore in discharging his office bravely but prudently: 'Well do soldiers know that all have their eyes on the banner, enemies as well as friends; and if its men see it retreat in the battle, they lose heart, while the enemies' courage waxes; and if they see it stand firm or go forward, they do the same'.[54] When, on Jersey in 1406, a combined force of Castilians, Bretons and Normans were heavily engaged with the English and Jerseymen, his commander Pero Niño detatched a company to attack the standard of St George. 'Friends', he said, 'so long as this flag flies, these English will never allow themselves to be beaten'. The banner was cast down, and the resistance of the main defending lines ebbed away into flight.[55] Standards were, indeed, principal signals of battle dispositions, but the almost mystical attachment which is still accorded to a regiment's colours perhaps echoes medieval religious sentiment focussed on them. The English soldiers – and Welsh and other soldiers serving with them – who could no longer see the banner of St George borne aloft may have been struck by fear that the saint had withdrawn his favour from the English – at the behest of the Mother of God, with whom, as we have seen, he was closely associated in the national hagiography. Another potent banner, in the north of England, was that of St Cuthbert, which was taken out of Durham Cathedral on campaign to bolster the morale of armies opposing the Scots. At Flodden it was with the men from the bishopric under the command of Lord Lumley. Bishop Ruthall wrote that the 'banner men [the colour party?] won great honour and gained the King of Scots' banner, which now stands before the shrine [of the saint]... All believe it [the victory] has been wrought by St Cuthbert, who never suffered anything to be done to his Church unrequited'.[56] In 1536 the Pilgrims from the bishopric of Durham displayed their saint's banner. It was white and crimson velvet, embroidered in gold and silk, with St Cuthbert's cross in the middle.[57]

Other attempts were made to associate regional cults with campaigns. Bolingbroke, after landing with a small armed company in 1399, linked himself to Yorkshire cults as he tried to rally support for his enterprise. He had come ashore some thirty miles south of Bridlington, in whose Augustinian priory lay the tomb of Prior John Thwenge (d. 1379), who had gained a widespread reputation for holiness – he was to be canonised in 1401. According to a hostile account, Bolingbroke swore to the Earl of Northumberland and his son Sir Henry Percy 'on the relics of Bridlington' that he would not strive for the crown – possibly the relics of the prior were brought to Doncaster for the purpose. Propaganda favourable to Bolingbroke spread the story that oil seeped from St John of Beverley's marble tomb in the Minster there continually day and night for thirty-one days after he had landed – presumably a sign that the saint wished Bolingbroke to be anointed as king.[58]

Welsh armies had a potent secular symbol. They probably flew the standard of the red dragon – Henry Tudor did so in 1485.[59] This related to a dearly-held national myth, centring on the 'Prophecies of Merlin'. The text of this, circulating in both Wales and England, was attributed to this awesome magician, closely associated with King Arthur. The triumph of the red dragon over its rival in the prophecies was held in Wales to foreshadow a reversal of fortunes in the old struggle between the Britons and the Saxons, in which the descendants of the former would once more wrest the mastery of Britain from those of its conquerors. It is likely that there was a distinctive animus current among Welsh soldiers in the Wars, especially when, as in 1485 and under William Herbert in 1469, they were operating on English soil. Beside this momentous forecast, linking all the soldiers with the heroic deeds of their forbears' warbands, the chivalrous culture the Welsh gentry shared with the English appears tame.[60]

Soldiers scoured the horizon and peered at relics in search of signs, and their commanders were eager to exploit any manifestation in order to boost morale. There are two well-known instances in the Wars of the Roses, and doubtless there were others. According to a pro-Yorkist chronicler, describing the future Edward IV's victory at Mortimer's Cross in 1461:

> About ten o'clock before noon, were seen three suns in the firmament shining full clear, whereof the people [i.e. Edward's soldiers] had great marvel and thereof were aghast. The noble Earl Edward them comforted and said, 'Be of good comfort and dread not; this is a good sign, for these three suns betoken the Father, the Son and the Holy Ghost, and therefore let us have good heart, and in the name of Almighty God go we against our enemies.[61]

The sentiment does not sound characteristic of an eighteen-year-old, pleasure-loving youth; perhaps it was put into his mouth by a quick-thinking chaplain. The parhelion appeared on the vigil of Candlemas (the Feast of the Purification of the Blessed Virgin Mary), protector of England against invasion. In the battle, according to one chronicler, the Yorkists 'slew of the Welshmen the number of 4,000', and there were merciless executions afterwards of captured gentlefolk, one justification for which may have been their defiance of the Trinity.[62] The God-given nature of the victory, which was to be the prelude to the usurpation, probably made a big impression on Edward and his soldiers, since he adopted a sun as one of his principal badges, a perpetual reminder of the miraculous appearance. After the coinage was reminted in 1464, a sun sometimes appeared on various denominations of his coins. A livery collar was devised for Edward's servants consisting of alternate suns and white roses – roses were associated in iconography with the Blessed Virgin. Notable surviving examples of the collar's use are on the figure of the comptroller of Edward's household, Sir Robert Wingfield (d.1480), in stained glass in East Harling church (Norfolk), and on that of one of the King's most trusted retainers, the Welshman Sir John Donne, on the altarpiece which Donne commissioned from Hans Memling.

When Mortimer's Cross was fought, the circumstances were critical for the Yorkist cause. The same was true in 1471, after Edward invaded the realm, when he was at Daventry (Northamptonshire), on the road to London, with Warwick's army to his rear, and the capital being held against him. According to the official account of Edward's campaigns in 1471, in his recent period of exile in the Low Countries, St Anne had been one of the saints to whom he had prayed especially for help: he promised to make an offering at the first image of her which he encountered. In Daventry parish church there was a little alabaster statue of the saint affixed to a pillar in front of the place where he knelt for Mass on Palm Sunday. When he went in the procession around the church, the shutters enclosing her statue, closed since Ash Wednesday, of their own accord opened slightly, then closed, then opened fully. 'The king, seeing this, thanked God, and St Anne, taking it for a good sign, and token of a good and prosperous aventure that God would send him in that he had to do'.[63] One may be sure that news of the miracle was soon spread round the host. Maybe there were speculations among the soldiers that it betokened that, just as Christ had entered Jerusalem in triumph, so Edward would be received in London. Perhaps some recalled how, after Agincourt, Henry V had been received in the city in one of the most remarkable series of English civic pageants of the century, in which it was projected as Jerusalem.[64] St Anne was one of the most popular saints, frequently depicted nurturing and teaching her daughter, the Blessed Virgin. It may have been in gratitude for the miracle of Daventry that the daughter born to Edward in 1475 was christened Anne; from at least the following year his sister Margaret duchess of Burgundy was a sister of the Guild of St Anne at Ghent.[65]

Besides having the saints marching with them, soldiers valued the spiritual ministrations of leading clergymen who accompanied them too. There were bishops with Queen Isabella's army when she rebelled in 1326.[66] Before combat at Neville's Cross, the archbishop of York, William Zouche proclaimed the forgiveness of the soldiers' sins, and commanded them to oppose vigorously the great malice of the Scots and to defend their country (*pais*).[67] In 1399 the presence in Bolingbroke's army of Thomas Arundel, former archbishop of both York and Canterbury, and a vigorous personality, is likely to have been a comfort to those rebelling against a king who had made much of his God-given authority. In the 1405 rising Archbishop Scrope preached in York Minster, exhorting the people to help reform the bad government of the realm. The text of his sermon was put up in the vernacular on the city gates, and he ordered parish priests in neighbouring villages to preach on similar lines.[68] The monk-chronicler of St Albans says that he promised forgiveness and plenary remission to those who died in the cause, and that, as a result, the common people (*populares*) and almost all the citizens of York who could bear arms flocked to support him.[69] On the morrow of the Ascension he celebrated Mass before a crowd of supporters on Shipton Moor, and once more preached on his reforming intentions, solemnly swearing that he was not rising against the King, nor had any evil intentions towards him.[70]

The weightiest ecclesiastical support any army of the Wars of the Roses received (or, for that matter, most previous armies of rebels in England) was enjoyed by the Yorkists on their successful campaign in 1460, prior to York's raising of his claim to the throne in parliament, which precipitated the long-lasting dynastic conflict. The previous year an envoy from Pope Pius II had arrived in England, charged with promoting the campaign against the Turks. Francesco Coppini, bishop of Terni was small of stature and undistinguished in appearance, but had a strong personality and possessed energy, vivacity and eloquence. Back on the continent in 1460, he showed himself to have been won over to the Yorkist cause: he joined Salisbury, Warwick and March when they were embattled in Calais, and went with them on their invasion of England. After their admission to London, he wrote to Henry VI, justifying their appearance in arms along lines similar to those on which York (soon to return from his refuge in Ireland) had justified publicly his previous risings: 'They offer obedience and loyalty to your Majesty provided they can state their cause in safety. They say they cannot do this unless they come strongly armed, as is notorious, but they will abstain from using arms if they have facilities for an audience'. Coppini told Henry in a somewhat minatory way: 'You can prevent this [war] if you will, and if you do not you will be guilty in the sight of God in that awful day of judgment in which I also shall stand and require of your hand the English blood, if it is spilt'.[71] Native of a land where *signori* were frequently denigrated and overthrown, Coppini seems to have had no real sense of the majesty of an anointed English king. In addressing Henry in this way he displayed deep disrespect and outrageous partisanship. What is more, the tenor of this missive, likely to encourage violence rather than reconciliation, was read out at Paul's Cross, next to St Paul's Cathedral, where government on occasion communicated important messages to the crowd. Pius II was to react with fury at this bombastic fantasist's biased interventions, and his insinuations that he had powers more appropriate to a legate. In 1462, after he had returned to Rome, he was denounced by the pope for having grievously exceeded his instructions: 'he raised the standard of the Roman Church in battle against Christ's faithful, gave plenary absolution of all their sins to those who fell in arms against the King [presumably, before the battle of Northampton], and on the other hand excommunicated all who were fighting for the King's side, [and] forbade burial to those who died in the fighting'.[72] Coppini was deprived of his bishopric, and endured a sojourn in a papal prison before being allowed to become a monk. It is not clear whether all the charges were true. In a letter of January 1461 to a member of Margaret of Anjou's household, Coppini had denied that he had carried out the excommunications – though his blatantly disingenuous protestations of his support for the queen in the letter strain his credibility.[73] Writing the following March to Francesco Sforza, Duke of Milan, the latter's ambassador in France, Prospero di Camulio, reported that it was being said that the reason for Coppini's recent departure from England (not much more than a week before the battle of St Albans) was 'because he promised Warwick to go into the camp and excommunicate the enemy [the queen's supporters advancing southwards], and give the benediction to the followers of Warwick' – but then reneged. 'Seeing the bad weather, and the queen's power, and not feeling well, he did not go. At this Warwick took offence' – as well he might have![74] It seems likely that in 1460 the Yorkist lords had exploited Coppini's self-important pliancy to use his supposed eminence to win over recruits and deter support for the King – and, moreover, that Coppini was willing to boost their soldiers' morale and depress that of their opponents before the battle of Northampton, by providing some or other spiritual services. However, the queen's victory at Wakefield appears to have given him a severe case of cold feet. After the death of York in that battle (an unnerving divine judgment for his followers), it would not be surprising if Warwick had urgently wanted him to provide ecclesiastical sanctions in favour of his soldiers – and that they were cast down when the ebullient little bishop failed to appear in their midst and boost their courage. Earlier the Yorkists may have discovered him to be the most priceless gift of Holy Church for a domestic campaign since the papal banner which William the Conqueror flew at the battle of Hastings. That made it more of a downturn for them that, shortly before their hour of need at St Albans, he had vanished abroad. He preferred to trust divine protection at sea at an unseasonable time of year rather than among the rampant English.

6

Memories

Abate the edge of traitors, gracious Lord,
That would reduce these bloody days again,
And make poor England weep in dreams of blood!

King Richard III, Act V, Scene IV

Henry's prayer was doubtless echoed by both its author and his audiences, well rehearsed in how the looming rocks of English dynastic conflict in the sixteenth century had been up till then miraculously negotiated, in contrast to the foundering in civil wars which history taught had darkened much of the fifteenth century. Among the principal foundations of Elizabethan – and Shakespearean – historiography of that century were two works published in Henry VIII's reign: the *New Chronicles of England and of France* by Robert Fabyan (d. 1513), draper and alderman of London, published in 1516, and the *Anglica Historia* of Polydore Vergil of Urbino (1470–1555), archdeacon of Wells, first published in 1534. Neither of these substantial works, which draw on anonymous eyewitnesses as well as literary sources for the events of the later fifteenth century, can be dismissed as merely 'Tudor propaganda'. They were, indeed, both mainly composed in Henry VII's last years (in Vergil's case with some encouragement from the King). Neither author was a mouthpiece for Henry – Vergil was sharply critical of his recent domestic policies. 1 Their views of the civil wars reflect a weight of sour opinion in a nobility and civic elite with unpleasant memories of how the stability of family fortunes had been profoundly shaken over several decades by episodes of rebellion and coup. Henry Tudor's rebellion was, by contrast, lauded because he had fulfilled to a remarkable extent his claim in 1485 that his reign would restore frequently shattered harmony.

This interpretation was endorsed in the first history which took the civil wars as its subject. *The Union of the two noble and illustre famelies of Lancastre and Yorke* was composed by Edward Hall, a lawyer who rose high in London's administration. It was published in 1548, the year after his death.[2] This was the last major history which included a good deal of new orally relayed anecdote about the Wars. For instance, Hall appears to have relied in part on family tradition to colour his account of the Yorkist debacle at Wakefield (1460). His forbear Davy Halle, the Duke of York's 'old servant and chief counseller', advised him to stay in his quarters at Sandal Castle in face of the Lancastrian advance. 'In a great fury he [the Duke] said, a Davy, Davy, hast thou loved me so long, and now wouldest have me dishonoured: Thou never saw me keep fortress when I was Regent in Normandy, when the Dauphin [Charles VII] himself, with his puissance came to besiege me, but like a man, and not like a bird included in a cage, I issued forth and fought with mine enemies, to their loss ever (I thank God) and to my honour...'. Davy was to die in the battle. Hall gives a vivid account of the death of York's son Rutland, aged seventeen, in the rout, 'a fair gentleman and a maidenlike person', citing as source the boy's chaplain and schoolmaster, Robert Aspall. As Rutland knelt, speechless with fear before Lord Clifford, the latter spurned Aspall's plea for his life, and, proclaiming revenge for his father's death, thrust his dagger into the boy's heart.[3] Though Hall depicts York as dying like a chivalrous hero, his praise is tempered for a magnate who had shown such 'ambition of pre-eminence'. In Henry VIII's later years Hall may have shared widespread concerns about the uncertain succession, the ambitions of leading magnates – and growing tendencies among the common folk to riot and rebel. He is at pains to emphasise the interventions of the latter during the Wars.[4]

Preoccupations with these various threats to stability were to characterise the reigns of HenryVIII's children. In the light of these tendencies, and the arresting features of Hall's narrative, it is not surprising that it was soon accepted as authoritative, and was used as a foundation in the best-selling histories of England published by Richard Grafton and Raphael Holinshed. Shakespeare doggedly reproduced Holinshed's version. He did not introduce any material which can be identified as deriving from oral memories of the Wars in Warwickshire, though people's forbears there had had especially direct and vivid experiences of them, through the passage of armies, Warwick the Kingmaker's recruitment of tenants for his retinues, and Coventry's provision of military companies. The authority of Shakespeare's history plays rested on their concordance with the received literary version and interpretation of events. However, it is to be surmised that his vivid depictions of the horrors of civil war, though reflecting perceptions of contemporary warfare in France and the Netherlands, were consonant with traditions in noble families, and with popular memories of the domestic conflicts.

Local folklore about the Wars had been occasionally noted by John Leland (*c.*1503–52) on his antiquarian travels, recorded in his *Itineraries*. He notes the location of the battle of Northampton, saying that many Welshmen were drowned in the River Nene, and that the dead were buried either at Delapré Abbey or St John's Hospital. This memory of the frantic flight of Henry VI's soldiers echoes the story behind the compensation of 3s 4d authorised by the governors of Beverley for John Welles, gentleman: 'for his horse taken out of the wood killed at Northampton race [presumably, the mill race] by Henry Rawlin soldier'.[5] Leland's version of the death of Rutland had a different emphasis from Hall's, recalling in a somewhat confused way the terror of local people during the rout of the Yorkists. 'When the Duke of York's men turned to flight, either the duke himself, or his son the Earl of Rutland, was killed just up from the bars beyond the bridge leading up the slope to the town of Wakefield... The popular version of the story in Wakefield is that the Earl was trying to take refuge in the house of a poor woman, but in fright she shut the door and immediately the Earl was slain. Because of the slaughter of men that occurred in this battle, Lord Clifford was dubbed "the butcher".[6]

Hall and Leland both drew on local anecdotage about the battle of Towton which repeated the contemporary stress on the unusually large scale of the slaughter. Hall says that many of the Lancastrian fugitives drowned in Cock Beck, 'in so much that the common people there affirm that men alive passed the river upon dead carcasses, and that the great river of Wharfe, which is the great sewer of the brook, and all the water coming from Towton, was coloured with blood'.[7] Leland seems to have derived information from the Hungate family, one of whom lived at Saxton (in which parish the battle was fought), about how one of their forbears had gathered together bones of the slain and had them reburied in the churchyard at Saxton. He mentions five great pits, half a mile away in Saxton fields, where the remains of those killed had previously lain.[8] When Leland visited York, he saw another memorial of civil conflict. In this case, it was apparently one of the assault and brief occupation of the city by rebels in 1489: '... and so to Fishergate, which has been blocked up ever since the mob burned it during Henry VII's reign'.[9]

As the historiography of ballads amply demonstrates, oral memorialising can swiftly lose accuracy and develop a legendary vitality and momentum of its own, as it mutates in response to changing circumstances and expectations. However, the historian needs to take seriously such fragments of hoarded reminiscence which remain embedded in text – not least because, in respect of the Wars, they recall events some of which were still within living memory as late as the 1540s, if only just so. What was apparently a much longer feat of accurate oral memory is found in Thomas Habington's record of the lore of Evesham folk at the time of the Great Civil War, in his *Survey of Worcestershire*

– about the death of Simon de Montfort in battle there in 1265: 'it is reported the dead body of the earl of Leicester being fouly and barbarously deformed with wounds was there discovered'. This is consonant with reports in contemporary chronicles, and probably reflects anecdotage told to pilgrims who visited his tomb in Evesham Abbey before the Reformation.[10]

In the second half of the sixteenth century, social and economic factors may have combined to erase many oral memories of the Wars. If some of the increasing volume of printed ballads hawked at markets and fairs were about episodes in the Wars, they would have tended to replace oral recollections. However, though there is a vast lost corpus of ballads, it is doubtful whether the Wars were one of their major subject areas. Heroic battles with the Scots, such as Otterburn (1388), Humbleton Hill (1402) and Flodden (1513) provided more enduring subjects for celebratory ballads. Joseph Addison, reinforcing the thrill expressed by the Elizabethan poet and soldier Sir Philip Sidney, wrote in 1711 that 'The old song of *Chevy-Chase* is the favourite Ballad of the common People of England'.[11] Three ballads focussing on the battle of Bosworth, were, however, printed in the late sixteenth and early seventeenth centuries. The texts preserve authentic features of the original compositions. They extol the roles of the Stanleys in Henry VII's reception of the Crown – somewhat besmirched ten years later by the treason of Sir William Stanley. The importance of their stance in 1485 is also recalled in the two ballads about Flodden, intended to defend their part against the Scots, and that played by the men of Cheshire and Lancashire. In *Flodden Feilde*, which may have been composed in 1515, the victorious commander, Thomas Howard, Earl of Surrey, sends a report to Henry VIII blaming the conduct of the soldiers from these shires. Reproached by the King, Thomas Stanley, Earl of Derby says that nothing like that would have happened if he had been present. However, a message comes from the queen declaring that the Lancashiremen and Cheshiremen had won the victory. Surrey is blamed for his falsehood, which is attributed to his desire for revenge on Derby, whose uncle, according to the poem, had slain Surrey's father, the Duke of Norfolk, at Bosworth. Thirty years after the official end of the Wars of the Roses, the composer of a ballad thought it would be generally accepted as plausible that a feud stemming from them was a significant factor in politics.[12]

Literate commoners (a growing body) are likely to have regarded texts as more authoritative sources of historical information than oral traditions. A seventeenth-century apprentice, Arise Evans, when aged twenty-two, while working his way to London, stayed for three months at Coventry 'by reason of an old Chronicle that was in my master's house that showed all the passages in Britain and Ireland from Noah's Flood to William the Conquerour… It was a great volume and by day I bestowed what time I could spare to read and bought candles for the night, so that I got by heart the most material part of it'.[13] Arise's rote-learning suggests the sort of processes (among illiterate auditors too) by which 'genuine' folk traditions were superseded or distorted by oral transmission originating from text. Literary men, who *sui generis* preferred to reconstruct the past from books rather tradition, had good reason to distrust the ramblings of rustics. Vergil (and Thomas More for his *History of King Richard the Third*) had sought out witnesses (though, preferably, among persons of authority), because of the dearth of literary sources. By contrast, Shakespeare's contemporary Samuel Daniel was keen to stress his adherence to the authority of historical works in his poem on *The Civil Wars*. 'I have carefully followed that truth which is delivered in the History; without adding to, or subtracting from, the general received opinion of things as we find them in our common Annals'.[14]

Moreover, in some regions economic changes and their social consequences may have obliterated folk memories about the Wars. Long-term economic developments and concomitant changes in social structure went through a period of acceleration in rural England in the 1590s. In prosperous agrarian areas, new farming complexes were consolidated, possibly obliterating some landmarks by enclosures of common fields, and certainly reducing many smallholders to mere labourers, who, when surplus to the requirements of rich stock farmers, perforce emigrated in search of employment to towns and woodland regions. Such uprootings may have sapped the preservation of folk memories closely related to senses of environment and community. Warwickshire and Leicestershire were both heavily affected by these trends, and commoners from both shires were strongly involved in 1607 in the Diggers' Revolt, in which protesters keenly cast down fences erected by farmers to enclose what had been common grazing.[15]

Yet in this period, in the Vale of Berkeley (Gloucestershire), vivid memories of a skirmish which had taken place in the period of the Wars were recorded by a passionately antiquarian steward of estates, John Smyth of Nibley (1567–1640). He had long been in the service of the Berkeley family; he was steward of the hundred of Berkeley and of the manors of the family's estate. His access to their well-preserved muniments formed the basis of his history of the family. Writing early in the seventeenth century, he was prepared to record local oral traditions too about the skirmish which took place in 1470 at Nibley Green between the forces of Lord Berkeley and Thomas Talbot, Viscount Lisle, though he displays the contemporary antiquarian's hesitations about using countryfolk's tales, and a need to justify their use. Here is what he says:

And if traditions might be here allowed. I would assure this noble family, That within thirty two yeares last, by reason of my dwelling at Nibley, and my often resort to Wotton and to the villages adjoyning, I have often heard many old men and weomen in those places, as… [eight men named, and three women], and others, many of whose parents lived in the time of king Edward the fourth, and most of themselves were born in the time of king Henry the seaventh, as their leases and copies [copyholds] declared, some of them one hundred and ten years old, divers an hundred, and none under fourscore, relate the reports of their parents kinsfolks and neighbours present at this skirmish, some with one lord, and others with the other; and of such as carryed

victualls and weapons to some of those companies, as this lords
party lay close to the utter skirts of Michaellwood chace, out of
which this lord Berkeley brake, when hee first beheld the lord
Lisle and his fellowship discending down that hill from Nibley
Church… And how the lord Berkeley's number was about one
thousand, and exceeded the other in greatness: That the place of
stand was at fowleshard, whence the lord Welliam sent upon the
lord Lisle the first shower of his arrowes. That one black Will
(soe called) should shoot the lord Lisle, as his beaver was up; And
that Thomas Longe father of the said William was servant to one
of them who helped to carry lord Lisle when hee was slayne,
and of many other perticularyties (which I purposely omit) not
possible almost by such plaine Country people to be fained. And
that a spetiall man of lord Lisles company was then also slaine,
and buryed under the great stone tomb which yet remaines in
the south side of Nibley Church yard: insomuch that I cannot
but deliver them as truths… And much the rather for the full
discourse thereof which old Mr Charles Hiet … had with the
lord Henry Berkeley at Berkeley Castle the 25th of September
1603, which my self then heard soe particularly delivered from
the relation of his father and grandfather as if the same had been
but yesterday: The said lord Henry himselfe seconding most of
what Mr Hiet related, from the reports of divers others made to
himselfe in his youth, some of whom were then born and of the
age of discretion, as his Lordship then affirmed.

One is carried along by Smyth's conviction, and inclined to
believe the truth of his precisely articulated reconstruction,
because of the care with which he presents the oral, topographical and monumental evidence – as well as the documentary
evidence (Lisle's challenge to Berkeley, and the reply). Indeed,
the veracity of the 'plain country people''s traditions about the
battle receives some reinforcement from the account which
Leland had written up in the 1540s, likely to have been based
on oral communications collected on his visit to the Vale. His
text is unlikely to have been familiar to Smyth and his rustics.

This is Leland's account:

> Lord Berkeley and Lord Lisle engaged in a passionate dispute
> over the ownership of Wotton under Edge, so much so that they
> arranged to fight, and met in a meadow in a place called Nibley.
> Lord Lisle raised the visor of his helmet just as Berkeley's arch-
> ers fired a massive volley, and the arrow of an archer from the
> Forest of Dean entered his mouth and passed out through the
> neck. There were several other casualties, and Lisle's men fled.
> Immediately Berkeley and his men ransacked the manor house
> at Wotton, and occupied the building.[17]

Smyth was to write that many men from Bristol, the Forest of
Dean and Thornbury (Berkeley's residence) came to Berkeley's
support. The killing of Lord Lisle was clearly an incident which
remained of interest to the Berkeleys and which stood out in the
popular memory. Maybe memories were tinged with lingering
bitterness. Smyth concluded, remarkably, that 'the bloud now
spilt [in the skirmish] was not cleane dryed up till the seaventh
year of king James' [1609–10] – presumably meaning that the
enmity of families of those killed or maimed was only assuaged
by then, either through reconciliation or extinction.[18]

Precise memories of greater conflicts as well as of this local
skirmish during the Wars perhaps lingered on even as late as
the seventeenth century and beyond. William Burton, writing
in 1622, relied principally on literary sources for his account of
the battle of Bosworth, but used local knowledge in order to
fix its location, 'by reason that some persons thereabout, which
saw the battle fought, were living within less than forty years,
of which persons myself have seen some, and have heard of
their discourses though related by the second hand'. Burton
mentioned the little hill where it was commonly reported that
Henry Tudor had made his oration to the soldiers before the
battle; Dickons Nook, where Richard was said to have made his
oration; Crown Hill, where Henry was crowned, and Hollow

Meadow, where the soldiers cheered his crowning.[19] However, by Burton's time the common local memory may have been affected by the print-driven fame of the battle. This was certainly the case when the antiquary John Nichols visited the putative site of the battle with his friend Mr Robinson in June 1789, 'at that precise season when the blossom of the hawthorn, assuming its deepest vermeil tincture, was on the point of expanding into bud; when the red and white rose, full-blown, were literally entwined beauties in embrace'. Nichols' mention of the hawthorn was a coy allusion to the legend that the crown was found on a bush. He and his friend took refuge from a thunderstorm in a farmhouse at Shenton. There they heard reminiscences about what was found in manuscripts which had been discovered in pulling down an old wainscot and subsequently burnt by the cook, and about finds of weapons and coins.[20] There were garrulous natives near other battle sites. F.R. Twemlow, in his book on the battle of Blore Heath, published in 1912, recorded a local tradition that Margaret of Anjou had viewed the battle from the tower of Mucclestone church, and that, when the Lancastrians were defeated, she had her horse's shoes reversed by a blacksmith named Skelhorn! His descendant was the blacksmith there in 1855.[21] At Wakefield, three willow trees were said by tradition to be the place where York had died, and J.G. Nicols recorded in 1847 that where Losecoat Field had been fought there was a place called Bloody Oaks, and surmised that there the Lincolnshiremen were hard pressed by their pursuers.[22] These possible memories were doleful ones. No other battle of the Wars of the Roses became a cause of lasting celebration like Bosworth, which in the longer perspective came to be regarded as having brought them to an end. There appears to have been little public celebration of the battles at the time. New kings, when they then made their customary first entry into cities in the period, were greeted with speeches and pageants which celebrated their triumphs, but there were no receptions explicitly designed to rejoice at victories, such as the city of London had laid on in 1415 for Henry V in thanks for Agincourt to God.

A sombre pall over Henry V's wars is cast by his son's foundation charter of 1438 for Archbishop Chichele's All Souls College, Oxford. The Warden and twenty scholars were to pray for Henry VI and Chichele in life and death, for the souls of Henry V, Thomas, Duke of Clarence (his brother, killed at the battle of Baugé in 1421), the dukes, earls, barons, knights and esquires and the others who had ended their lives in the wars in the kingdom of France – and for all the souls of all the faithful departed.[23] Concern for the war dead in the later Middle Ages was probably intensified by the vividly envisaged beliefs in the period in the torments of Purgatory. This laid a heavy burden on kinsfolk and neighbours to say and provide prayers for the deceased, especially on the anniversaries of their deaths. Occasionally, commanders made provision for the souls of those who had died on service in their armies. Thomas of Woodstock, Duke of Gloucester, included those who had succumbed on his expedition to France in 1380–1 in the prayers to be said in perpetuity by the priests of the college which he founded at Pleshey (Essex).[24] Henry VI had a concern for the souls of those who died in the first battle of St Albans. As part of his attempt to reconcile the factions in 1458, he laid down that, within two years, York, Warwick and Salisbury were to grant property to St Albans Abbey in perpetuity, worth £45 p.a., for Masses and prayers for the souls of Somerset, Northumberland and Clifford, killed there and buried in the abbey, and for the souls of all the others killed. William Herbert, Earl of Pembroke, in the will he made a few days before the battle of Edgcote in 1469, laid down that two priests were to be found to sing before the image of the Trinity at Llandeilo 'for my soul, and for all their souls slain in the field for two years'.[25]

Related concerns of soldiers and their families, were that, if they succumbed in battle, funeral rites should be performed, and that they should be buried in consecrated ground, in a churchyard or church. These concerns are reflected in the wills of two Yorkshire landowners, Sir Hugh Hastings and Sir John Constable, which they made when intending to go on Gloucester's invasion of Scotland in 1482. Hastings laid down, 'my body to be buried in Christian burial where as shall please Almighty God', and Constable used an almost identical phrase.[26] It would have been a matter of utmost anxiety if, at the battle of Northampton in 1460, as Bishop Coppini was to be charged (but had already implicitly denied), he had 'excommunicated all those who were fighting on the King's side, [and] forbade burial to those of them who died in battle'.[27] Remains of some of those who had been killed at Otterburn in 1388 were buried or reinterred in the appropriate parish church, at Elsdon, though it was three miles from the battle site. In 1810, 'during the removal of great accumulations of earth against the north wall of the nave, the bones of one hundred or more persons were discovered, in double rows, with the skulls of one row within the thigh bones of the other, packed within the smallest possible compass. These were evidently only part of a great interment which had once taken place, for in 1877 a large number of other skeletons in a similar attitude were found extending right under the north wall into the church, to all appearances the remains of young and middle-aged men.'[28]

When, after exceptional slaughter, gravepits were dug a distance from a churchyard, they were on occasion hallowed by the foundation of a religious institution on the site explicitly to provide prayers for the deceased in the battle, as well as the founders.[29] In 1406–8 Battlefield church was built where Henry IV had had his bloody victory over the Percy rebels in 1403 (the battle of Shrewsbury). Richard Husse, a local landowner, had received royal licence to assign two acres for the purpose of founding a chapel in which prayers were to be said for those who had died. In 1410 the priest there, Roger Ive, received a royal charter creating a perpetual chantry. Husse and his heirs were to be patrons, Ive was to be the first master of the college, and there were to be six chaplains. Prayers were to be said for the King, the founders and their families and for the souls of those who had died in the battle. Henry endowed the college generously with advowsons, and gave it the right to hold an annual fair. In 1433 a papal indulgence to the college described it as a place 'where many died in battle and were buried', so it is probable that one reason for its inception was to transform the area of grave pits into hallowed ground.[30]

It is probable that many local men were buried on the battlefield of Towton; this may help account for the long-lasting concerns shown for commemoration there. An attempt was made, apparently commencing two decades after the battle, to set up a chapel amidst grave pits. This might have developed in the mode of Battlefield college, in more propitious circumstances. Successive archbishops of York showed concern about its endowments and upkeep. In 1486 Thomas Rotherham granted an indulgence to those who gave alms for the completion of the building, graphically describing its location where 'the bodies of the first and greatest in the land as well as great multitudes of other men were first slain and then buried and interred in the fields around'. In 1502 his successor Thomas Savage lamented that the chapel 'was not sufficiently endowed with possessions and rents as to sustain it and have divine service celebrated therein', and tried to rally support for it'.[31] Nevertheless, the foundation still did not flourish. Leland says that 'Towton village, a mile from Saxton, has a large unfinished chapel begun by Richard III. The father of Sir John Moulton [landowner at Towton] laid the first stone of the chapel, and there too were buried many of the battle casualties'.[32] Richard may well have wished to ingratiate himself with Yorkshire folk, who probably recalled that his family had a prime responsibility for the deaths of their kinsfolk there. Savage's efforts in 1502 suggest the existence of ongoing concerns for the provision of Masses for the souls of long-deceased kinsfolk and neighbours at Towton. The gentry may have been less concerned than the commons, for they could better afford to make private provision for the spiritual health of their ancestors. The Tudor dynasty, lacking the close links with Yorkshire society that Richard had had, did not have his special incentive to patronise the foundation. None of Henry VII's close relatives had died at Towton. After 1485, Richard's association with the chapel may have hampered its chances of gaining the necessary further patronage and endowment by the Crown and gentry. Moreover, the determination of the manorial lords of Saxton to make the parish church a cult centre for the battle diverted the focus of commemoration from Towton chapel.

There may have been another form of commemoration at some other battle sites. It is possible that wooden or stone crosses were set up in the period of the Wars of the Roses, to solicit prayers, especially for an individual among the deceased – but the evidence is mostly weak. Leland says that a cross was erected at Wakefield to mark the spot where Rutland was killed. Twemlow, the historian of Blore Heath, mentioned 'Audley's Cross', supposedly marking the spot where that Lancastrian noble had been killed. The cross, repaired in 1765, had been noted as an 'antiquity' in 1686.[33] However, this may have been one of the many wayside crosses peppered over the realm, which might have become associated in the popular mind with a battle fought nearby. In the eighteenth and nineteenth centuries, as a result of the romanticisation of the Middle Ages, and the popularity of Shakespeare's 'history plays', commemorative stones were set up at some of the battle sites of the Wars. For instance, a monument to what its inscription described as the 'obstinate bloody and decisive battle' of Mortimer's Cross was set up at Kingsland in 1799, paid for by public subscription.[34] A memorial stone was set up at Wakefield in the nineteenth century commemorating the death of the Duke of York. A medieval cross by the wayside at Towton was repaired in 1929, and given an inscription commemorating the battle.[35]

Whatever a soldier's status was, the usual preference was doubtless for a resting-place, be it tomb, churchyard or charnel-house, within one's own or one's family's cult-centre. However, even nobles and knights had to accept that, if they died abroad, it was likely that they would be buried there, as the terms of wills show. Sometimes noble families had remains repatriated. John, Lord Mowbray, was killed by Muslims in 1368 and buried in the Dominican convent in Galata outside Constantinople. His son Thomas, Earl Marshal, negotiated in 1396 for the return of his father's bones to England: they were reinterred in Whitefriars, the Carmelite church in Fleet Street, London.[36] It was not always feasible for noble families to recover the bodies of their fallen kinsmen from domestic battlefields, to be buried amidst their ancestors, particularly if they were on the losing side, when the kin might be in flight or reduced to penury. They were unable initially to provide a worthy burial if the deceased's dismembered body was subsequently being displayed in order to reinforce the lessons of treason. This was the immediate fate of the corpse of the first Earl of Northumberland, killed in battle while rebelling in 1408 (as, similarly, of his son Hotspur's corpse five years before). However, their remains were eventually collected for burial in York Minster, though maybe without the construction of grandiose tombs appropriate to their station.[37] After the first battle of St Albans in 1455, Abbot Whethamstede was shocked that corpses were being left where they lay, including those of the three nobles killed defending the King – the Duke of Somerset, the Earl of Northumberland and Lord Clifford. Since these lords had been hated by the victor, York, no one touched them or performed exequies over them. The abbot went to York and persuaded him to allow honourable burial. Whethamstede arranged for the lords to be buried in the splendid Chapel of the Blessed Virgin at the east end of the abbey church, not far from the shrines of St Alban and St Amphibalus. He wrote grandiloquent memorial verses to commemorate them as victims of war. The Percy family do not seem to have transferred the second earl's remains to the fine chantry chapel which he had founded at Tynemouth priory in Northumberland. The priory was the abbey's cell, patronage of which by the Percys had long given them amicable ties with the monks of St Albans.[38] For them, and the kinsmen of the other two lords, burial in a pre-eminent abbey and centre of pilgrimage near where they had died fighting for their lord probably seemed fitting, as did later burials of lords in other abbeys in similar circumstances. However, we do not know whether common soldiers were given the like privilege of burial within monastic precincts; at St Albans in 1455 their remains are more likely to have been laid in the churchyard of the town church in whose parish the battle had been fought, St Peter's.

York and his son Rutland, slain in the debacle of Wakefield in 1460, were buried a few miles away at Pontefract. In 1461, Edward IV had their heads brought down from Micklegate Bar, York and taken there. It is not clear where their fellow victims, Salisbury and his son Sir Thomas Neville lay, but in 1463 Warwick had the remains translated to Bisham Abbey (Berkshire), the ancestral abbey of the earls of Salisbury. The House of York seem to have been content to let their kinsmen lie in Pontefract for years – presumably honourably so, and therefore, probably, in the Cluniac priory, where lay the shrine of the executed Thomas of Lancaster, widely reputed a martyr and a saint. The bodies were exhumed in 1476 and taken on progress with great pomp to be buried in the House of York's principal centre of private devotion, Fotheringhay collegiate parish church in Northamptonshire.[39]

Somerset's burial in a religious house near the scene of his death in battle proved an unfortunate precedent for his family. In 1464, his son Duke Henry, captured in the fight near Hexham by the Yorkists, was beheaded, probably in the marketplace, and buried in the Augustinian priory overlooking it, a hallowed place to lie, especially because of the well-remembered holy glories of its Anglo-Saxon bishops. Henry's brothers Edmund and John, killed at Tewkesbury in 1471, were buried together in the abbey there before the altar of St James. A monk of the abbey listed thirty-six peers, knights, esquires and others killed in the battle, or executed afterwards, who were buried in the abbey, most apparently scattered all over the nave (which was the parish church), and six knights in the churchyard. Two nobles beside the Beauforts had the privilege of burial in the monastic part of the church, but pride of place went to Henry VI's young son Edward, Prince of Wales, 'slain and buried in the midst of the monastic choir'. The monk did not know the names of all who were buried in the church, probably a token of the haste with which many were interred: he lists 'Master Fildynge esquire, Master Hervy, recorder of Bristol… with many others.' Alternative arrangements were made in some cases. Lord

Wenlock's body was taken from the battlefield elsewhere. The body of Sir John Langstrother, Prior of the Order of St John of Jerusalem, who had been executed, was encased in lead and taken for burial in the Order's church at St John, Clerkenwell, outside London. Henry Baron, esquire, was buried in the parish church in the abbey, before the image of St Clement, but 'afterwards fetched from hence to his own country'. Tewkesbury Abbey thus became, through the accident of battle, the mausoleum of Henry VI's lost cause. There lie gathered the bones of most of the last of the Lancastrian nobility (and, probably, some commons). This suited all parties. For Edward, the abbey was conveniently placed to house the remains, whose impressive gathering-in was a reminder of God's savage judgment on the cause. For those who had been about to be executed (after having been dragged from sanctuary in the abbey), and for the relatives of the dead, it provided a fittingly sacred resting-place, an ancient Benedictine abbey dedicated to the Blessed Virgin Mary, with prestigious past royal and noble associations. For the monks, the burials provided prospects of future patronage by the kinsfolk of the dead. Investment in the body of a prince (however discredited), who had died by violence, could produce long-term yields, as the monks of Gloucester Abbey had found after they took off the body of Edward II. There is evidence from 1502 and 1513 of the practice of pilgrimage to Prince Edward's tomb – in the first case, on behalf of Henry VII's queen Elizabeth of York, whose father, Edward IV, had been the principal beneficiary of the prince's death.[40] Can one surmise that she must have been frustrated by the disappearance of the remains of her brothers, Edward V and Richard, Duke of York, by her inability to have them properly entombed, and make appropriate offerings? What a prize their remains would have been for a religious house! However, her husband is unlikely to have been keen on the prospect of a cult of the 'Princes in the Tower', since it might have detracted from his efforts to promote that of Henry VI, and advertised an episode widely viewed as a sordid one in the recent history of a monarchy whose dignity and magnificence he was determined to put on an awesome and worshipful footing. Henry VII had no incentive to institute a search for the remains of the princes.

Other leading families were able to retrieve the bodies of the fallen from unpropitious localities. The third Earl of Northumberland and his brother Sir Richard Percy, killed at Towton, lie in the vault under the family's former chapel (the north aisle) in the parish church of St Denys, Walmgate, in York.[41] The Welshman Herbert, leading his army through the 'foreign' English Midlands in 1469, willed that 'my body be sent for home in all haste by Mr Leisone and certain friars', to be buried in the priory at Abergavenny. He was executed after his capture at the battle of Edgcote, and was indeed buried in Wales, but in the grand Cistercian abbey of Tintern, of which he was a benefactor.[42] John Howard, Duke of Norfolk, who died fighting for Richard III at Bosworth, was at first buried, like the King, at Leicester, but was to be translated to the family's place of burial, Thetford priory (Norfolk). The Howards may have been uncomfortable about his continued juxtaposition with the sinisterly painted master whom he had served only too well.[43] By contrast, the family of Ralph, Lord Dacre, who died fighting for Henry VI at Towton, did not have him interred with his forbears in Lanercost priory (Cumberland), but in a distinctive way at Saxton. A tomb was erected for him in the churchyard, not in a more honourable and hallowed setting within the church. He may have been placed where he was so that he might be surrounded by his fallen Border fighters, and his monument conspicuous to those who came to pray for the dead of Towton. It was certainly intended to highlight his chivalrous loyalty; the inscription on it recorded his death 'as a true knight, valiant in battle in the service of King Henry VI'.[44]

A vogue for mentioning in funeral inscriptions the achievements of the deceased, occasionally military ones, but, more usually, office-holding, had developed in the fourteenth century. A notable example of one recording a military career was that copied in translation from French by Leland on the brass

of Sir Matthew Gournay, crusader, and professional soldier in
the Hundred Years War, in the church of Stoke-sub-Hambdon
(Somerset):

> Here lies the noble and valiant Maheu de Gurney, formerly sene-
> schal of Landes and commander of Castel Daques [Dax] for Our
> Lord the King in the Duchy of Guyene. During his life he fought
> at the battle of Beuamazin [Benmarin in Morocco], and later
> took part in the siege of Dalgezire [Algeciras, 1343–44] against the
> Saracens, also the battles of Le Scluse [Edward III's naval victory
> at Sluis, 1340], Crécy [1346], Ingenesse, Poitiers [1356], Nazarre
> [the Black Prince's victory at Nájera, 1367], Dozrey [Auray, 1365],
> and many other battles and sieges, in which he honourably won
> great praise and credit over a period of 56 years. He died on the
> 26th day of September in the year of Our Lord Jesus Christ 1406.
> May God have mercy on his soul. Amen 1406.[45]

There were other ways of commemorating participation in
battles. The memorial brass of Sir William Molyneux (d.1548)
and his two wives in Sefton church (Lancashire) depicts two
Scottish banners, which he had captured at Flodden – an unusual
feature, perhaps included with the slurs on the conduct of the
Lancashiremen in mind.[46] Stained-glass windows in churches
might be used to project secular achievements as well as sacred
themes. The great east window of Gloucester Abbey may have
been given as a memorial to some of the lords and knights who
had fought in the battle of Crécy by one of the commanders, Lord
Bradeston.[47] In St Leonard's church at Middleton (Lancsashire)
there is the stained-glass window of Sir Richard Assheton and
his wife Anne, dating from 1524, which also depicts seventeen
archers, with their names written above them. They presumably
formed his company at Flodden, or were the members of it who
died there. The window is the most striking remaining memorial
to the English common soldier surviving from our period.[48]

Fulsome tomb inscriptions like Gournay's, alluding to participation in battles, do not seem to have been favoured with

regard to the Wars of the Roses; few are known which make any reference to them. Here are some rare examples. The joint epitaph of Ralph Babthorpe and his son Ralph, formerly in St Peter's church, St Albans, which describes the former as Henry VI's esquire, and the latter as his steward, says that they were both true to their prince, for whose sake they gave their lives. The date given for their deaths was that of the first battle at St Albans. The Babthorpe family had a record of service in estate administration to the House of Lancaster, and they had held the offices of constable and porter of the king's castle at Scarborough (Yorkshire).[49] Thomas Barret esquire's inscription in the church of St Martin's in the Fields, London, recorded how in 1460 he had been taken from sanctuary at Westminster Abbey and cruelly killed by impious people contrary to the laws of England and the privileges of the Church. He was an esquire of Henry VI who had fought in the French wars, lynched by the King's enemies.[50] In Westminster Abbey, the verse epitaph of Humphrey Bourchier, cupbearer to Queen Elizabeth Wydeville, laments his death in the battle of Barnet.[51] The memorial brass of John Sacheverell esquire and his wife Joan in Morley church (Derbyshire) depicts him kneeling in full plate armour, and records that 'he died in the battle of Richard the third near bosworth in the year of the lord 1485' – an unusual monumental allusion to service to the king, apparently erected forty years after the event.[52]

The most remarkable known inscription focussing in part on episodes in the Wars was one written in English on a 'table' which was fixed to the tomb of Thomas Howard, Duke of Norfolk (d.1524), who was buried before the high altar in Thetford priory (Norfolk). To a large extent the inscription was an apologia for his role in the Wars, arguing that he had always acted as an honourable and brave subject, and implying that a magnate should stay true to the oath of allegiance he had made to whichever king was ruling. It is unclear when this brief chivalrous biography was composed, or by whom, but its content and turns of phrase suggest that it was derived from Howard's self-imaging. The inscription records that he supported Edward IV at

the battles of Losecoat Field (1470), at the time of the battle of
Edgcote (1469), and in opposition to Warwick's renewed rebel-
lion in 1470. When Edward fled abroad, he took sanctuary at
Colchester. He was badly wounded when fighting for him at
Barnet the following year, and was wounded and captured fight-
ing for Richard III at Bosworth. Imprisoned in the Tower of
London by Henry VII, he demonstrated his new found loyalty
to him by turning down a chance to escape during the Earl of
Lincoln's invasion in 1487.[53]

This account (which assumes that readers had a good deal of
knowledge about the Wars) is consonant with other known facts
about the Duke's career. Perhaps its most remarkable notice was
the admission that he had fought until incapacitated for Richard
at Bosworth. Indeed, this was notorious, and it may be the key
as to why the Duke, or members of his family, felt the need to
mount this very public posthumous defence of his honour, putting his behaviour in the context of loyalty to the Crown. Since
the Howards had emerged as the dominant family in Norfolk
in the sixteenth century, they may have felt the need to set
the record straight in a prominent and appropriate location,
reassuring their 'well-willers' and refuting their denigrators by
proclaiming that the victor of Flodden had a career unblemished
by treason.

By contrast, the inscription on the tomb of Sir Marmaduke
Constable (d. 1520) in Flamborough church (Yorkshire) is,
where Richard III is concerned, a masterly case of economical
truthfulness:

> Here lieth Marmaduke Cunstable, of fflaynborght, knyght,
> Who made aduento[re] into ffrance, and for the right of the
> same
> Passed over with kyng Edwarde the fourtht, yt noble knight;
> And also with noble king Herre, the seuinth of that name.
> He was also at Barwick, at the winnyng of the same,
> And by ky[n]g Edward chosy[n] Captey[n] there first of any
> one;

And rewllid and gouernid ther his tyme without blame.

Bot for all that, as ye se, he lieth under thys stone,

At Brankisto[n] feld, wher the kyng of Scottis was slayne,

He, then beyng of the age of thre score and tene,

With the gode duke of Northefolke yt jorney he hay tayn

And coragely avau[n]cid hy[m]self emo[n]g other, ther and then,

The ki[n]g beyng i[n] Frau[n]ce with grete nombre of Y[ngleshmen[n],

He, nothing hedyng his age ther but jeopyde hy as on

With his sonnes, brothe[r], sarvantt[s], and kynnismen,

Bot now, as ye se, he lyeth under this stone.[54]

As far as it goes, this is an accurate account of a military career, emphasising, as did the Duke of Norfolk's inscription, loyal and chivalrous service to the Crown. Constable, it records, took part in Edward IV's expedition to France in 1475 and Henry VII's in 1492; he was at the Earl of Northumberland's siege of Berwick in 1482 (during Richard of Gloucester's invasion of Scotland) and was appointed captain of the garrison. At an advanced age he led a company in the army commanded by Howard which defeated and killed James IV at Flodden, near the village of Branxton. However, a vital chapter of his career was glossed over. A knight of the body to Richard III, he was one of the leading northern knights on whom the King relied to hold sway in potentially recalcitrant shires, first Kent and then Leicestershire. He received important offices in the duchy of Lancaster, notably the stewardship and constableship of Tutbury (Staffordshire). It seems likely that Constable campaigned for Richard against the rebels of 1483 and in the Bosworth campaign.[55]

We have been concerned here with commemoration of the Wars in ecclesiastical settings. It may be that episodes in them were commemorated in secular buildings, in the sculpture and stained glass windows of great houses, and in their furnishings, such as tapestries and panel paintings. In Stowe School (Buckinghamshire) there is a carved stone relief depicting the triumph of Henry Tudor over Richard at Bosworth. It is thought to date from the late sixteenth century, and was discovered in 1736 in a farmhouse at Halstead (Essex), not its original settings. It has been conjectured that it came from nearby Hedingham Castle, residence of the de Veres, earls of Oxford, in which case it may have been intended to point up the role of John de Vere in commanding Henry's vanguard in the battle.[56]

Norfolk's inscription is the nearest we have to a biographical account of participation in the Wars. Yet chivalrous biography was flourishing in the fifteenth century – no more so than in court circles of the Valois dukes of Burgundy, which had close ties with English courtly culture during the reign of Edward IV. Among earlier English examples of the genre were lives of Henry V written in Latin, for which there was a demand among well-educated nobles. An Italian, Tito Livio of Forli (d.1442), who became a member of the household of Henry's brother Humphrey, Duke of Gloucester (d.1447), wrote a life of the King at his request. Another biography of the King was commissioned by Walter, Lord Hungerford (d.1449). This is lost, as is the life of Henry composed by an anonymous author who wrote after 29 June 1455, and incorporated reminiscences derived from James Butler, Earl of Ormonde (d.1452). Ormonde had also served in France under Henry.[57] We know that William Worcestre (d.c.1485) wrote a military biography of the veteran of the French wars whom he had served as secretary, *The Deeds of Sir John Fastolf* – also now apparently lost.[58] A mainly pictorial life of one of Henry V's chivalrous companions, Richard Beauchamp, Earl of Warwick (d .1439), dating from between 1485 and 1490, was commissioned either by his daughter Anne Neville, (d.1493), widow of Warwick the Kingmaker, or another member of the family.[59] Heroism in chivalrous adventures and in the French wars may have been the subject of other sorts of pictorial commemoration. Henry VII's mother, Margaret Beaufort owned a tapestry, which she inherited from her father the Duke of Somerset (d.1444), which told the story of the Welsh captain Matthew Gough.[60]

Even taking into account manuscript losses, there is a marked contrast between the numbers of biographical narratives known to have been written which centred on successes in the wars in France, and the dearth of any lauding leading figures in the Wars of the Roses. All we have are Blacman's Latin hagiography of Henry VI, the 'propaganda pieces' describing Edward IV's suppression of rebellion in 1470 and conquest of the realm in 1471, and the eulogy of Henry VII written in humanist vein by his French chaplain Bernard André.[61] If the future Richard III modelled himself on his father in the ways in which Dr Michael K. Jones has suggested, why did he not commission a life of York from one of the highly competent Italian humanists who sought patronage at the Yorkist court?[62] Why did Edward IV, victor of more battles than any other English king, and avid collector of lavishly embellished historical works, not fix his heroics for posterity with a biography emulating the ones in which Henry V's had been projected? It may be that, for many nobles who had fought in the Wars, and their descendants, memories of disloyalties, humiliations and internecine bloodshed were too painful to be trumpeted abroad. Henry VII could contemplate a panegyric with equanimity because he had been involved very little in the strife. He had not changed dynastic horses, and probably in his own eyes invaded Wales and England as a peacemaker and reconciler, not as yet another magnate lusting for a crown. The chivalrous biographical genre was to reappear in England only in 1513–14, when an anonymous author composed the first life of Henry V to be written in English. The dedication was to Henry VIII, and the work should be related to enthusiasm and nostalgia for the wars in France, revived among the nobility by the determination of a young king of warlike mien to renew them.[63]

Occasionally, anecdotage about the vicissitudes suffered in the Wars by individual nobles and their families surfaces from the sixteenth century, sometimes preserved orally in family tradition down to the seventeenth century. Tragic memories among noble families are likely to have been frequent, since, as we have seen, participation by their forbears had been more likely to lead to death in battle, execution or exile afterwards, and forfeiture, than by the forbears of commoners. Some nobles endured death at the hands of mere footmen, a fate which had once been more prevalent for misguided French nobles faced by their 'rightful' English rulers' archers. Richard III may have been deliberately slain by a common English or Welsh subject, a truly shocking assault on an anointed English king.[64] Mortifying stories spread and were sometimes handed down about the plight of the dispossessed, reduced to demeaning circumstances. The chronicler Ellis Gruffydd was to recall how, when Henry VI's half-brother Jasper Tudor had to flee from Wales in 1464, he was 'constrained to carry a load of pease-straw on his back as he went to the ship lest he should be recognized'.[65] Edward Hall relayed stories about the death of Lord Clifford in 1461 and the fate of his son and heir: 'Putting on his gorget, suddenly with an arrow (as some say) without a head was stricken into the throat, and incontinent rendered his spirit... whose young son Thomas Clifford was brought up with a shepherd, in poor habit, and dissimulated behaviour ever in fear to publish his lineage or degree.' He was able to emerge and claim his inheritance after the victory of Henry Tudor.[66] It is a tale with resonances from Arthurian romance.

However, pride was taken by noble families to preserve in particular memories of warlike deeds and of sacrifices in Henry Tudor's cause. Forbears who rose in arms in 1483 and 1485 had had a 'good war', memories of which might have some social cachet and political value. They might help to counterbalance descendants' offences and shortcomings, as we have seen in the tenor of the ballads which extol the support which the Stanleys gave to Henry Tudor, and their roles in inaugurating the dynasty.[67] The Wyatt family of Allington Castle (Kent), originally from Yorkshire, had good reason to recall the sterling service of the founder of their courtly fortunes, Sir Henry (*c.*1460–1536), since his son, the courtier-poet Sir Thomas, on occasion fell spectacularly from Henry VIII's grace, and the latter's son of the same name was beheaded for his rebellion against Mary Tudor in 1554. In a letter of 1537, the poet asserted that the grace of God had preserved his father 'in prison from the hands of the tyrant [Richard III] that could find in his heart to see him racked'.[68] Family anecdotes about Henry's vicissitudes were written down *c.*1612 by one of the descendants, Thomas Scott – doubtless having gained dramatic, improbable highlights in the retellings. Here is Scott's dialogue about his imprisonment in the Tower of London:

> Richard III (to Wyatt, on the rack): Wyatt, why art thou such a fool? thou servest for moonshine in the water, A beggarly fugitive, forsake him, and become mine, who can reward thee and I swear unto thee, Will.
>
> Wyatt: If I had first chosen you for my Master, thus faithful would I have been to you, if you should have needed it, but the Earl [of Richmond, i.e. Henry Tudor], poor and unhappy, though he be, is my Master and no discouragement or allurement shall ever drive, or draw me from him by God's grace.[69]

If Wyatt did reply in that vein, it is puzzling that he survived! According to family legend, he was fed in prison by a cat. She kept him warm, and brought him pigeons, which his keeper dressed for his meat. 'Sir Henry Wyatt in his prosperity would ever make much of cats, as other men will of their spaniels and hounds'.[70] Moving from family piety to documented fact, we find that Henry did, indeed, participate in the revolt of 1483; he was to show administrative talents and to prosper mightily in the service of the Tudors. Soon after Bosworth, he was appointed keeper of Norwich Castle and its gaol. He fought for the King at Stoke in 1487, and was rewarded with the offices of bailiff and constable of Conisborough Castle (Yorkshire). He became a royal councillor in 1504, and was a knight banneret on Henry VIII's French expedition of 1513. The pinnacle of his career was the post of Treasurer of the King's Chamber, which he held from 1524 to 1528.[71]

Richard Carew of Antony (1555–1620), in *The Survey of Cornwall*, whose first version was written in the period 1585–94, recorded stories about the vicissitudes in the Wars suffered by some of the shire's leading families, to whom he was related. One of his wife's forbears, Sir John Arundell of Lanherne, when sheriff of Cornwall in 1473, was ordered by Edward IV to take the shire levies to besiege St Michael's Mount, which had been seized by the incorrigible Lancastrian, John deVere, Earl of Oxford. Carew says that 'It is received by tradition that [Arundell]... was fore-warned by I wot not what calker [fortune-teller] how he should be slain on the sands... but, despite shunning sandy dwelling... there, in skirmish in the sands, lost his life'. He was buried in a particularly sacred place, the chapel on the Mount, overlook-ing the scene of his chivalrous death in his lord's service. The Benedictine priory on the Mount was a place of pilgrimage.[72]

In 1484 Richard III appointed a commission to enquire into the treason of Sir Richard Edgecombe of Cotehele and others; Edgecombe was the great-grandfather of Carew's wife Elizabeth. He had led a conspiracy to send money to a neighbour, Sir Robert Willoughby, and Peter Courtenay, bishop of Exeter, who had fled to Brittany, Henry Tudor's refuge, after the failure of the 1483 rebellion. Edgecombe now made good his escape, too. Carew has a dramatic tale to tell about it: he

> was driven to hide himself in those his thick woods which over-look the river [the Tamar, at Cotehele], what time being suspected of favouring the Earl of Richmond's party against King Richard the Third, he was hotly pursued and narrowly searched for, which extremity taught him a sudden policy, to put a stone in his cap and tumble the same into the water while these rangers were fast at his heels, who looking down after the noise and seeing the cap swimming thereon, supposed that he had desperately drowned himself, gave over of their farther hunting, and left him liberty; for a grateful remembrance of which he afterwards builded a chapel, not yet utterly decayed.[73]

A brief reminiscence of the rebellious adventures in this period of Henry Ley, much lower down in the social scale than Edgecombe, survives in a document, the 'Declaration of the Family of Ley', commissioned *c.*1610 by Robert Ley, first Earl of Marlborough. Henry had been a servant of Sir Robert Willoughby at his manor of Bere Ferrers, near Plymouth. He took part with his master in the 1483 rebellion, and fled with him to Brittany, returning in 1485 in Henry Tudor's army. At Bosworth he served under Henry in the main 'battle': he 'was a man at Arms, on the part of the Earl against the King, and was near about the Earl's person, At such time as the King was slain by one Thomas Woodshawe'.[74] Here we seem to have an echo of an authentic voice from the ranks.

In Wales, the preservation of family history was promoted by the strong sense of the kin and by the legacy of a bardic culture which had continually shaped and refreshed secular values by reference to incidents in the past. This led to the hoarding of memories of the Wars, such as those about Sir Rhys ap Thomas (*c.*1449–1525), collated with written sources in the biography composed by his descendant Henry Rice (*c.*1590–1651).[75] Let us take some examples recorded in another biographical narrative. Sir John Wynn of Gwydir (1553–1627) wrote a family history which traced the family's descent from the princely family of Gwynedd. Wynn preserved vivid memories of William Herbert's campaign in Gwynedd in 1468 to capture Harlech Castle. He 'wasted with fire and sword all Nanconwey and all the country lying between Conwey and dyvye [Denbigh], he granted the same time a protection or safeconduct to Jeuan ap Robert ap meredyth and to his followers to come to parle[y] with him which I have to show, under his seal of arms' [the text of this then given; dated 4 November 1468]. Wynn writes eloquently of the menace of Herbert's soldiers, but says that 'he was a most goodly man of personage, of great stature as may appear by the welsh songs made unto him and most valiant with all... he sustained deadly feud... at home in his door; a war far more dangerous than the other.'[76] He says that Edward IV had sent Herbert with a great army to waste the 'mountainous countries' of Caernavonshire and Merionethshire and gain Harlech, in revenge for the Lancastrian captains' recent campaign, in which they had 'wasted with fire and sword the suburbs of the town of Denbigh and all the lordship of Denbigh.'

Wynn told a family anecdote about this devastating Welsh war:

> In that expedition Jeuan Robert lay one night at the house of Rees ap Engion at henblas married to his cousin Katherine verch Robyn vaughan and setting forth very early before day unwittingly carried upon his finger the wrest of his cousin's harp whereon as it seemeth he had played overnight as the manner was in those days to bring himself to sleep. Which he returned by a messenger unto his cousin he came not into Denbigh land to take from his cousin as much as the wrest of her harp, whereby it appears that by his means neither her house or any of her goods was burnt, wasted, hurt or despoiled Both her houses henblas and brynsylltu [Bryn Sylldy, like Henblas, just to the east of Llanrwst] escaped the earl of Herbert's desolation though the same consumed the whole borough of llanrust and all the vale of Conwey beside… the very stones of the ruins of many habitations in and along my demaines, carrying yet the colour of the fire.[77]

This reminiscence has an authentic echo of troubled emotions in a land at war – the soldier and his cousin concerned at the threat of sack, he assuaging his sleepless anxiety in the still of night with familiar, comforting chords.

We have very little in the way of reminiscences stemming from the common soldier. We have to be content with one highly dubious source for an anecdote about the battle of Barnet. William Bullein (d .1575/6), rector of Blaxhall (Suffolk), published in 1564 a *Dialogue Against the Fever Pestilence*, the year after a terrible visitation of plague in London. This sprawling rag-bag, its elements comprising, among others, moralising and satire as well as prescriptions against the plague, proved popular, being reprinted four times up to 1578. It takes the form of discussions involving twelve interlocutors, personifications including Death

(*Mors*). The action, conveyed through the dialogue, starts in a plague-stricken London, with the beggar, *Mendicus*, knocking on the door of *Civis*, the chief speaker. In the latter part of the work, *Civis* and his wife *Uxor* (alias *Susan*) are travelling north from the city; they have various encounters. *Mors* appears with three darts in his hand, a black one for pestilence, a blood-red one for war and a pale one for famine He strikes down *Civis*.[78] *Civis* and *Uxor* are accompanied by their servant *Roger,* aged forty. Early on their journey, before it turns nasty, they reach Barnet:

Civis. But how like you this Heath? Here was fought a fearful field called Palm Sunday battle in king Edward the fourth's time; many thousands were slain on this ground: here was slain the noble Earl of Warwick.

Roger. If it please your mastership, my grandfather was also here with twenty tall men of the Parish where I was born, and none of them escaped but my grandfather only. I had his bow in my hand many a time; no man can stir the string when it was bent; also his harness was worn upon our St. George's back in our church many a cold winter after; and I heard my Grandame tell how he escaped.

Civis. Tell me, Roger, I pray thee, how he did escape the danger.

Roger. Sir, when the battle was pitched and appointed to be fought near unto this Windmill, and the Summons given by the Heralds of Arms that Spear, Poleaxe, black Bill, Bow and Arrows should be set a work the day following, and that it should be tried by bloody weapon, a sudden fear fell on my Grandfather, and the same night, when it was dark, he stole out of the Earl's camp for fear of the king's displeasure, and hid him in the Wood; and at length he espied a great hollow Oak Tree with arms somewhat green, and climbed up partly through cunning, for he was a Thatcher, but fear was worth a Ladder to him; and then by the help of a writhen arm of the Tree he went down and there remained a good while, and was fed there by the space of a Month with old Acorns and Nuts which Squirrels had brought in, and also did in his Sallet keep the Rain water for his drink, and at length escaped the danger.

Civis. So he might for any stripes that he had there; he was well
harnessed with a Tree, but I never read this in any Chronicle.
Roger. There be many things (and it shall please your Mastership)
which are not in the Chronicles, I do think are as true as John
your man do read into unto me when we do go to bed almost
every night. I shall never forget them : fare well, good John![79]

It would be easy to dismiss this just as an Elizabethan merry tale,
which counterpoints a grim drama. Yet Bullein is making a serious
point, in *Roger's* last remarks, about the inadequacies in current
history-writing. He may be dipping into folklore with a basis in fact.
Bullein came from Northumberland, where Warwick had exercised
military authority as Lieutenant of the Marches. Roger says that
he had travelled to Wolpit fair (probably Woolpit, near Stowmarket
in Suffolk), and recalls being on the road between Godminchester
(Godmanchester, south of Huntingdon) and Gogmanshille (Gog
Magog Hills, near Great Shelford, south of Cambridge).[80] Levies
from these parts of England had been among those under the command of the Duke of Exeter, the Earl of Oxford and Lord Bardolf
who had retreated from Newark in face of Edward's southward
advance. However, the 'battle' under Oxford's command performed
well at Barnet, routing the opposing wing. The Lancastrian debacle
was precipitated by their return to the field, when they were mis-
takenly attacked by Warwick's men, and fled.[81] Many particulars in
the story are circumstantially correct or plausible. Twenty men from
a parish would have corresponded to the basic unit of the shire array,
the *vingtaine*. The weapons described, and the type of helmet (the
sallet) were characteristic of those used by arrayed men in the later
fifteenth century. There were areas of deciduous woodland near the
encampments at Barnet field, such as on Hadley Common and in
Enfield Chase, and there was a windmill in the vicinity of the battle
site in 1584.[82] The night before the battle was exceptionally dark,
and there was thick fog in the early morning, giving good cover
for desertion. In the battle, casualties were, indeed, high.[83]

Even if the episode was wholly invented, stemming from
Bullein's musings as he passed through through Barnet, it does give

us plausible information about modes of transmission of ordinary soldiers' reminiscences, and about inherited attitudes towards the Wars among the Elizabethan commons. We may deduce, as regards transmission, that there were military heirlooms, both weapons and armour, which were kept in the families of husbandmen and artisans as well as gentlefolk, and that they might be used as aids to preserve memory of stories about the activities on campaign of their earlier owners. Moreover, widows (and, presumably, other womenfolk) also had roles in keeping such memories alive. The reference to Warwick as 'noble' may be an echo of his contemporary popularity among the commons. The most notable feature of the story is the approval of desertion. This is not attributed to cowardice. The soldier is categorised as tall, powerfully built, skilled in archery, and highly resourceful in applying his peacetime skills to living off the land in an unpropitious nemoral environment. His motive for desertion was one of which every politically correct Elizabethan would approve: it was 'for fear of the king's displeasure'. Deep-seated hatred and horror of civil war are symbolised by the conversion of the sallet into a drinking vessel, and of the armour into a theatrical costume, used for the annual parochial play of St George and the Dragon. These plays, commonly enacted in parishes throughout England on the saint's feast day, for which bits of real old armour were often stored to equip the player-saint, symbolised the unity of the local and the national community.

One of the most poignant and powerful scenes in Shakespeare's 'history plays' is the one in which, at Towton, a son bears the body of the father he has slain, and a father does likewise to his son:

> Son. O heavy times, begetting such events!
> From London by the king [Henry VI] was I press'd forth;
> My father, being the Earl of Warwick's man,
> Came on the part of York, press'd by his master…

The other father is shown in the act of uncomprehendingly killing his son:

> Thou that so stoutly hast resisted me,
> Give me thy gold, if thou hast any gold;
> For I have bought it with an hundred blows
> (*King Henry VI, Third Part*, Act II, Scene V).

Though these horrific images may have echoed comparatively rare occurences in the Wars, their tenor surely accorded with bad memories of them among the common folk. In these thumbnail sketches Shakespeare accurately reflected familiar compulsions, incentives and outcomes in the civil wars – impressment to serve king and magnate, ambition to find loot on the bodies of opponents, and enforced conflict between kinsfolk.

However, we must not exclude the possibility that there were nostalgic memories of the Wars, too.

> Shallow. O, Sir John, do you remember since we lay all night in the windmill in Saint George's Fields?
> Falstaff. No more of that, good Master Shallow, no more of that.
> Shallow. Ha, it was a merry night. And is Jane Nightwork alive?
> (*King Henry IV, Second Part*, Act III, Scene II).

Shallow was recalling, or inventing, 'the wildness of his youth' in peaceful times as an apprentice at law in London; there were surely other old men who recalled their escapades on campaign. Recollections of derring-do in the Wars may have given the prospect of domestic strife a dangerous allure for new generations of would-be firebrands. Such exhilarating tales were less likely to enter literary tradition, because they did not accord with the soberness young men were exhorted to cultivate, or with political moralising about the Wars in the sixteenth century. Yet Professor Hicks has pointed out how Warwick continued to be given a favourable literary profile.[84] One might not expect an earl who pulled down and plucked up monarchs to have been a role-model! The favourable treatment may have echoed a vein of popular nostalgia for a noble with a legendary reputation for affability to the commons, and largesse. This contrasted with the less benign and benevolent strands in some nobles' attitudes towards the commons in the sixteenth and seventeenth centuries. These stemmed from tensions over rents and fears of popular rebellion. Other developments in noble living probably tended to make relations between nobles and commons more distant and occasional. The trend for noble families to live privately may have led to more restricted and regulated access to them and their households. The attractions for nobles of living in London and provincial cities increased absenteeism from country estates. There was nostalgia among the folk for the 'good old days', such as those imagined in the seventeenth century as having characterised the castle at Newcastle-under-Lyme (Staffordshire) in the later fourteenth century:

> there be manie that need be tould what John of Gaunt his Newcastle was, and will sore lament it now is not, to give the needy sojourner largess of bread, beef, beer. Our grandames doe say that their grandames did delight to tell what it had been, and how well it was counted off before theire days.[85]

During the period of the Wars of the Roses, when nobles envisaged that they might need to conjure up a goodly array at short notice, it would surely have been prudent for them to emulate Warwick's search for popularity, and to doff their caps and provide largesse in their 'countries'. Indeed, there are not, apparently, many magnates in the period who acquired an evil reputation. Some did, like Clifford and Herbert, because of their behaviour in the Wars. Could it be that the Wars were in one sense a golden age, one of social harmony between lords and commons? Even though the most exalted in the land were gravely at risk in the campaigns of being slaughtered by rustics and artisans! However, if a kind of harmony existed, it is unlikely to have survived intact in the rapidly changing economic and social conditions of the sixteenth century. In the new climate of tensions between gentlefolk and commons, that characteristic of the Wars of the Roses may have taken on a roseate glow.

7

The Legacy of the Wars

... those opposed eyes
Which, like the meteors of a troubled heaven,
All of one nature, of one substance bred,
Did lately meet in the intestine shock
And furious close of civil butchery,
Shall now, in mutual well-beseeming ranks,
March all one way, and be no more oppos'd
Against acquaintance, kindred and allies:
The edge of war, like an ill-sheathed knife,
No more shall cut his master.

King Henry IV, Part 1, Act 1, Scene I

English and Welsh lords and gentlefolk repeatedly planned and participated in rebellions in the second half of the fifteenth century. They sometimes did so with the intention of recruiting large numbers of commoners to their cause. The kings whom they aimed to control or topple tried to recruit in the same way, pre-emptively. The arraying organisation provided an organisational bedrock for recruitment on a regional basis, a system which had been honed during the long confrontations with the Scots and the French Crown during the Hundred Years War, and whetted once more in the 1440s and '50s, to meet the challenges of the renewal of French raids on southern English coasts, and warfare with Scotland. Changes in economic and social relationships between landlords and tenants, and between masters and men, since the Peasants' Revolt of 1381, had probably eased the fears of elites about the involvement of the commons in large-scale rebellion.

Why did the commons participate in the Wars of the Roses? Short answers are that they sometimes felt pressured into doing so by the threat of disfavour from landlords and masters, or of punishment for disobedience to the statutes for array and the king's commands. However, that does not account for the eagerness they sometimes displayed, like the men of Kent in their assaults on London in 1471. London chronicles hint that economic grievances lay behind such attacks.[1] Local or regional grievances and predatoriness were doubtless frequent motivations, often unrecorded, for participation in the Wars – and had been staples in popular participation in past rebellions. Moreover, rebellions assumed traditional modes in England. They had been decked out in an ideology, appealing alike to gentlefolk and commons, which legitimised them as justifiable for the rescue and reform of the commonwealth. Some noble leaders of rebellions had become hallowed as saints, who had died for the liberties of the community. English risings had come to assume characteristic modes in the fourteenth century – they were short in duration, they did little to disrupt or damage society, and, with the exception of the battle of Shrewsbury, they did not lead to large-scale spilling of commoners' blood. Kings and their opponents were generally eager to keep to these conventions, in order to sustain and widen the basis of support.

Political, social and military circumstances militated against the long-entrenched maintenance of dynastic war, such as had characterised the reign of King Stephen (d.1154), when there had been a continuously maintained 'Eighteen Years War' with the partisans of Queen Matilda (but with only two major battles). Then, when loyalties were divided, and before his Angevin successor Henry II tightened up the control of the state over society, it was possible for magnates, such as Matilda's half-brother Robert, Earl of Gloucester, to maintain 'parallel kingdoms', in which they effectively combined the exercise of royal and their own feudal power. In Stephen's time, a multitude of castles could be quickly thrown up, constructed of earth and timber, and garrisons could be kept in them with less concern than later for the concomitant hardships of the civilian population. Dr Keith Stringer has noted that castles were the decisive weapon of territorial power, and that the technology of defence had outstripped that of attack.[2] However, the mining of the keep of Rochester Castle by King John in 1215 showed that later massive stone defence systems had become vulnerable to improved siegecraft. If military architects once more gained the edge in the thirteenth century, as supremely exemplified by James of St George's designs for Edward I's castles in Wales, it was at the cost of high investment, the option of the wealthiest, and justifiable only in lands where war was expected to continue as a normal condition. The castles of the English nobility in the fifteenth century, in a land where peace was expected to be the customary condition, tended to have antiquated defences, ill-equipped for an age of rapidly advancing gunpowder technology. Modern additions had been designed mostly for peaceful, luxurious living. These castles could have been turned only at vast expense into fortresses defending a region – and then would have been dependent on the uncertain support of powerful gentry, and urban and rural elites for the costly maintenance of garrisons.

So, English society could anticipate with more equanimity than communities in many parts of Western Christendom the recurrence of rebellion, such as in the Wars of the Roses, because there were expectations that it would be as marginally disruptive as in earlier rebellions – and because, to a remarkable extent, these expectations were fulfilled in the Wars. The common soldier's outlay on arms and equipment was, indeed, burdensome. However, there was usually the prospect of brief and mobile campaigning, minimising the risks from the soldier's greatest enemy, disease. The time of the year often held the promise of mild weather, fair ways, and plentiful supplies. The routes taken were mostly within easy reach of an abundance of markets, alehouses and women. Local inhabitants, generally used to the flow of merchants, pilgrims and minstrels from other parts of the realm, shared cultural norms with most fellow countrymen. Indeed, there was a high risk of combat, since campaigns often involved a pitched battle, but the terrible hazards involved in that might be softened by the prevailing doctrine in English civil wars that the defeated commons should be spared.

Such optimistic prospects doubtless excited young men eager for companionship and adventure, and helped to reassure the more cautious and fearful. Moreover, there was the temptation to gamble the possibility of large gains against losing one's clothes or health or life itself. Commanders channelled the urge to rob and despoil indiscriminately, by their incitements to kill opposing nobles and gentlefolk. Their proclamations urging this contained the implicit inducement of stripping dead and stricken peers, knights and esquires of the valuables their status required them to hazard on the battlefield. This inducement helps to account for the large numbers of gentlefolk listed as killed in the battles of the Wars, and the attribution of the deaths of some great men – notably Warwick and Richard III – to commoners. The great battles are likely to have provided a bonanza in chattels and horses for common soldiers, and a brisk market in second-hand goods in the vicinity.

There were other possible motives for the participation of commoners besides particular grievances, tolerant and complacent attitudes towards rebellion, adventurousness and covetousness. Up-and-coming tenant farmers, who often styled themselves 'yeoman', and aspired to lifestyles which aped gentelfolk's, might have felt special incentives to parade, well equipped, in arms, concerned to lead their communities in war, and display their involvement with nobles and the issues of high politics. Just as much as gentlefolk and yeomanry, the poorest digger and his wife, living on the margins of subsistence, might be concerned about the momentous dynastic issue raised in 1460, for it might threaten, as a result of God's wrath, their precarious lives. A ruler whose title to the throne was wrongful was even more of a threat to the commonweal than the influence of 'evil' royal councillors.

Concern among layfolk (as well as clerics) about the rightful succession to the English throne (and English kings' claims to other thrones) is reflected in what appears to be a proliferation of genealogical rolls tracing the succession of the kings of England, dating from the reigns of Henry VI and Edward IV. The ease with which they could be exhibited, their pictorial form, with brief accompanying notes, sometimes mainly in English, suggest that they were often drafted for the use of layfolk as well as clerics, and could be used as an aid in instructing the illiterate about the fundamentals of English history and royalty, such as groups of servants in a household, or young children still struggling with their primers. (One recalls the cigarette cards of English and British monarchs which children used to collect and paste into booklets in the mid-twentieth century). Some of these medieval genealogies start with Adam, and progress to English kings via Biblical figures. The mythical ancient British kings, whose sway had been so influentially hyped by Geoffrey of Monmouth in the twelfth century, figure prominently in some genealogies. In a roll commencing with Adam and ending with Edward IV, it was declared that Richard Duke of York was 'ryght eyre of Brute fraunce and spayne'.[3] Here, the rule of the whole of Britain was being claimed for Edward IV as the successor of Brutus, the Trojan warrior who, according to Geoffrey, conquered Albion, after whom it was renamed Britain. The House of York for long maintained a claim to the throne of Castile, one not shared by the Lancastrians.[4]

One roll, deposited in Somerset Record Office, starts with William the Conqueror, and goes down to Henry VI, ending with a mention of his coronations at Westminster in 1429 and in Paris in 1430. There follows a note tracing Edward III's claim to the French throne. A marginal note added that Henry was slain by his enemies, buried at Chertsey, and afterwards transferred to Windsor [1484], concluding, 'Now every man may know what he was' (i.e. a saint). This roll was probably preserved under the Yorkist kings by a family of covert Lancastrian loyalists. It has a crudely drawn figure of each king in a roundel, underneath which are short verses in English about the reign. Another version of this roll, starting with the Conqueror, and identical in its format and sets of verses, has recently been deposited in the Library of the University of

St Andrews. This lacks the last section covering the Lancastrian kings, which appears to have been carefully unstitched – perhaps by a nervous owner in time of Yorkist rule. A note at the top suggests ownership by a prior of the Gilbertine house of Watton (Yorkshire). Indeed, this roll is produced in a more sophisticated manner, appropriate to clerical circles. The figures are drawn delicately, and there are additional marginal notes in Latin. An illuminated initial introduces a Latin note recording the Black Death (*magna pestilencia*), the pandemic of 1369 (*secunda pestilencia*), and the great storm (*magnus ventus*) the same year.[5]

The popularity of such rolls seem to have declined under Henry VII, though this was not because he desired to trumpet forth his distinguished ancestry and the rightfulness of his claim to the throne less than his predecessors. Perhaps cynicism had set in about regarding such rolls as 'proofs'. By the late 1480s gentlefolk and commons were becoming increasingly deaf to the siren voices of would-be dynastic rebels. What were the possible reasons for this? One may have been bewilderment over who was the true king. There are likely to have been others in a puzzle about it besides Master Butlar, who got into trouble, after fighting for Henry VII against the West Country rebels in 1497, for saying 'for why tis hard to know who is the Rightwise king'.[6] The sensational justifications which Richard, Duke of Gloucester, had put forward to support his claim of 1483 to be the 'rightwise' king had muddied the Yorkist right which, though contentious, had been generally accepted after the death of Henry VI. Some ambitious great men, after the events of the early 1480s, may have seemed to many too transparently cynical in their preparedness to back any horse they considered suitable who had a plausible pedigree. When Henry VII was ill (*c.* 1503), Sir Hugh Conway, treasurer of Calais, according to his confession, fell into conversation with 'many great personages' about the succession, if the King died. 'Then he said that some of them spake of my lord of Buckingham, saying that he was a noble man and would be a royal ruler. Other were that spake, he said, in like wise of your traitor, Edmund de la Pole, but none of them, he said, spake of my lord prince'. Perhaps they had in mind the desirability of dismissing the claim of a child to reign, in favour of an adult, as had been done in 1483. In 1504 Henry, Prince of Wales (the future Henry VIII) reached the age of thirteen, the same age that Edward V attained, or would have attained, in 1483. Richard III cast a long shadow.[7]

However, for both lords and commons, revolt in the cause of dynastic rebellion largely went off the political agenda, though dreaming about 'kingmaking' did not go entirely out of fashion. In 1553 the highly unpopular John Dudley, Duke of Northumberland, dominant in government, persuaded the dying Edward VI to alter the succession as laid down by his father Henry VIII, in favour of Henry Grey, Duke of Suffolk's daughter Jane (granddaughter of Henry VIII's sister Mary), hastily married to Dudley's son Guildford. Despite the adherence of councillors to Edward's 'devise', after the King's death the arrogant Dudley found that support was universally behind the claim of Henry's designated heir, his daughter Mary; his attempts to rally support failed miserably. Suffolk, incorrigibly, engaged in plotting the new queen's downfall. In 1554 he planned rebellion with a few gentry from different regions, with the objectives of marrying Edward Courtenay, Earl of Devon (great-grandson of Richard, Duke of York) to Mary's sister Elizabeth, and placing them on the throne together. No other peers joined in the plotting, and, when it came to arms, Courtenay and his kinsmen failed to show. Suffolk's band of about 140 horsemen in the Midlands consisted mainly of kinsmen and servants, with a few humble townsmen: his belief that he would get support from Leicester and Coventry proved wide of the mark, and he had to disband. In Devon, despite the sedulous propaganda of Sir Peter and Sir Gawain Carew against the queen's intended marriage to Philip of Spain, only about seventy would-be rebels turned up to their assembly at Mohun's Ottery. However, anti-Spanish feeling ran high in south-east England, and in mid-Kent Sir Thomas Wyatt was able to raise some gentlefolk, and, besides them, tradesmen from Rochester and Maidstone, and yeomen, husbandmen and labourers from neighbouring villages. Wyatt put together a well-disciplined force, which loyal peers and gentry in Kent could not find sufficient arrayed men to oppose. A militia force sent into Kent from London had no stomach to fight him. He advanced to Southwark, crossed Kingston Bridge and marched his men to assault London, without opposition, despite the queen's determination to stay in the city. However, when his attack on Ludgate was repulsed, the queen's retainers and the civic militia (hitherto spectators, very much in the manner of many in the Wars of the Roses) closed in on Wyatt's hopelessly outnumbered men at Temple Bar. Cardinal Pole (another great-grandson of Richard, Duke of York) thought that Wyatt was ultimately repulsed more because of fear of sack rather than any antipathy to his cause.[8] Maybe there were recollections in the city of fears there in 1497 that the Cornishmen would sack it, and in 1471 that the Kentishmen would.

There was to be one more resurgence of dynastic plotting among magnates, stimulated by Mary Queen of Scots' flight to England in 1568. The fact that she had a plausible alternative claim to the throne, attractive to Roman Catholics, raised in more acute form the problem of the succession. Some nobles, notably Robert Dudley, Earl of Leicester (son of that aspiring 'kingmaker', the Duke of Northumberland), hoping to overthrow the ascendancy of William Cecil and his anti-Spanish policies, toyed with arranging a marriage between Queen Mary and Thomas Howard, Duke of Norfolk. When Elizabeth heard about these schemes, she was infuriated. Norfolk continued to prevaricate, ultimately to his downfall. Most nobles prudently backed off, but his arrest in 1569 flushed out those with an undoubtedly treasonable agenda. Thomas Percy, Earl of Northumberland, and Charles Neville, Earl of Westmorland, wished to replace Elizabeth with Mary. Indeed, characteristically of Tudor magnates, they were reluctant to take up arms, but felt that they would lose honour among those close to them if they failed to pursue the cause they had undertaken. Their rebellion had some ephemeral successes in the bishopric of Durham. They appealed to strong religious conservatism – the banner of the Five Wounds of Christ was raised, as in 1536. They called on their traditional ties with gentry and commons, neighbours and tenants, some of which retained an old-fashioned strength. However, their cause did not have such resonances generally in England. Having fled into exile, they posed no further threat – and it was the commons who now suffered for treason. Over 400 were executed.

They were not the last English dynastic rebels. There were the artisans and labourers in the West Country who followed Charles II's illegitimate son James, Duke of Monmouth, in rebellion against James II and VII in 1685, with equally dire consequences for themselves. There were yet to be faint echoes of medieval-style rebellion in the eighteenth century. In 1715 the Earl of Derwentwater, local gentry and their servants gathered in arms at Warkworth to hear 'James III' proclaimed. In the '45, when the Highland Army entered Manchester, two or three hundred young artisans and labourers were recruited, to form a regiment under the command of a local gentleman. During the Wars of the Roses, Sir Thomas Malory had criticised the tendency of people in the North to rebel; over 200 years later, there were still parts of society there in which highly localised and traditional ties could lead to faint simulacra of such stirs.

As we have seen, the Wars of the Roses did not kill off rebellion. There were formidable rebellions comparable to earlier ones in the sixteenth century, yet changing social and economic conditions affected the nature of rebellion and popular protest, undermining perceived congruities of interest between lords and commons, which had underpinned risings and sustained their dynamic in the previous period. Characteristically of this period, in 1553 Northumberland could not hope to raise the commons, since he had alienated them through his government's support for enclosures. In 1554 the Carews could not raise the commons in Devon. They and the other gentry, generally of Protestant persuasion, had, in vain, opposed the rising of the religiously conservative populace in Cornwall and Devon in 1549, a protest movement focussed on the abolition of the Mass and the introduction of the Book of Common Prayer. The Cornish rebels had besieged the gentry who had taken refuge on St Michael's Mount.[9]

Demographic growth, rising remorselessly from the 1520s, increased commodity prices, inducing landlords to maximise rents and profits. Especially in the second half of the century, and into the seventeenth century, landowners sought to profit from more intense grain and stock production, by enclosing wastes, commons and woodlands, curtailing their immemorial use as a vital resource by smallholders. Some of the growing tensions between lords and peasants over rent appear in the Pilgrimage of Grace, in the main a grand old-style gathering of the commons in arms under the leadership of their gentry. However, tenants from the estates in Craven and Westmorland of Henry Clifford, Earl of Cumberland, rioted in protest at his harsh seigneurial policies. The formidable risings in Norfolk and Suffolk in 1549, and disturbances in neighbouring shires, which started with a riot at Wymondham (Norfolk), were specifically aimed against the policies of the gentry. The well-disciplined rebels who encamped outside Norwich, captained by the prosperous tanner Robert Kett, arrested and detained some gentlemen. Their loyal articles of complaint stated their grievances about the ways in which the Norfolk gentry exploited tenures and offices for commercial gain. Though the rebellion, like that in the West Country in the same year, ended in defeat and disaster for the participants, it was long remembered by the common folk with a certain relish. In 1595, it was said in Norfolk that there should be 'suche as Kettes Campe was and ther men shold fytt [fight] for corne'.[10] The terrible times of dearth in the 1590s provoked seditious talk of a violent nature against those lords and gentry whose tenurial and farming policies were blamed for hardships. In 1596 Bartholomew Steer, carpenter, was the ringleader of an attempted rising in Oxfordshire, where there had been a growth in larger holdings in the hands of yeomen, and a corresponding increase in the numbers of indigent rural labourers and cottagers. Steer tried to recruit poor people to pull down enclosures, and to animate his followers by threats to kill gentlemen. He hoped to link up eventually with London apprentices. Only a handful of followers turned up for his assembly on Enslow Hill. They disbanded and were arrested. Punishments were exemplary.[11]

The Oxfordshire rising shows how difficult it had become to mount regional popular risings, in face of lack of support and, indeed, vigilant hostility from many of the 'better sort' – gentlefolk, yeomen, well-to-do artisans. Professor Manning has shown that the characteristic form of popular protest in the Elizabethan and early Stuart period remained the highly localised riot, directed to right what was perceived as the flouting of custom and right within a community. Gentry, often of lesser status, played a declining part in instigating anti-enclosing riots – which were, indeed, often protests against the policies of particular enclosing gentry. Popular protest rarely developed a wider significance. The most notable exceptions were the agrarian risings in the Midlands in 1607, which began in Northamptonshire, and spread to Warwickshire and Leicestershire. Large crowds of men, women and children, of up to 1,000, congregated. There were some signs of organisation along traditional lines. A manifesto was produced by the 'Diggers of Warwickshire to all other Diggers', in which they protested their loyalty to the King, and eloquently denounced 'incroaching Tirants which would grinde our flesh upon the whetstone of poverty'. The Northamptonshire risings even threw up an effective leader, John Reynolds, 'a base fellow' – supposedly a tinker or peddlar. He apparently kept good order in his company, forbidding swearing, and violence to those encountered. He asserted that he had the King's authority to throw down enclosures, 'and that he was sent of God to satisfie all degrees whatsoever'. Here one has an echo of the assurance of divine favour which had buoyed up some medieval risings – and Reynolds also had a charismatic object he carried, an equivalent of the crosses and sacred banners which had once been such potent and inspiring symbols for rebels. He was known as 'Captain Powch'. The suggestion was that his pouch contained a talisman, but when it was opened, after his capture, all that was found in it was a piece of mouldy cheese.[12]

The reason the Midland risings rolled on largely undisturbed for well over a month was the sympathy felt for them by members of the trained bands, which forced the exasperated gentry to temporise. Yet the diggers' lack of a sophisticated leadership meant that they never attained any coherent military and political momentum. They devoted their energies just to digging, grubbing up hedges and fences. Indeed, traditions of popular protest were to remain vigorous in the seventeenth century (exemplified by the opponents of the drainers of the Fenlands, and by the Clubmen of the Great Civil War), but we may take Captain Powch's mouldy cheese as a symbol of the disintegration and disappearance of the conditions and conventions of medieval rebellion. There are indications that they were unravelling as a result of the Wars of the Roses, but novel religious, economic and social developments were to undermine them further in the sixteenth century. No longer could the commons, as in Lincolnshire in 1536, hope to look to the gentry to guide and cosset them in rebellion – instead, there was the expectation, if they overstepped the accepted limits of rioting, that they would face the provost marshal or the magistrate, with the probablity of the hangman's noose. Moreover, there was a stark contrast to the uprooted and restless Anglo-Welsh establishments of soldiers, well-connected and motivated to engage in domestic strife during some periods of the later fifteenth century. The growing fiscal power of the state in the sixteenth and seventeenth centuries gave it what came to be a monopoly of hiring and keeping the services of large bodies of professional soldiers. The overwhelming violence that the state could command was starkly demonstrated on the men of Devon at Sedgmoor in 1685.

It is likely that memories of the Wars and other risings of the later fifteenth century, and myths about them, strongly influenced the aims and conduct of major rebellions in the first half of the sixteenth century, whose outcomes in turn provided stark warnings and lessons for future would-be risers. As we have seen, dynastic issues were mostly eschewed. When government under Henry VIII and Edward VI momentarily seemed to be at the mercy of the rebels, they did not budge from their regional bases in order to take king or capital by surprise, according to the strategy often employed in the Wars and in previous risings. Like Archbishop Scrope in 1405, they wanted to use their strength to negotiate with government. Perhaps they feared that to move poorly funded and potentially unruly forces far beyond their own 'countries' would rapidly lose them any goodwill that they enjoyed elsewhere. This is most striking in the case of the forces in Yorkshire which were the nexus of the Pilgrimage of Grace. Their leaders would not stir out of the shire, despite the fact that there were widespread echoes of their complaints about government in southern England, and that the royal commander, the Duke of Norfolk, considered that his forces were so outclassed that he persuaded Henry VIII of the necessity of negotiating. The battles of 1461 were still within living memory. Yorkshiremen may have remembered apprehensively how Margaret of Anjou's army, moving from their shire on London, had stirred up hatred in the South, and how a terrible revenge had been exacted by an army coming thence, at Towton a few months later. In 1549 the rebellious commons of Devon and Cornwall encamped at Clyst St Mary, near Exeter, and besieged the city. Though the government could not offer effective opposition immediately, the rebels did not advance beyond the West Country, as the rebels of 1497 had boldly done. Similarly, the Norfolk rebels of 1549 stayed within their own 'country'. On religion, their views were diametrically opposed to those of the westerners: the Reformation had produced diverse regional trends in worship which made it harder to concert widespread rebellion, so strengthening the authority of central government. Maybe the Wars had already left a legacy of intercommunal distrust which hampered the co-ordination of risings. Edward Hall, writing about the battle of Edgcote in the 1540s, asserted 'the whiche battaile euer synce hath bene, and yet is a continuall grudge betwene the Northernmen and the Welshemen'.[13]

In many parts of England and Wales, families and communities preserved memories of the Wars in the sixteenth century – perhaps they were only eclipsed by the dramas of the Great Civil War, which were to fill the historical horizons of Richard Gough, writing his history of Myddle (Shropshire), replete with orally transmitted traditions.[14] Those memories of the Wars that have been preserved support the litany of distress and disaster with which discursive writers of the sixteenth century embellished them. Families proudly recalled the alleged chivalrous deeds or heroic suffering of an ancestor in the cause of Henry Tudor. Communities in the vicinity of battles preserved traditions about the place where a great man had fallen or there had been slaughter or drowning. Such memories probably induced caution about joining protesting magnates – better to trust a well-respected local man of lower status, like the provincial lawyer Aske, the tanner Kett, and even the tinker, Captain Powch. Among the commons, risings were to become the last resort of the dispossessed and the desperate, rather than the assertions by communities of their right to adjust the ordering of the commonwealth, sometimes within a cosmic and numinous context.

The family and folk memories of the Wars which have been recorded were mostly gloomy ones. The commemorative institutions – obits and chantries – set up to minister to the souls of some of the individuals who died in them kept alive the memory of their violent deaths. However, the dissolution of the chantries in 1547 by Edward VI's first parliament is likely to have blurred these memories. Moreover, we cannot assume that unhappy memories of the Wars predominated. Veterans often blank out or stay silent about the moments of terror which may invade their dreams, and the lifelong pain of losing mentors and youthful comrades. They prefer to look back with nostalgia on military service performed when they were young, at full strength, eager for new experiences. They remember the fun they had with pals – and they remember the lasses. They hold their audiences of younger folk with tales of exciting sights (like those witnessed by the boys up the trees at Nibley Green) or amazing and comical escapades, like hiding in the hollow of a tree, or fooling pursuers by floating a cap as a decoy. Their audiences of young ploughmen and apprentices may have wished that they, too, could experience such excitements, and awe alehouse cronies by recalling them.

Notes

CHAPTER 1: INTRODUCTION: THE WARS OF THE ROSES TODAY

1. Schama, S., *A History of Britain*, London, 2000, 266–68.
2. *Rotuli Parliamentorum*, ed. Strachey, J. et al., 6 vols, London, 1767–83, vol.5, 463–64.
3. *The Nobility of Later Medieval England*, Oxford, 1973.
4. For general accounts, Gillingham, J., *The Wars of the Roses*, London, 1981 and Weir, A. *The Wars of the Roses*, London, 1994; for concise accounts, Ross, C., *The Wars of the Roses. A Concise History*, London, 1976 and Pollard, A.J., *The Wars of the Roses*, London, 1988. Lander, J.R., *The Wars of the Roses*, London, 1965 has a narrative largely carried forward by extracts from contemporary chronicles and documents. For a refreshing variety of approaches, Pollard, A.J., ed., *The Wars of the Roses*, Basingstoke, 1995.
5. Watts, J., *Henry VI and the Politics of Kingship*, Cambridge, 1996; Carpenter, C., *The Wars of the Roses. Politics and the constitution in England, c. 1437–1509*, Cambridge, 1997.
6. Richmond, C.R., 'Fauconberg's Kentish Rising of May 1471', *EHR*, 85, 1970; Dockray, K., 'The Yorkshire Rebellion of 1469', *The Ricardian*, 6, 1983; Pollard, A.J., *North–East England during the Wars of the Roses*, Oxford, 1990.
7. Dockray, K., 'The Battle of Wakefield and the Wars of the Roses', *The Ricardian*, 9, 1992.
8. Pollard, T. and Oliver, N., *Two Men in a Trench*, London, 2002.
9. Fiorato, V., Boylston, A. and Knüssel, C., *Blood Red Roses*, Oxford, 2000.

CHAPTER 2: ATTITUDES TO WAR

1. Vaughan, R., *Charles the Bold. The Last Valois Duke of Burgundy*, London, 1973, 217.
2. Commynes, 353.
3. *Two Memoirs of Renaissance Florence*, trans. Martines, J., ed. Brucker, G., New York, 1967, 42–3.
4. *Gesta Henrici Quinti*, 92–3.
5. 'The Siege of Rouen', *The Historical Collections of a London Citizen in the Fifteenth Century*, ed. Gairdner, J., 1st Camden ser., 109, London,

1876, 1-46. For the siege of Rouen, Allmand, C.T., *Henry V*, Newhaven and London, 1997, 122-27.

6. *CSP...Venice*, 1, ed. Brown, R., London, R.S., 1864, 8-9.

7. *Foedera*, vol.7, 407.

8. *Westminster Chronicle*, 212-13.

9. *CPR*, 1401–1405, 261, 352, 354.

10. 'Bale's Chronicle', *Six Town Chronicles of England*, ed. Flenley, R., Oxford, 1921, 148.

11. 'Chronicle of the Rebellion in Lincolnshire in 1470', ed. Nicols, J.G., *Camden Miscellany* 1, London, 1847, 10.

12. For society in Ireland, Lydon, J., *Ireland in the Later Middle Ages*, Dublin, 1973. For a map of the comparative distribution of tower houses in the British Isles from the fourteenth to the seventeenth century, Griffiths, R.A. ed., *Short Oxford History of the British Isles. The Fourteenth and Fifteenth Centuries*, Oxford, 2003, 213.

13. Du Boulay, F.R.H., *Germany in the later Middle Ages*, London, 1983, 71-2.

14. Storey, R.L., *The End of the House of Lancaster*.

15. Blacman, J., *Henry the Sixth*, ed. James, M. R., Cambridge, 1919; *The Miracles of King Henry VI*, ed. Knox, R. and Leslie, S., Cambridge, 1923, 53, 79.

16. Head, C., 'Pius II and the Wars of the Roses', *Archivum Historiae Pontificae*, 8, 1970, 145.

17. 'Annales Ricardi Secundi et Henrici Quarti', 337-38.

18. Pounds, N.J.G., *The Medieval Castle in England and Wales. A social and political history*, Cambridge, 1990, 257-60; Goodman, A., 'The Defence of Northumberland: a Preliminary Survey', *Armies, Chivalry and Warfare in Medieval Britain and France*, ed. Strickland, M, Stamford, 1998, 170 and n.43-44; Brooke, C., *Safe Sanctuaries. Security and Defence in Anglo-Scottish Border Churches*

1290–1690, Edinburgh, 2000.

19. See below, 187.

20. Evans, J., *English Art 1307–1461*, Oxford, 1949, 133-34.

21. Barnes, H.D. and Simpson, W.D., 'Caister Castle', *The Antiquaries' Journal*, 32, 1952.

22. *Paston Letters*, 2, nos.620, 627-28; Worcestre, 186-91 ; Richmond, C., *The Paston Family in the Fifteenth Century*, Cambridge, 1996, 192-207.

23. Smyth, John, of Nibley, *Lives of the Berkeleys*, ed. Maclean, J., 2, Gloucester, 1883, 109-15.

24. Keen, M., *The laws of war in the late Middle Ages*, London, 1965.

25. Barbour, John, *The Brus*, Spalding Club, Aberdeen, 1856, 403-5. Barbour alleged that of the 1,000 or more Englishmen killed, 300 were priests.

26. *Chronicon Angliae*, ed. Thompson, E.M., R.S., London, 1874, 151-52.

27. PRO, E403/464, m6 (Issue Roll for second part of Easter term, first year of Richard II). For arrays of the clergy, McHardy, A.K., 'The English clergy and the Hundred Years War', *The church and war*, ed. Shiels, W.J., Oxford, 1983, 171-78.

28. *Chronicon Angliae*, 239-40.

29. Pearce, E.H., *The Monks of Westminster*, Cambridge, 1916, 107.

30. *Gesta Henrici Quinti*, 85-89.

31. Goodman, A., *Introduction to Richard II. The Art of Kingship*, ed. Goodman, A. and Gillespie, J.L., Oxford, 1999, 11-12.

32. For Bowet's array of the clergy, Goodman, A., *Margery Kempe and Her World*, London, 2002, 144-45.

33. 'Herald's report', Bennett, M., *Lambert Simnel and the Battle of Stoke*, Gloucester, 1987, 127-9.

34. Bennett, M., 'Henry VII and the Northern Rising of 1489', *EHR*, 105, 1990, 41-42.

35. Griffiths, *The Reign of King Henry VI*, 815; Goodman, A., *The Wars of the Roses*, London, 1981, 60-63.

36. *The Anonimalle Chronicle 1333 to 1381*,

ed. Galbraith, V.H., Manchester, 1970, 44-46.

37. Pearsall, D., *The Life of Geoffrey Chaucer. A Critical Biography*, Oxford, 1992, 40-41.

38. *Lines* 2000, 2002, 213-16.

39. Goodman, A., *John of Gaunt*, London, 1992, 225; Bower, Walter, *Scotichronicon*, ed. Watt, D., 8, Aberdeen, 1987, 34-37. Knighton, 334-35, says that Gaunt's army burnt several villages and homes ('plures uillulas et domos') – the latter possibly fortalices – and that they cut down and burnt woods extensively.

40. *Gesta Henrici Quinti*, 68-69.

41. Ibid., 70-71.

42. Keegan, J., *The Mask of Command*, London, 1988, 219-20.

43. Keen, *The Laws of War.*

44. Rogers, A., 'Hoton versus Shakell: a Ransom Case in the Court of Chivalry, 1390-5', *Nottingham Mediaeval Studies*, 6 (1962), 74-75, 75, n.8, 86.

45. The Villena collection in the Archivo del Reino de Valencia has relevant documents.

46. *Historia Anglicana*, ed. Riley, H.T., R.S., vol.1, 319n; *Anonimalle Chronicle*, 115-16; A.R. Valencia, *Maestre Racional*, 11, 599 – schedule about the imprisonment in England of the count of Denia.

47. Northumberland County Record Office, ZSW/4/45; ZSW/4/60, Swinburne of Capheaton MSS; Thomson, P., *Sir Thomas Wyatt and His Background*, London, 1964, 6.

48. Froissart, vol.8, 38-45.

49. Keegan, *The Mask of Command*, 149-50.

50. le Baker, Geoffrey, extract from chronicle, *The Life and Campaigns of the Black Prince*, ed. and trans. Barber, R., Woodbridge, 1979, 43; *Gesta Henrici Quinti*, 90-93 and 92, n.1; Macdougall, N., *An Antidote to the English. The Auld Alliance 1295-1560*, East Linton, 2001, 73.

51. Bridge, J.S.C., *A History of France from the death of Louis XI*, 1, 1483-1493, Oxford, 1921, 165-67.

52. Crow, M.M. and Olson, C.C. ed., *Chaucer Life-Records*, Oxford, 1966, 23-25.

53. Froissart, vol. 9, 137-8.

54. 'The Prologue', lines 390-410.

55. 'Bale's Chronicle', 152.

56. Vaughan, R., *John the Fearless*, London, 1966,100.

57. Commynes, 203-04; Vaughan, *Charles the Bold*, 77-78.

58. Ibid., 80-81.

59. Ibid., 354-56, 362-63, 370.

60. Ibid., 33-35; Bower, *Scotichronicon*, ed. Watt, 7, Aberdeen, 1996, 254-57, 260-1.

61. Commynes, 65; Vaughan, R., *Philip the Good*, London, 1970, 383.

62. Fortescue, Sir John, *The Governance of England*, ed. Plummer, C., Oxford, 1885.

63. Citations in Nicholson, R., *Scotland. The Later Middle Ages*, Edinburgh, 1974, 341.

64. Ibid., 359-60, 364. Ranald Nicholson described the sack of Stirling as demonstrating an antiquated attitude and political ineptitude.

65. Ibid., 204-05.

66. Wyntoun, Andrew, *The Orygynale Cronykil of Scotland*, 3, Paterson, W., ed., 1879, 55.

67. Lloyd, J.E., *Owen Glendower*, Oxford, 1931, 86-87 (ravaging of Shropshire); 'Gloucester Annals', Kingsford, C.L., *English Historical Literature in the Fifteenth Century*, Oxford, 1913, 356-57 (rejoicing at Herbert's execution).

68. Lloyd, 34 (royal force's sack of Franciscan house at Llanfaes), 42-43 (Henry IV's rough treatment of monks of Strata Florida), 60-61 (Prince Henry's plundering expedition), 89-90 and 90, n.1 (Glyn Dŵr's burning of Cardiff and the destruction of its Benedictine priory), 126, n.2; Williams, G., *Renewal and Reformation. Wales c.1415-1642*, Oxford, 1993, 16-30.

69. Ibid., 199-201.

70. Loomis, R. and Johnston, D, ed. and trans., *Medieval Welsh Poems. An Anthology,* Binghampton, New York, 1972, 165-68; Williams, 201-02.

71. Commynes, 297, 340. In 1456, in a campaign between two rival brothers of the Wettin family of Saxony, sixty villages were burnt in one day (Du Boulay, *Germany in the Later Middle Ages,* 182).

72. Gragg, F.A. trans. and Gabel, L.C. ed., *Memoirs of a Renaissance Pope. The Commentaries of Pius II,* London, 1960, 201; Cohn, H.J., *The Government of the Rhine Palatinate in the Fifteenth Century,* Oxford, 1965, 11-12.

73. *Memoirs of a Renaissance Pope,* 187.

74. Ibid., 225.

75. Mallett, M., *Mercenaries and their Masters. Warfare in Renaissance Italy,* London, 1974, 191-92.

76. Mallett, 192.

77. O'Callaghan, J.F., *A History of Medieval Spain, Ithaca and London,* 1975, 553-77.

78. Ibid., 563, 573, 581; Gamez, Guttiere Diaz de, *The Unconquered Knight. A Chronicle of the Deeds of Don Pero Niño,* ed. and trans. Evans, J., London, 1928,

79. I owe thanks for information about this campaign to Harry Schnitker.

80. Given-Wilson, C. ed., *The Chronicle of Adam Usk 1377–1421,* Oxford, 1997, 52-55.

81. Ibid., 54-57.

82. Cron, B.M., 'Margaret of Anjou and the Lancastrian March on London, 1461', *The Ricardian,* 11, 1999, 590-615; Whethamstede, vol.1, 171-73.

83. 'Annales rerum anglicanum', *Letters and Papers Illustrative of the Wars of the English in France during the Reign of Henry the Sixth, King of England,* ed. Stevenson, J., 2, pt 2, R.S., 777; Poulson, G., *Beverlac; or, The Antiquities and History of the Town of Beverley,* 1, London, 1829, 234, 239.

84. See below, Chapter 6.

85. Dunn, A., 'Henry IV and the Politics of Resistance in Early Lancastrian England, 1399–1413', *The Fifteenth Century II. Authority and Subversion,* ed. Clark, L., Woodbridge, 2003, 13-14.

86. Walker, S., 'The Yorkshire Risings of 1405: Texts and Contexts', *Henry IV: the Establishment of the Regime, 1399–1406,* ed. Dodd, G. and Biggs, D., York, 2003, 161-84.

87. Goodman, A. and MacKay, A., 'A Castilian report on English affairs, 1486', *EHR,* 88, 1973.

88. 'Annales Ricardi Secundi et Henrici Quarti', 322-30, 337-38; McFarlane, K.B., *John Wycliffe and the Beginnings of English Nonconformity,* London, 1966, 167; Pugh, T.B., *Henry V and the Southampton Plot of 1415,* Southampton, 1988.

89. Wolffe, B.P., *Henry VI,* London, 1981, 338-39, 347.

90. Brown, M., *James I,* Edinburgh, 1994, 186-88; Shirley, John, trans., 'The Dethe of the Kynge of Scotis', *Death and Dissent. Two Fifteenth-Century Chronicles,* ed. Matheson, L.M., Woodbridge, 1999.

91. Scarisbrick, J.J., *Henry VIII,* New Haven and London, 1977, 121.

92. Hutton, R., *The Rise and Fall of Merry England. The Ritual Year 1400–1700,* Oxford, 1994, 9; Dobson, R.B., *The Peasants' Revolt of 1381,* London, 1970, 389-91.

93. Fryde, N., *The tyranny and fall of Edward II 1321–1326,* Cambridge, 1979, 185-90; Tuck, A., *Richard II and the English Nobility,* London, 1973, 71, 103-04.

94. Knighton, 402-03; Tuck, 117-19; Saul, N., *Richard II,* New Haven and London, 1997, 186-89.

95. Given-Wilson, C., ed., *Chronicles of the Revolution 1397–1400,* Manchester, 1993, 32-39.

96. Fryde, 190.

97. For Henry's campaign, Given-

Wilson, op. cit.

98. Griffiths, *Reign of King Henry VI*, 867-88.

99. *Historie of the Arrivall of King Edward IV*, ed. Bruce, J., Camden Soc., London, 1838; Goodman, *Wars of the Roses*, 75-83.

100. See discussion below, 84ff.

101. Dunn, A., *The Great Rising of 1381*, Stroud, 2002.

102. Text in Chrimes, S.B. and Brown, A.L., *Select Documents of English Constitutional History 1307-1485*, London, 1961, 290.

103. Griffiths, 860-61; Ross, C., *Edward IV*, London, 1974, 129-30.

104. Thornley, I.D., 'Treason by Words in the Fifteenth Century', *EHR*, 32, 1917, 556-61; Allen, H.E. and Meech, S.B., ed., *The Book of Margery Kempe*, Early English Text Soc., Woodbridge, 1997, 102.

105. *Paston Letters*, 3, no. 916; Bennett, M., 'Henry VII and the Northern Risings of 1489', *EHR*, 105, 1990, 34-59.

106. Denholm-Young, N., ed., *Vita Edward Secundi*, London, 1957, 18.

107. Goodman, *John of Gaunt*, 39, 252, 259, 270, n.100; *Testamenta Eboracensia. A Selection of Wills from the Registry at York*, 3, Surtees Soc., 45, 1864, 273-78 Leland, 522.

108. 'Annales Ricardi Secundi et Henrici Quarti', 218-19; McKenna, J.W., 'Popular canonization as political propaganda: the cult of Archbishop Scrope', *Speculum*, 44, 1970, 608-23.

109. Hammond, P.W., Sutton, A.F. and Visser-Fuchs, L., 'The Reburial of Richard, Duke of York, 21-30 July 1476', *The Ricardian*, 10, 1994, 145-47.

110. *The Miracles of King Henry VI*, ed. Knox and Leslie; Hanham, A., 'Henry VI and his Miracles', *The Ricardian*, 12, 2000, 638-52.

111. Ibid., 642.

112. Dodds, vol.1, 238; ibid., vol.2, 17. For the use of the symbols of the Five Wounds, and of a chalice with a

Host by the Lincolnshire rebels, ibid., vol.1, 129.

CHAPTER 3: SOLDIERS

1. Allmand, C., *The Hundred Years War*, Cambridge, 1988; Fowler, K., *Medieval Mercenaries*, 1, Oxford, 2001.

2. Given-Wilson, C. and Prestwich, M., 'Introduction', *The Age of Edward III*, ed. Bothwell, T.S., York, 2001, 2.

3. Ayton, A., *Knights and Warhorses. Military Service and the English Aristocracy under Edward III*, Woodbridge, 1994; idem., 'English Armies in the Fourteenth Century', *Arms, Armies and Fortifications in the Hundred Years War*, ed. Curry, A. and Hughes, M., Woodbridge, 1994, 21-38.

4. Hatcher, J., *Plague, Population and the English Economy 1348-1530*, London, 1977; text about Archer's company, Harding, A., *The Law Courts of Medieval England*, London, 1973, 175.

5. Dyer, C., *Standards of living in the later Middle Ages*, Cambridge, 1989, 227-28.

6. *Anonimalle Chronicle*, 121-22, 190; *Chronicon Angliae*, 207-11, 241-22; A.R. Valencia, Maestre Racional, 9, 600, 'Record of the reasons why the count of Denia is not bound by the obligations which he was forced to make by the English and Gascons', n.d.

7. Rodgers, 'Hoton versus Shakell', 75, n.8, 86; *CCR*, 1377-1381, 482-83; *CPR*, 1381-1385, 302.

8. Fowler, K., 'Sir John Hawkwood and the English condottieri in Trecento Italy', *Renaissance Studies*, 12, 1998, 131-48.

9. Froissart, vol. 9, 407-09; *Chronicon Angliae*, 172-73; Fowler, K., 'Introduction: War and Change', *The Hundred Years War*, ed. idem, London, 10, 25, n.35. I owe thanks to K.B. McFarlane for the reference to Salle's

servile origins.

10. Knighton, 224; cf *Chronicon Angliae*, 305.

11. For instance, Leland said that Lord Sudeley built Sudeley Castle with the profits of war from France (op. cit., 170).

12. For Gournay's funeral inscription, see below, 218-19.

13. Norfolk Record Office, MR 314 242 X 5; Goodman, A., 'The military subcontracts of Sir Hugh Hastings, 1380', *EHR*, 95, 1980, 116-17 and 117, n.1. For Nowell's military and criminal careers, Fowler, *Medieval Mercenaries*, 1, 20-21. I owe thanks to Professor Michael Bennett for his tentative identification of Jankyn Nowell as John son of Lawrence Nowell of Read, Lancs., citing *Victoria History of the County of Lancashire*, vol. 7, 339-40, 504; Lancashire Record Office, Towneley MSS, DD 40; CPR, 1385–1389, 126; Lancashire Inquisitions Post Mortem, vol. 2, 38.

14. Guto'r Glyn, 'The Drinking Bout', in *Medieval Welsh Poems. An Anthology*, 146-47.

15. Tuck, op. cit., 165-68; Froissart, vol. 16, 3; Williams, B. cd., *Chronique de la Traison et Mort Richart Deux*, London, 1847, 117-21.

16. Saul, op.cit., 393-94. Richard II also retained knights and esquires heavily from Cheshire and Lancashire in his final years.

17. The fact that many of them were only interested in plunder suggests this (Usk, 54-55).

18. Grummitt, D., 'William Lord Hastings and the Defence of Calais, 1471–83', *Social Attitudes and Political Structures in the Fifteenth Century*, ed. Thornton, T., Stroud, 2000, 151. In the 1470s the garrison at Calais in time of truce was c.780 (Lander, J.R., *Crown and Nobility, 1450–1509*, London, 1976, 240n); in 1513, there were c.700 soldiers in

Calais itself, 99 in Guines Castle, 40 in Hammes Castle, 17 at Ruysbank and 13 at Nieulay, a total of c.869 (Cruickshank, C.G., *Army Royal. Henry VIII's Invasion of France 1513*, Oxford, 1969, 9).

19. *Calendar of Documents relating to Scotland*, ed. Bain, J., 4, 1327–1509, Edinburgh, 1888, 118-19, 140, 182. There was also the garrison of the royal castle at Carlisle. Early in 1383 it had been garrisoned (at a time of mounting tension with the Scots) by 50 men-at-arms and 100 mounted archers (ibid., no. 320).

20. For the reputation of English archers' skills abroad, see below, 101ff.

21. Vaughan, *John the Fearless*, 61.

22. Perroy, E., *The Hundred Years War*, London, 1951, 231; Kirby, J.L., *Henry IV of England*, London, 1970, 236-37, 244-45.

23. Conocer al Pueblo, A., *Historia de Catalunya y de la Corona de Aragon*, 3, Barcelona, 1862, 435-38.

24. Zurita, G., *Los cincos libros primeros de la Segunda parte de la Corona de Aragon*, Saragossa, 1579, 92 r-d.

25. Archivo Municipal de Sevilla, Mayordomazgo, 1413, no.47. I owe thanks for this reference to Professor Angus MacKay.

26. *CSP... Venice*, 1, 64.

27. Curry, A., 'English Armies in the Fifteenth Century', *Arms, Armies and Fortifications*, 51-60.

28. Calmette, J., *The Golden Age of Burgundy*, trans. Weightman, D., London, 1962, 223; Vaughan, *Philip the Good*, 358-72.

29. For Richard III and the Turks, Visser-Fuchs, L., 'Review Article; What Niclas von Popplau really wrote about Richard III', *The Ricardian*, 11, 1999, 527-28; for Henry VIII's attitude to them and crusading, Scarisbrick, *Henry VIII*, 24, 28, 105-06, 106n; for James IV's crusading plans, Macquarrie, A., *Scotland and the Crusades 1095–1560*, Edinburgh, 1985,

108-12.

30. Griffiths, *Reign of King Henry VI*, 516, 519-21, 612-13. By Privy Seal letter, dated 25 August 1450, the King wrote to the Treasurer and Chamberlains of the Exchequer: 'We wol and charge you to thentent that oure houshold may be discharged of the souldeours which dayly resort to the same unto oure greet charge and costes ye delivere unto oure ryghte trusty and welbeloued the lorde Scales. l. li. [£50] of oure Tresore to be employed after his discrecion for and aboute the sustenance of the said souldeours for xv dayes' (PRO, E 404/66).

31. *Paston Letters*, 1., no.99.

32. Griffiths, 499-500, 520-21, 615; Carr, A.D., 'Welshmen and the Hundred Years War', *Welsh History Review*, 4, 1968-9, 39-41.

33. Worcestre, 356-57.

34. Dorset County Record Office, Bridport Muster Roll, 1457, B3/FG3.

35. *Testamenta Eboracensia*, vol. 3, 278.

36. Surtz, E and Hexter, J.H. ed., *The Complete Works of Sir Thomas More*, New Haven and London, 1965, 60-62.

37. For examples of captains of condottieri of the fifteenth century who recovered from serious head wounds, Mallett, *Mercenaries and their Masters*, 200.

38. *Blood Red Roses*, 246-47.

39. Worcestre, 190-91.

40. Ibid., 202-05; Williams, *Renewal and Reformation*, 188.

41. Worcestre, 202-07.

42. Williams, 172; see below, 228-29.

43. All those mentioned except York and Kyriel died in Henry VI's cause.

44. Commynes, 252.

45. Ibid., 72, 124, 237.

46. Ross, *Edward IV*, 221.

47. *Westminster Chronicle*, 214-15 and 215n.

48. Ibid., 210-11.

49. The question of the extent to which soldiers who enrolled for Arundel's expedition joined the Appellants in arms is discussed by Dr Adrian R. Bell in his PhD thesis, 'Anatomy of an Army: The Campaigns of 1387-1388' (University of Reading, 2002).

50. 'Annales Ricardi Secundi et Henrici Quarti', 242.

51. Grummitt, 'William Lord Hastings and the Defence of Calais 1471-1483', 151-54; Hicks, *Warwick*, 138-48.

52. Waurin, Jehan de, *Recueil des Croniques et Anchiennes Istoires de la Grant Bretagne, a present nomme Engleterre*, 5, ed. Hardy, W. and E.L.C.P., R.S., 276-77.

53. Goodman, *Wars of the Roses*, 30-35; Hicks, 173-77.

54. Goodman, 41-42, 56, 123, 127.

55. Hicks, 271-77, 286-87.

56. 'The Life of Sir Thomas More', *Complete Works*, ed. Sylvester, R.S. and Harding, D.P., New Haven and London, 1962, 208.

57. Grummitt, 158-67; Elton, G.R. ed. *The Tudor Constitution*, Cambridge, no.4.

58. Goodman, 189.

59. Cf ibid., 145-46. Weever.

60. In 1508, Sir William Conyers contracted to be captain in the next year of the town of Berwick with a garrison of 230, and lieutenant of the castle there with one of 32 soldiers (*Calendar of Documents... Scotland*, 2, no.1751).

61. Macdougall. N., *James III. A Political Study*, Edinburgh, 1982, 188-89, 199, 217.

62. Commynes, 71-72, 237.

63. Weever, J., *Ancient Funerall Monuments (etc.)*, London, 1631, 834.

64. Ballard, M., 'An Expedition of English Archers to Liege in 1467, and the Anglo-Burgundian Marriage Alliance', *Nottingham Mediaeval Studies* 34, 1990, 167-69.

65. Ibid., 165.

66. I owe thanks to Harry Schnitker

for information about Duchess Margaret's guard.

67. Vaughan, *Charles the Bold*, 18-19, 216-17.

68. Ibid., 198-200.

69. Ibid., 221.

70. Ibid., 385; Commynes, 294-96.

71. Vaughan, *Charles the Bold*, 393.

72. Meek, E.L., 'The career of Sir Thomas Everingham, 'Knight of the North', in the service of Maximilian duke of Austria, 1477–81', *Historical Research*, 74, 2001, 241. Everingham was in Charles the Bold's service in 1474 and 1476.

73. Ibid.

74. Ibid., 242-47.

75. Wernham, R.B., *Before the Armada. The Growth of English Foreign Policy 1485–1588*, London, 1966, 35. Morley was married to Elizabeth, daughter of John de la Pole, Duke of Suffolk and Edward IV's sister Elizabeth (*CP*, vol.9, 20).

76. Vaughan, *Charles the Bold*, 392.

77. Meek, 241, 243.

78. Ibid., 243, 247.

79. Horrox, R., *Richard III. A Study of Service*, 204, n.81, 288-89, 291.

80. Ross, *Richard III*, 205; *Miracles of King Henry VI*, 77, in which Everingham is described as 'a captain of great renown'.

81. Vaughan, *Charles the Bold*, 324.

82. Ibid., 383.

83. Ibid., 198-203.

84. Ibid., 18-19, 322.

85. Meek, 246.

86. Goodman, *Wars of the Roses*, 187-88.

87. Macdougall, *James III*, 154-55, 168-69.

88. See below, 110.

89. See below, 114.

90. Barr, N., *Flodden 1513*, Stroud, 2000, 46-48.

91. Vergil, P., *Anglicae Historiae libri viginti septem*, Basel, 1555, 563.

92. *The History of the King's Works*, vol.3, 1485–1660, pt 1, ed. Colvin, H.M., Ransome, D.R., and Summerson, J., London, 1975, 233-34.

93. 'The History of King Richard III', ed. Sylvester, in *Complete Works*, 2, 1963, 10-11.

94. Pulgar, F. del, *Crónica de los Reyes Catolicos, 2, Guerra de Granada*, ed. Mata Carriazo, J. de, Madrid, 222, 226-27.

95. Ross, *Edward IV*, 206.

96. Ross, *Richard III*, 45, n.4.

97. Mancini, D., *The Usurpation of Richard the Third*, ed. Armstrong, C. A. J., Oxford, 1969, 80-81, 84-87, 122-23.

98. Ross, *Richard III*, 195-99.

99. Palencia, Alonso de, *Décadas*, 5, ed. Paz y Mélia, A., Madrid, 1909.

100. *The Crowland Chronicle Continuations 1459–1486*, ed. Pronay, N. and Cox, J., London, 1988, 181; Bennett, M., *The Battle of Bosworth*, Gloucester, 1985, 134.

101. Ruano, E. Benito, 'Un Cruzado Inglés en la Guerra de Granada', *Anuario de Estudios Medievales*, 9, 1974–1979, 588-91, 589, n.21.

102. Ibid., 589-90.

103. Ross, *Edward IV*, 112-13, 206-08, 214.

104. Wernham, 32-33; *Paston Letters*, 3, no. 904.

105. Wernham, 33-36. Pulgar noted Wydeville's expedition of 1488 and his death (op.cit., 346).

106. PRO, E101/41/5, Muster Roll of Earl of Arundel's expedition, 1387.

107. I owe thanks for this information to Professor Christopher Allmand.

108. *The Historical Collections of a London Citizen in the Fifteenth Century*, ed. Gairdner, J., Camden Soc., new ser., 17, 1876, 213-14.

109. Ross, *Edward IV*, 50-54.

110. Warkworth, J., *A Chronicle of the First Thirteen Years of the Reign of King Edward the Fourth*, Camden Soc., original ser., 10, 1839, 13. For a reassessment of this work, Thomson, J.A.F., 'Warkworth's Chronicle' Reconsidered', *EHR*, 116, 2001, 657-64.

111. Ross, *Edward IV*, 169; *Paston Letters*, 3, no.671.

112. *Epistolas y otros varios tratados de Mosén Diego de Valera*, ed. Balenchina, J.A. de, Madrid, 1878, 91-96; B L Harleian 433, ed. Horrox, R. and Hammond, P., Gloucester, 1980, 209, 213-14, 216-17, 228. For Salaçar s career after Bosworth, Bennett, *Lambert Simnel*, 61.

113. E.g., Jones, M.K., *Bosworth 1485. Psychology of a Battle*, Stroud, 2002.

114. Bennett, *Simnel*, passim; for Schwarz, ibid., 60-61, 63.

115. Arthurson, I., *The Perkin Warbeck Conspiracy 1491–1499*, Stroud, 1994, 108, 110, 118, 158.

116. Flemings were killed by the rebels in London in the Great Revolt of 1381, and aliens were among the targets of rioters on 'Evil May Day' there in 1517. Cf for common attitudes to aliens, Griffiths, *Reign of King Henry VI*, 167-71.

117. Dodds, vol.1, 128.

118. Powicke, M., *Military Obligation in Medieval England*, Oxford, 1962. For arrays of the clergy, see above, 37-38.

119. Orme, N., *From Childhood to Chivalry*, London and New York, 1984, 202.

120. *Foedera*, vol. 11, 501-02.

121. Ibid., 523-24.

122. For examples of rebel manifestos, see above, 71, 73.

123. Dodds, vol.2, 43; cf ibid., 51, 79-80.

124. Ibid.,vol.1, 100, 142, 144-45, 147-48; ibid., vol.2, 66-6.

125. *Foedera*, vol.11, 624.

126. Dodds, vol.1, 100, 175.

127. Ibid., 122.

128. *Arrivall*, 7-8; *Paston Letters*, 2, no.664.

129. Dodds, vol.1, 100.

130. *Paston Letters*, 2, no.384.

131. Dodds, vol.1, 146-48.

132. *Foedera*, vol.11, 444-45.

133. Ibid., 680-81.

134. Child, F.J. ed., *English and Scottish Popular Ballads*, 5, Boston, 1859, 94.

135. Ibid., 157-58.

136. *Gesta Henrici Quinti*, 88-89.

137. Child, vol.5, 144-45.

138. See above, 110.

139. *Chronicon Angliae*, 168-69.

140. *CPR*, 1452–1461, 406-10.

141. Griffiths, R.A., *Sir Rhys ap Thomas and his Family. A Study in the Wars of the Roses and Early Tudor Politics*, Cardiff, 1993, 179.

142. Thomas, A.H. and Thornley, I.D. ed., *The Great Chronicle of London*, London, 1938, 218.

143. Manning, R.B., *Village Revolts. Social Protest and Popular Disturbances in England 1509–1640*, Oxford, 1988, 96-98.

144. Oliver, A.M. ed., *Northumberland and Durham Deeds from the Dodsworth MSS in Bodley's Library, Oxford*, Newcastle, 1929, 222.

CHAPTER 4: CAMPAIGNING

1. Whethamstede, vol.1. 175-76.

2. *Gesta Henrici Quinti*, 67, 75, 77, 81.

3. 'Annales Ricardi Secundi et Henrici Quarti', 345-46.

4. Ibid., 383-84; Wylie, J.H., *History of England under Henry the Fourth*, vol.1, 1399–1404, London, 1884, 434-48.

5. Orme, *From Childhood to Chivalry*, 184-85.

6. Goodman, *John of Gaunt*, 31; Usk, 60-61.

7. Dodds, vol.1, 204.

8. See below, 218-19.

9. Pizan, C. de, *The Book of Deeds of Arms and of Chivalry,* trans. Willard, S. and ed. Willard, C.C., University Park, Pennsylvania, 1999, 33.

10. Orme, 303.

11. Chester, A.G. ed., *Selected Sermons of Hugh Latimer*, Charlottesville, 1968, xiii, 67 – First Sermon before King Edward VI, 8 March 1549.

12. See below, 207-08.

13. Knighton, 424-45 ('unum puerum').

14. Rogers, A., 'Henry IV and the Revolt of the Earls, 1400', *History Today*, 18, 1968, 282.

15. *Historical Collections of a London*

Citizen, 204; Dodds, vol.1., 232.

16. Nicolas, N.H., *History of the Battle of Agincourt*, London, 1832, Appendix VIII, 37. Apropos the army with which Edward IV invaded France in 1475, Commynes remarked, with surprise, 'in the whole army there was not a single page' (op.cit., 237). Maybe in the recent campaigns of the Wars of the Roses, the presence of lads had caused unruliness and added to victualling problems to an extent which had exasperated the king.

17. Gamez, *The Unconquered Knight*, 173.

18. Commynes, 70. At Flodden, the Scots were said to have been 'so plainly determined to abide battle and not to flee, that they put from them their horses and also put off their boots and shoes, and fought in the vampis [foot coverings] of their hoses' (Laing, D., ed., 'A Contemporary Account of the Battle of Flodden 9 September 1513' [etc.], *Proceedings of the Society of Antiquaries of Scotland*, 7, 1867, 153).

19. Monstrelet, Enguerrand de, *The Chronicles*, trans. Johnes, T., 1, London, 1840, 340.

20. Knighton, 92-95.

21. Boccaccio, G., *Famous Women*, ed. and trans. Brown, V., Cambridge, Mass. and London, 2001; 'The Knight's Tale', lines 875-83.

22. Warner, M., *Joan of Arc. The Image of Female Heroism*, London, 1981, 255-56.

23. Ibid., 201.

24. *A Chronicle of London from 1189 to 1483*, London, 1827, 118; Froissart, vol.3, 421-24; ibid., vol.4, 15-29; Hampton, W.E., *Memorials of the Wars of the Roses*, Gloucester, 1979, 82.

25. 'Annales Ricardi Secundi et Henrici Quarti', 383; Child, *English and Scottish Popular Ballads*, vol.5, 133-34.

26. Vaughan, *Charles the Bold*, 79.

27. Knox, J., *History of the Reformation in Scotland*, vol.1, ed. Dickinson, W.C.,

London, 1949, 318-19.

28. Vaughan, op.cit., 325.

29. *English and Scottish Popular Ballads*, vol.7, 257-59.

30. Adie, K., *Corsets to Camouflage. Women and War*, London, 2003, 3-5.

31. Mallett, *Mercenaries and their Masters*, 190.

32. Vaughan, op.cit., 209.

33. Warner, 153-54.

34. Hale, J.R., *Artists and Warfare in the Renaissance*, New Haven and London, 1990, 9-10.

35. Knighton, 330-31.

36. *Chronicon Angliae*, 249-51; *Anonimalle Chronicle*, 131-32.

37. Karras, R.M., *Common Women. Prostitution and Sexuality in Medieval England*, New York and Oxford, 36.

38. 'Annales Ricardi Secundi et Henrici Quarti', 341.

39. Nicolas, *Battle of Agincourt*, Appendix VIII, 41-44.

40. Hughes, P.L. and Larkin, J.F. ed., *Tudor Royal Proclamations, 1, The Early Tudors (1485–1553)*, New Haven and London, 1964, 113.

41. *CSP…* Venice, 2, ed. Brown, Rawdon, R.S., 1867, 260-1. For St Cuthbert and Flodden, see below, 194.

42. Jones, M.K. and Underwood, M.G., *The King's Mother. Lady Margaret Beaufort Countess of Richmond and Derby*, Cambridge, 1992, 101.

43. *Tudor Royal Proclamations*, vol.1, 13-15.

44. 'Herald's report', Bennett, *Lambert Simnel*, 127-29.

45. Kettle, A.J., 'Ruined Maids: Prostitutes and Servant Girls in Later Medieval England', *Matrons and Marginal Women*, ed. Edwards, R.R. and Ziegler, V., Woodbridge, 1995. For the provision of commercial sex in cities and towns, especially in York, Goldberg, P.J., 'Pigs and prostitutes: streetwalking in comparable perspective', in *Young Medieval Women*, ed. Menuge, K.J. and Phillips, K.M., Stroud, 1999.

46. A locus classicus for the growth, treatment and uses of cannabis in early modern peasant society is Marcandier, A., *A treatise on hemp*, London, 1764, reprinted Lyme Regis, 1996.

47. Dodds, vol.1, 106.

48. Vegetius, *Epitome of Military Science*, ed. and trans. Milner, N.P., Liverpool, 1996, 10–11; Allmand, C., 'Fifteenth-Century Versions of Vegetius', 'De Re Militari', in *Arms, Chivalry and Warfare in Medieval Britain and France*, ed. Strickland, 30–45; cf. Pizan, C. de, *The Book of Deeds of Arms and of Chivalry*, 50–51.

49. Ross, *Edward IV*, 52.

50. *Calendar of Inquisitions Post Mortem*, vol.18, ed. Kirby, J.L., London, 1987, nos 908–926; *CCR*, 1399–1402, 30, 102, 209, 381; 'Annales Ricardi Secundi et Henrici Quarti', 369–70.

51. *CPR*, 1452–1461, 595.

52. See above, 41.

53. *Gesta Henrici Quinti*, 55.

54. Commynes, 156; Vaughan, *Charles the Bold*, 209; *Tudor Royal Proclamations*, vol.1., 113.

55. Froissart, vol.1, 133–34. This is based on the eyewitness account of Jean le Bel.

56. *Deeds of Arms and of Chivalry*, 110–11.

57. Enclosed wooden carts are depicted in the *Mittelalterliches Hausbuch* (*c*.1480), reproduced in the end pages of Vale, M., *War and Chivalry*, London, 1981.

58. Goodman, *Margery Kempe and her World*, 149, 247, n.126, 252, n.87.

59. *Tudor Royal Proclamations*, vol.1, 13–15.

60. *Arrivall*, 26.

61. Froissart, vol. 10, 382–87; *Westminster Chronicle*, 122–23.

62. Williams, *Renewal and Reformation in Wales*, 204–205.

63. Dyer, *Standards of living in the later Middle Ages*, 167; *The Book of Margery Kempe*, III.

64. Dodds, vol.1, 107.

65. Ibid., 151, 160–61, 183.

66. See above, 59–60.

67. Commynes, 254–55.

68. *Chronique de la Traison et Mort Richart Deux*, 238–42.

69. 'Annales Ricardi Secundi et Henrici Quarti', 371.

70. 'Bale's Chronicle', 149–50.

71. Muniments of the Borough of King's Lynn, KL/C7/4, Hall Book, vol.2, 284; Haward, W.I., 'Economic Aspects of the Wars of the Roses in East Anglia', *EHR*, 41, 1926, 179, 185.

72. Commynes, 186–87.

73. I owe thanks for the suggestion that Edward stayed at Middleton Tower to Mrs Katherine Parker. For Middleton Tower, Emery, A., *Greater Medieval Houses of England and Wales 1300–1500*, 1, East Anglia, Central England and Wales, Cambridge, 2000, 126–27.

74. Bennett, *Battle of Bosworth*, 91, 94.

75. Dodds, vol.1, 179.

76. 'Annales Ricardi Secundi et Henrici Quarti', 343; Lloyd, *Owen Glendower*, 54–55.

77. *An English Chronicle of the reigns of Richard II, Henry IV, Henry V and Henry VI*, ed. Davies, J.S., Camden Soc., 64, 1856, 97; *Historical Collections of a London Citizen*, 207.

78. *Arrivall*, 18, 25.

79. *Gesta Henrici Quinti*, 80–81.

80. 'Herald's report', Bennett, *Lambert Simnel*, 128.

81. *Tudor Royal Proclamations*, vol.1, 13–15.

82. Dodds, vol.1, 178.

83. Ibid., 151, 161–62.

84. *Epitome of Military Science*, 67.

85. *Deeds of Arms and of Chivalry*, 41.

86. *Arrivall*, 28.

87. 'Short Kirkstall Chronicle', *Chronicles of the Revolution*, ed. Given-Wilson, 132–34.

88. *Historical Collections of a London Citizen*, 212.

89. *Gesta Henrici Quinti*, 66–67; Commynes, 92.

90. 'Annales Ricardi Secundi et Henrici Quarti', 364.

91. 'Annales Rerum Anglicarum', 2 pt 2, 775.

92. See above, 59-60.

93. Dyer, *Standards of living in the later Middle Ages*, 263, 265.

94. Ibid., 271.

95. Goodman, *John of Gaunt*, 225; PRO, E 403/511/10.

96. Idem, *Wars of the Roses*, 59-65.

97. For the siege of Alnwick, ibid., 61-62.

98. Davies, R.R., *The Revolt of Owain Glyn Dŵr*, Oxford, 1995, 146-47.

99. Saul, *Richard II*, 219-21.

100. Knighton, 351; Walsingham, *Historia Anglicana*, vol.2, 148.

101. PRO, C1/31/516. William Blakwell of Totteridge, Middlesex, 'yoman', was granted goods at Barnet and elsewhere in 1463 (*CCR, 1461–1468*, 197).

102. *Tudor Royal Proclamations*, vol.1, 114-15.

103. Ibid., 121.

104. *Gesta Henrici Quinti*, 59.

105. Goodman, *Wars of the Roses*, 154.

106. See above, 63.

107. 'Herald's report', Bennett, *Simnel*, 128.

108. Poulson, G., *Beverlac*, 240-1. For hiring of harness (armour) in disturbed times, *Paston Letters*, 2, no.384. For Richard III's order for smiths to manufacture 2,000 'walshe [Welsh] billes or glayves', BL Harleian 433, vol.2, 8-9.

109. Edward, P., *The Horse Trade of Tudor and Stuart England*, Cambridge, 1988.

CHAPTER 5: HOPES AND FEARS

1. 'Chronicle of the Rebellion in Lincolnshire', 6.

2. Goodman, *Wars of the Roses*, 145-46, 154.

3. *Paston Letters*, 1, no.367; Dodds, vol.1, 248.

4. Vaughan, *Charles the Bold*.

5. Dodds, vol. 1, 248.

6. Muniments of the Borough of King's Lynn, KL/C7/7, Hall Book, vol.2, 285-86. See also above, 158.

7. *Arrivall*, 22.

8. *Collections of a London Citizen*, 223.

9. See below, 183.

10. For the conjoined cults of the Blessed Virgin and St George, Goodman, 'Introduction', in *Richard II. The Art of Kingship*, ed. Goodman and Gillespie, 10-13.

11. Holt, *Robin Hood*, 58-59.

12. Knighton, 423.

13. *CPR 1401–1405*, 258.

14. *CSP, Letters and Papers, Foreign and Domestic, of the reign of Henry VIII*, 1, pt 2, ed. Brewer, J.S. and Brodie. R.H., London, 1920, no.2283 (30 Sept. 1513). After Bosworth, Henry Tudor 'mandolo conbrir de la cinta aboxo con un peno negro asaz pobre' (Valera, *Epistolas*, 91-96).

15. Hutton, *The Rise and Fall of Merry England*, ch.1; Usk, 14-17.

16. Hall, *The Union*, 588-90. For the Oxford trials in 1400, see above, 137-38.

17. *The Surgery of Theodoric of Lucca ca. A.D. 1267*, ed. Campbell, E. and Colton, J., New York, 1955. I owe thanks for this reference to Dr Simone Macdougall.

18. *Treatises of Fistula in Ano… by John Arderne*, ed. Power, Sir D'Arcy, Early English Text Soc., original ser., 139, Oxford, 1910, xv, 1; *The Scrope and Grosvenor Controversy*, ed. Nicolas, N.H, I, London, 1832, 239-41.

19. Arderne, 5-6. For the retained physicians whose services when they were abroad were anticipated by Edward III's sons the Black Prince and John of Gaunt, Rawcliffe, C., *Medicine and Society in Later Medieval England*, Stroud, 1995, 110.

20. Warkworth, 16-17.

21. *Miracles of King Henry VI*, 77-84 (no.37). No.167 concerns William Sir, who suffered from chronic pain as a result of a wound received from a small artillery piece (a petard). Copland's poem, based on a French

one issued in 1505, is cited in Orme, N. and Webster, M., *The English Hospital 1070–1570*, New Haven and London, 1995, 151–55. For Richard at Scarborough, Ross, *Richard III,* 176n, 180n, 205.

22. Commynes, 187.

23. *Westminster Chronicle*, 223.

24. *An English Chronicle*, ed. Davies, 97. When Edward IV defeated the Lincolnshire rebels in 1470, he is said to have used 'plentifully his mercy in saving of the lives of his poor and wretched commons' ('Chronicle of the Rebellion in Lincolnshire', 10).

25. Commynes, 187.

26. *An English Chronicle*, 97.

27. *Blood Red Roses*.

28. Ibid., 15, 24.

29. Commynes, 195.

30. Ibid., 196.

31. Vergil, *Anglicae Historiae libri*, 564; *Crowland Chronicle Continuations*, 182–83.

32. Jones, M.K., 'The Battle of Verneuil (17 August 1424): Towards a History of Courage,' *War in History,* 9, 2002, 395–98.

33. *Historical Collections of a London Citizen*, 212–13.

34. Warkworth, 13.

35. Commynes, 195. According to Warkworth, Warwick attempted to flee on horseback, but was spotted by one of the king's men while trying to extricate himself from a wood, and was killed by him (op.cit., 13).

36. Visser-Fuchs, 'Niclas von Popplau', 529.

37. *Paston Letters*, 2, no.464.

38. Vergil, *Anglicae Historiae libri*, 561, 564.

39. Campbell, W. ed., *Materials for a History of the Reign of Henry VII*, 1, R.S.,1873, 188, 201.

40. *Crowland Chronicle Continuations*, 180–81.

41. *Collections of a London Citizen*, 212.

42. *Paston Letters*, 2, no.385; *Chronicles of London*, ed. Kingsford, 175. *CSP…*

Milan, 1, 67.

43. See above, 71, 73.

44. Child, *English and Scottish Popular Ballads*.

45. 'Annales Ricardi Secundi et Henrici Quarti', 368.

46. 'Bale's Chronicle', 161.

47. *Anonimalle Chronicle*, 26.

48. Nicolas, *Agincourt*, 252n.; Vaughan, *Charles the Bold*, 201.

49. Ibid., 209; *CSP…* Venice, 2, 141-42 (no.333).

50. *Book of Deeds of Arms and of Chivalry,* 21-23. Christine de Pisan noted that Charles VI was aged fourteen when he was present at the victory over the rebellious Flemings at Roosebeke in 1382.

51. Bower, *Scotichronicon*, ed. Watt, 8, 59.

52. Monstrelet, *Chronicles*, 346. For other references to Henry V's wearing of his crown at Agincourt, Nicolas, *Battle of Agincourt*, 258, 261.

53. *Chronicles of London*, ed. Kingsford, 178, 318, n.23.

54. Gamez, *The Unconquered Knight*, 125-26.

55. Ibid., 174-77.

56. *Scotish Feilde and Flodden Feilde. Two Flodden Poems*, ed. Baird, I.F., New York and London, 1982, 11; *CSP,* Letters and Papers… Henry VIII, 1, pt 2, no.2283.

57. Dodds, vol.1, 238.

58. Clarke, M.V., *Fourteenth Century Studies*, ed. Sutherland, L.S. and McKisack, M., Oxford, 1937, 65-66.

59. Griffiths, R.A. and Thomas, R.S., *The Making of the Tudor Dynasty*, Gloucester, 1985, 187, 189.

60. Monmouth, Geoffrey of, *The History of the Kings of Britain*, ed. and trans. Thorpe, L., Harmondsworth, Middlesex, 1966, 170-73.

61. *English Chronicle*, ed. Davies, 10; cf Hodges, G., *Ludford Bridge and Mortimer's Cross*, Woonton Almeley, Herefordshire, 2001, 48-49.

62. *English Chronicle*, ed. Davies, 110; Worcestre, 202-03.

63. Arrivall, 13-14.

64. *Gesta Henrici Quinti*, 100-13.

65. I owe thanks to Harry Schnitker for information about Margaret of York's attachment to the cult of St Anne.

66. Fryde, The tyranny and fall of Edward II, 186-87. Adam Orleton, bishop of Hereford preached sermons in support of the queen's cause as her army advanced.

67. Anonimalle Chronicle, 26-27.

68. Eulogium (Historiarum sive Temporis) Chronicon (etc.), ed. Hayden, F.S., 3, R. S., 1863, 405.

69. 'Annales Ricardi Secundi et Henrici Quarti', 403-05.

70. The Historians of the Church of York and its Archbishops, ed. Raine, J., 3, R.S., 1894, 288-91.

71. Head, 'Pius II and the Wars of the Roses', 139-54; CSP... Milan, I, 23-26.

72. Head, 173.

73. Ibid., 163.

74. Ibid., 165-66 ; CSP... Milan, 1, 60.

CHAPTER 6: MEMORIES

1. Gransden, A., Historical Writing in England, 2, c.1307 to the Early Sixteenth Century, Ithaca, New York, 1982; Hay, D., Polydore Vergil, Renaissance Man of Letters, Oxford, 1952; McKisack, M., Medieval History in the Tudor Age, Oxford, 1971.

2. Ibid.,105. For Hall's family and career, see biography by Alan Harding, The History of Parliament. The House of Commons 1509–1558, ed. Bindoff, S.T., 3, London, 1982, 279-83.

3. Hall, 250-51. The remarks attributed to York allude to the Pontoise campaign of 1441 (for which, see Jones, Bosworth 1485, 49-51). They imply that Davy Halle took part in this, but I have been unable to find him listed in the muster roll for York's expedition, though there were several

named Halle in the retinues (PRO, E101/53/33).

4. Hall, 231, 251 (on York); ibid., 242, 245, 252-53, 274, 285, 291, 294, 297 (some references to roles of the commons).

5. Leland, 22, 325; Poulson, Beverlac, 228.

6. Leland, 529.

7. Hall, 256.

8. Leland, 568; *Blood Red Roses*, 5, 11-12.

9. Leland, 539, 542; cf Bennett, 'Henry VII and the Northern Rising of 1489', 45.

10. Fox, A., Oral and Literate Culture in England 1500–1700, Oxford, 2000, 222; Maddiccot, J.R., Simon de Montfort, Cambridge, 1994, 342. I owe thanks to Professor David Carpenter for information about contemporary sources for Montfort's death.

11. Citations by Reed, J., The Border Ballads, London, 1973, 124, from Sidney's Apology for Poetry and Addison's essay in The Spectator, 21 May 1711.

12. 'Bosworth feilde' and 'Ladye Bessiye', Bishop Percy's Folio Manuscript Ballads and Romances, ed. Furnivall, J.W. and F.J., London, 1868, 233-39, 319-63; 'The Rose of England', Child, F.J. ed., The English and Scottish Popular Ballads, 3, New York, 1957, 331-33; Scottish Feilde and Flodden Feilde. Two Flodden Poems, ed. Baird.

13. Wrightson, K., English Society 1580–1680, London, 1982, 197.

14. Daniel, S., The Civil Wars, ed. Michel, L., New Haven, 1958, 67.

15. Manning, Village Revolts, 229-46.

16. Ross, Edward IV, 138; Fox, 220-22; Smyth, Lives of the Berkeleys, 2, 114-15.

17. Leland, 190.

18. Smyth, 115.

19. Burton's account is cited in Nichols, J., *The History and Antiquities of the County of Leicester*, 4, pt 2, London,

1811, 549.

20. Ibid., 554 and n.

21. Twemlow, F.R.T., *The Battle of Blore Heath, 1459*, Wolverhampton, 1912, 25.

22. Knowles, 'The Battle of Wakefield: the Topography', 22; 'Chronicle of the Rebellion in Lincolnshire', 23-24.

23. Mallett, C.E., *A History of the University of Oxford*, 1, New York and London, 1924, 363.

24. Gough, R., *The History and Antiquities of Pleshy*, London, 1803, 179-80.

25. *Testamenta Vetusta*, ed. Nicolas, N.H., 1, London, 1826, 304.

26. *Testamenta Eboracensia*, 3, 273, 278-79.

27. Head, 'Pope Pius II and the Wars of the Roses', 163, 173.

28. Reed, *The Border Ballads*, 134-35.

29. Battle Abbey was founded on the site of the battle of Hastings by William the Conqueror; he had made a vow that, if God gave him victory, he would found a monastery on the place of battle.

30. Charlesworth, M., *St Mary Magdalene Battlefield Shropshire*, London, 1986; Pollard and Oliver, *Two Men in a Trench*, 57-63.

31. *Blood Red Roses*, 12-13, 163, 165, 166; Habberjam, M., 'Towton Memorial Chapel', *Ricardian Bulletin*, Autumn 2003, 26-28.

32. Leland, 531.

33. Ibid., 529; Twemlow, 6.

34. Hodges, *Ludford Bridge and Mortimer's Cross*, 54.

35. Knowles, 'The Battle of Wakefield: the Topography', 263; *Blood Red Roses*, 12. The monument at Wakefield was erected on the site of a cross destroyed in 1645.

36. Goodman, *John of Gaunt*, 163.

37. CP., vol.9, 712n, 714n.

38. Whethamstede, 1, 175-78. The Percy family did not have a single traditional place of burial.

39. Hammond, Sutton and Visser-Fuchs, 'The Reburial of Richard Duke of York', 122-65.

40. 'Tewkesbury annals', in Kingsford, *English Historical Literature in the Fifteenth Century*, 377-78. For the place of burial and the cult of Prince Edward at Tewkesbury, Rogers, N.J., 'The Cult of Prince Edward at Tewkesbury', *Transactions of the Bristol and Gloucestershire Archaeological Society* for 1983, 101, 1984, 188.

41. CP, vol.9, 717.

42. Nicolas, *Testamenta Vetusta*, 1, 304-05; CP, vol.10, 401.

43. Ibid., 12, pt 1, 612.

44. *Blood Red Roses*, 155; CP, vol.7, 18-20.

45. Leland, 420. For Gournay's career, Fowler, *Medieval Mercenaries*, 1, passim.

46. Barr, N., *Flodden 1513*, Stroud, 2001, 77.

47. Grimke-Drayton, T.D., 'The East Window of Gloucester Cathedral', *Transactions of the Bristol and Gloucestershire Archaeological Soc.*, 38, 1915, 78, 82, 90.

48. Barr, 77, 129.

49. Weever, *Ancient Funerall Monuments*, 579; *CPR*, 1452-1461, 248.

50. Weever, 447.

51. Ibid., 482.

52. Condon, M., 'Bosworth Field. A footnote to a controversy', *The Ricardian*, 8, 363, 365, n.3.

53. Weever, 833-41.

54. Pevsner, N., *The Buildings of England. Yorkshire: York and the East Riding*, Harmondsworth, 1972, 229-30

55. Horrox, *Richard III*, 191-92, 213-14; Bennett, *Battle of Bosworth*, 50, 67, 79, 90, 114, 171.

56. Day, I., 'The Battle of Bosworth at Stowe', *Ricardian Bulletin*, June 1993, 7-9.

57. Gransden, *Historical Writing in England*, 2, 194-219.

58. McFarlane, K.B., 'William Worcester, A Preliminary Survey', *Studies presented to Sir Hilary Jenkinson*, ed. Davies, J. and Conway, L., London, 1957, 208-10. Two soldiers who started out as archers, Peter

Basset, esquire, and Christopher Hanson, wrote an account of military events in France which was intended for Fastolf, and was used by Edward Hall (Rowe, B.J.H., 'A Contemporary Account of the Hundred Years War from 1415 to 1429', *EHR*, 41, 1926, 504–13).

59. Sinclair, A., ed., *The Beauchamp Pageant*, Donington, 2003.

60. Jones and Underwood, *The King's Mother*, 30. For Gough, see above, 90–91. The account by the two English soldiers eulogised him (Rowe, 512).

61. James, M.R. ed., *A Compilation of the Meekness and Good Life of King Henry VI gathered by Master John Blacman (etc.)*, Cambridge, 1919; André, Bernard, 'Vita Henrici Septimi', *Memorials of King Henry VII*, ed. Gairdner, J., R.S., London, 1858.

62. Jones, *Bosworth 1485*, passim.

63. Kingsford, C.L., ed., *The First English Life of King Henry the Fifth*, Oxford, 1911, vi, ix–x, xvi, xix.

64. Skinner, R.J., 'Thomas Woodshawe, "Grasiour" and Regicide', *The Ricardian*, 9, 1993, 417–25, citing 'Declaration of the Family of Ley', Wiltshire County Record Office, W.R.O, 366/1; Molinet, Jean de, *Chronique*, ed. Doutrepont, G., and Jodogne, O., 1. Brussels, 1935, 435.

65. Williams, *Renewal and Reformation*, 200.

66. Hall, 253.

67. See above, 192.

68. Thompson, P., *Sir Thomas Wyatt and His Background*, London, 1964, 3, 273.

69. Ibid., 4.

70. Muir, K., *Life and Letters of Sir Thomas Wyatt*, Liverpool, 1963, 1–2.

71. Thompson, 4–6, 9.

72. Carew, R., *The Survey of Cornwall*, ed. Halliday, F.E., London, 1953, 18–19.

73. Ibid., 15, 83; Horrox, *Richard III*, 275–76; Bennett, *The Battle of Bosworth*, 64, 83, 127, 134, 157.

74. 'Declaration of the Family of Ley', Wiltshire County Record Office,

W.R.O., 366/1.

75. For bardic commemoration, Williams, ch.6.

76. Wynn, Sir John, of Gwydir, *The History of the Gwydir Family*, ed. Ballinger, J., Cardiff, 1927, 28–29.

77. Ibid., 33–34.

78. McCutcheon, E., 'William Bullein's "Dialogue Against the Fever Pestilence": A Sixteenth-Century Anatomy', *Miscellanea Moreana*, 100, 1989, 342–59.

79. *Bullein, A Dialogue against the Fever Pestilence*, ed. Bullein, M.W. and A.H., Early English Text Soc., ser.8, no.33, 59–60.

80. Bullein, 113.

81. Goodman, *Wars of the Roses*, 78–80.

82. Pollard and Oliver, *Two Men in a Trench*, 98–99, 109.

83. Watson, P.J., 'A Review of the Sources for the Battle of Barnet, 14 April 1471', *The Ricardian*, 12, 2000, 57, 59–60.

84. *Warwick the Kingmaker*, ch.1.

85. Pape, T., *Medieval Newcastle-under-Lyme*, Manchester, 1928, 124–25.

CHAPTER 7: THE LEGACY OF THE WARS

1. See above, 124. Beerhouses in the suburbs of London, belonging both to aliens and natives, were said to have been attacked in 1470, especially by folk from Kent (*Chronicles of London*, ed. Kingsford, 181–82).

2. Stringer, K.J., *The Reign of King Stephen*, London and New York, 1993, 8–9, 15–16, 38–39.

3. Anglo, S., 'The British History in Early Tudor Propaganda' (etc.), *Bulletin of the John Rylands Library*, 44, 1961–1962; Allan, A., 'Yorkist Propaganda: Pedigree, prophecy and the "British History" in the Reign of Edward IV', *Patronage, Pedigree and Power in Later Medieval England*, ed. Ross, C., Gloucester, 1979;

Wagner, A.R., *A Catalogue of English Mediaeval Rolls of Arms*, London, 1950, 93, 97–98.

4. Goodman, A. and Morgan, D., 'The Yorkist claim to the throne of Castile', *Journal of Medieval History*, 2, 1985.

5. Somerset Record Office, DD/SF/836; Muniment Collection of the University of St Andrews, genealogical roll.

6. Arthurson, *Perkin Warbeck Conspiracy*, 167.

7. Elton ed., *Tudor Constitution*, no.4. Arthur, Prince of Wales died on 2 April 1502, and the future Henry VIII was created Prince on 18 February 1504.

8. Loades, D.M., *Two Tudor Conspiracies*, Cambridge, 1965.

9. Loach, J., *Edward VI*, ed. Bernard, G. and Williams, P., New Haven and London, 1999, 70–78, 82.

10. Manning, *Village Revolts*, 48–49; Loach, 78–82; Walter, J., 'A "Rising of the People"? The Oxfordshire Rising of 1596', *Past and Present*, 107, 1985, 92.

11. Walter, op.cit.; Manning, 221–29.

12. Ibid., 57, 64–65, 83–84, 94, 229–46.

13. Hall, 275.

14. The work by Richard Gough (1635–1723) was first published in 1834; reprint edition, London, 1981.

England and Wales in the Wars of the Roses

Genealogical Table of English Kings and their Kinsfolk in the Later Middle Ages

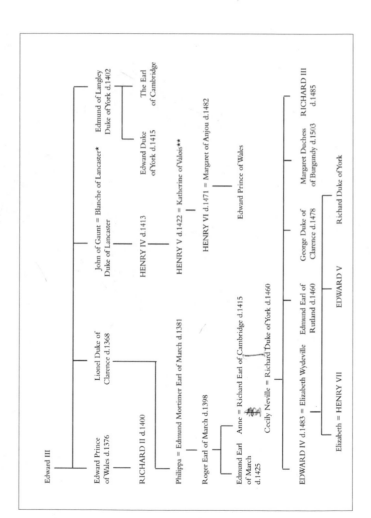

Genealogical Table of English Kings and their Kinsfolk in the Later Middle Ages (continued)

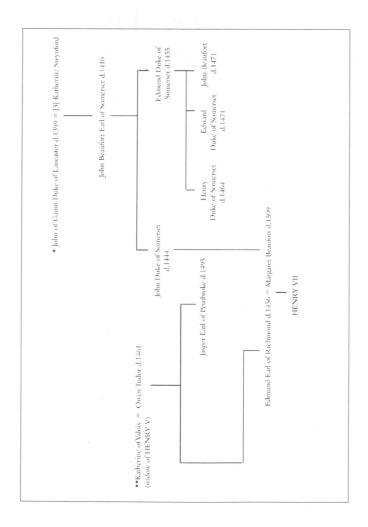

Illustration List

Select Bibliography

MANUSCRIPT SOURCES

DORCHESTER

Dorset County Record Office

B3/FG3 Bridport Muster Roll, 1457.

KING'S LYNN

Muniments of the Borough of King's Lynn

KL/C/7/4 Hall Book, vol.2.

LONDON

The National Archives (Public Record Office)

C1/31/516 Petition of William Blakwell to the Chancellor.
E101/40/33 Muster roll of the Earl of Arundel's expedition, 1387.
E101/41/5 Muster roll of the Earl of Arundel's expedition, 1388.
E101/53/33 Muster rolls for Richard, Duke of York's expedition to France, 1441.
E403/464 Issue Roll of the Exchequer, second part of Easter term, 1 Richard II.
E403/511/10 Issue Roll of the Exchequer, Michaelmas term, 9 Richard II.
E404/66 Privy Seal letter, 25 August 1450.

NEWCASTLE–UPON–TYNE

Northumberland County Record Office

ZSW/4/45 Swinburne of Capheaton collection: letter of Walter Ferrefort.
ZSW/4/60 Ibid.: contract of Walter Doget.

ST ANDREWS

Muniments of the University of St Andrews

Genealogical table of the kings of England, from William the Conqueror, 15th
century.

TAUNTON

Somerset County Record Office

DD/SF/836 Sandford of Nynehead Collection: genealogical table of the kings of
England, from William the Conqueror to Henry VI, 15th century.

TROWBRIDGE

Wiltshire County Record Office

W.R.O., 366/1 Declaration of the Family of Ley.

VALENCIA

Archivo del Reino de Valencia

Mestre Racional, 9,600 Villena collection: schedule of reasons why the count of
Denia was not bound by the obligations which he was forced to make by the
English and Gascons, n.d.
Mestre Racional, 11,599 Villena collection: record by the marquis of Villena of the
process of the imprisonment in England of the count of Denia, n.d.

Unpublished Dissertation

Bell, Adrian R., 'Anatomy of an Army: The Campaigns of 1387–1388', PhD,
University of Reading, 2002.

Published and Calendared Documents

Calendars of Close Rolls, H.M. Stationery Office, London.

Calendars of Patent Rolls, H.M. Stationery Office, London.

Calendars of State Papers, H.M. Stationery Office, London.

Foedera, Conventiones, Litterae… et Acta Publica (etc.), ed. Rymer, T., 20 vols, London, 1704–35.

Poulson, G., ed., *Beverlac; or, The Antiquities and History of the Town of Beverley*, 1, London, 1829.

The Miracles of King Henry VI, ed. Knox, R. and Leslie, J., Cambridge, 1923.

Tudor Royal Proclamations, 1, *The Early Tudors (1485–1553)*, ed. Hughes, P.L. and Larkin, J.F. New Haven and London, 1964.

LITERARY WORKS

An English Chronicle of the reigns of Richard II, Henry IV, Henry V and Henry VI, ed. Davies, J.S., Camden Soc., 64, 1856.

'Annales Ricardi Secundi et Henrici Quarti', Johannis de Trokelowe… Chronica et Annales, ed. Riley, H.T., R.S., London, 1866.

'Bale's Chronicle', *Six Town Chronicles*.

Bullein, William, *A Dialogue against the Fever Pestilence*, ed. Bullein, M.W. and A.H., Early English Text Soc., ser.8, no.33, London, 1888.

Carew, Richard, of Antony, *The Survey of Cornwall*, ed. Halliday, F.E., London, 1953.

'Chronicle of the Rebellion in Lincolnshire, 1470', ed. Nichols, J.G., Camden Miscellany 1, London, 1847.

Chronicles of London, ed. Kingsford, C.L., Oxford, 1905.

Chronicles of the Revolution 1397–1400, trans. and ed. Given-Wilson, C., Manchester, 1993.

Commynes, Philippe de, *Memoirs. The Reign of Louis XI 1461–83*, trans. and ed. Jones, M., Harmondsworth, 1972.

Froissart, Jean, *Oeuvres*, ed. Lettenhove, Kervyn de, 25 vols, Brussels, 1867–77.

Gamez, Guttiere Diaz de, *The Unconquered Knight. A Chronicle of the Deeds of Don Pero Niño*, trans. and ed. Evans, J., London, 1928.

Gesta Henrici Quinti. The Deeds of Henry V, trans. and ed. Taylor, F. and Roskell, J.S., Oxford, 1975.

Griffiths, R.A., *Sir Rhys ap Thomas and his Family. A Study in the Wars of the Roses and Early Tudor Politics*, Cardiff, 1993.

Hall, Edward, *The Vnion of the Two Noble and Illustre Famelies of Lancastre and Yorke (etc.), London, 1548* – edtn London, 1809.

Historie of the Arrivall of King Edward IV, ed. Bruce, J., Camden Soc., London, 1838.

Knighton's Chronicle 1337–1396, ed. Martin, G.H., Oxford, 1995.

Leland, John, *Travels in Tudor England*, ed. Chandler, J., Stroud, 1993.

Medieval Welsh Poems. An Anthology, trans. and ed. Loomis, R. and Johnston, D., Binghampton, N.Y., 1992.

Monstrelet, Enguerrand de, *The Chronicles*, trans. Johnes, T., 1, London, 1840.

Pizan, Christine de, *The Book of Deeds of Arms and of Chivalry*, trans. and ed. Willard, S. and C.C., University Park, Pennsylvania, 1999.

Six Town Chronicles, ed. Flenley, R., Oxford, 1921.

Smyth, John, of Nibley, *Lives of the Berkeleys*, 2, ed. Maclean, J., Gloucester, 1883.

The Crowland Chronicle Continuations: 1459–1486, ed. Pronay, N. and Cox, J., London, 1986.

The First English Life of King Henry the Fifth, ed. Kingsford, C.L., Oxford, 1911.

The Historical Collections of a London Citizen in the Fifteenth Century, ed. Gairdner, J., Camden Soc., ser.1, 109, London, 1876.

The Paston Letters 1422–1509, 4 vols, ed. Gairdner, J., Edinburgh, 1910.

'The Siege of Rouen', The Historical Collections of a London Citizen.

The Westminster Chronicle 1381–1394, ed. Hector, L.C. and Harvey, B.F., Oxford, 1982.

Valera, Mosén Diego de, 'A Spanish account of the battle of Bosworth', ed. Nokes, E.M. and Wheeler, G., The Ricardian, 2, 1976.

Vegetius, *Epitome of Military Science*, trans. and ed. Milner, N.P., Liverpool, 1996.

Vergil, Polydore, *Anglica Historiae libri viginti septem*, Basel, 1555.

Warkworth, John, *A Chronicle of the First Thirteen Years of the Reign of King Edward the Fourth*, ed. Halliwell, J.O., Camden Soc., 1839.

Whethamstede, John, 'Register', *Registra quorundam Abbatum Monasterii S. Albani*, ed. Riley, H.T., I, R.S., 1872.

Worcestre, William, *Itineraries*, ed. Harvey, J.H., Oxford, 1969.

Wynn, Sir John, of Gwydir, *The History of the Gwydir Family*, ed. Ballinger, J., Cardiff, 1927.

SECONDARY SOURCES

Adie, K., *Corsets to Camouflage. Women and War*, London, 2003.

Allan, A., 'Yorkist Propaganda: Pedigree, Prophecy and the "British History" in the Reign of Edward IV', *Patronage, Pedigree and Power In Later Medieval England*, ed. Ross, C., Gloucester, 1979.

Arthurson, I., *The Perkin Warbeck Conspiracy 1491–1499*, Stroud, 1994.

Ballard, M., 'An Expedition of English Archers to Liège in 1467, and the Anglo-Burgundian Marriage Alliance', *Nottingham Mediaeval Studies*, 34, 1990.

Barr, N., *Flodden 1513*, Stroud, 2001.

Bennett, M., *The Battle of Bosworth*, Gloucester, 1985.

Idem, *Lambert Simnel and the Battle of Stoke*, Gloucester, 1987.

Idem, 'Henry VII and the Northern Rising of 1489', *EHR*, 105, 1990.

Cron, B.M., 'Margaret of Anjou and the Lancastrian March on London, 1461', *The Ricardian*, 11, 1999.

Cruickshank, C.G., *Army Royal. Henry VIII's Invasion of France, 1513*, Oxford, 1969.

Curry, A., 'English Armies in the Fifteenth Century', Arms, Armies and Fortifications in the Hundred Years War, ed. Curry, A. and Hughes, M., Woodbridge, 1994.

Dockray, K., 'The Battle of Wakefield and the Wars of the Roses', *The Ricardian*, 9, 1992.

Dodds, M.H. and R., *The Pilgrimage of Grace 1536–1537 and the Exeter Conspiracy 1538*, 2 vols, Cambridge, 1915.

Dyer, C., *Standards of living in the later Middle Ages*, Cambridge, 1989.

Fiorato, V., Boylston, A. and Knüssel, C. ed., *Blood Red Roses. The archaeology of a mass grave from the Battle of Towton AD 1461*, Oxford, 2000.

Fowler, K., *Medieval Mercenaries, 1*, Oxford, 2001.

Fox, A., *Oral and Literate Culture in England 1500–1700*, Oxford, 2000.

Gill, L., *Richard III and Buckingham's Rebellion*, Stroud, 1999.

Goodman, A., *The Wars of the Roses*, London, 1981.

Gransden, A., *Historical Writing in England II c.1307 to the Early Sixteenth Century*, Ithaca N.Y., 1982.

Griffiths, R.A., *The Reign of King Henry VI*, London, 1981.

Griffiths, R.A. and Thomas, R.S., *The Making of the Tudor Dynasty*, Gloucester, 1985.

Grummitt, D., 'William Lord Hastings and the Defence of Calais, 1471–83', *Social Attitudes and Political Structures in the Fifteenth Century*, ed. Thornton, T., Stroud, 2000.

Hale, J.R., *Artists and Warfare in the Renaissance*, New Haven and London, 1990.

Hammond, P.W., Sutton, A.F. and Visser-Fuchs, L., 'The Reburial of Richard, Duke of York, 21–30 July 1476', *The Ricardian*, 10, 1994.

Hanham, A., 'Henry VI and his Miracles', *The Ricardian*, 12, 2000.

Hay, D., *Polydore Vergil*, Oxford, 1952.

Head, C., 'Pius II and the Wars of the Roses', *Archivium Historiae Pontificae*, 8, 1970.

Hicks, M., *Warwick the Kingmaker*, Oxford, 2002.

Horrox, R., *Richard III. A Study of Service*, Cambridge, 1989.

Jones, M.K., *Bosworth 1485*, Stroud, 2002.

Kingsford, C.L., *English Historical Literature in the Fifteenth Century*, Oxford, 1913.

Knowles, R., 'The Battle of Wakefield: the Topography', *The Ricardian*, 9, 1992.

Mallett, M., *Mercenaries and their Masters. Warfare in Renaissance Italy*, London, 1974.

Manning, R.B., *Village Revolts. Social Protest and Popular Disturbances in England, 1509–1640*, Oxford, 1988.

McKenna, J.W., 'Popular canonization as political propaganda: the cult of Archbishop Scrope', *Speculum*, 44, 1970.

Meek, E.L., 'The career of Sir Thomas Everingham, "Knight of the North", in the service of Maximilian duke of Austria 1477–81', *Historical Research*, 74, 2001.

Muir, K., *Life and Letters of Sir Thomas Wyatt*, Liverpool, 1963.

O'Callaghan, J.F., *A History of Medieval Spain*, Ithaca and London, 1975.

Pollard, A.J., *North–East England during the Wars of the Roses*, Oxford, 1990.

Idem, *The Wars of the Roses*, Basingstoke, 1988.

Ross, C., *Edward IV*, London, 1974.

Idem, *Richard III*, London, 1981.

Ruano, E. Benito, 'Un Cruzado Inglés en la Guerra de Granada', *Anuario de Estudios Medievales*, 9, 1974–1979.

Skinner, R.J., 'Thomas Woodshawe, 'Grasiour' and Regicide', *The Ricardian*, 9, 1993.

Storey, R.L., *The End of the House of Lancaster*, London, 1966.

Sutton, A.F., see Hammond.

The Complete Peerage of England, Scotland, Ireland and Great Britain and the United Kingdom, ed. G.E.C., new edtn by Gibbs, V. et al., 13 vols, London, 1910–59.

Thomas, R.S., see Griffiths.

Thompson, P., *Sir Thomas Wyatt and His Background*, London, 1964.

Twemlow, F. R., *The Battle of Blore Heath*, ed. Griffith, P., Nuneaton, 1995.

Vaughan, R., *John the Fearless. The Growth of Burgundian Power*, London, 1966.

Idem, *Philip the Good. The Apogee of Burgundy*, London, 1970.

Idem, *Charles the Bold. The Last Valois Duke of Burgundy*, London, 1973.

Viser-Fuchs, L., see Hammond

Weever, J., *Ancient Funerall Monuments* (etc.), London, 1631.

Williams, Glanmor, *Renewal and Reformation. Wales c.1415–1642*, Oxford, 1993.

Wolffe, B.P., *Henry VI*, London, 1981.

Index

TEMPUS — REVEALING HISTORY

 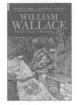

William II Rufus, the Red King
EMMA MASON
'A thoroughly new reappraisal of a much maligned king. The dramatic story of his life is told with great pace and insight'
John Gillingham
£25
0 7524 3528 0

William Wallace The True Story of Braveheart
CHRIS BROWN
'A formidable new biography... sieves through masses of medieval records to distinguish the man from the myth' **Magnus Magnusson**
£17.99
0 7524 3432 2

Elizabeth Wydeville
The Slandered Queen
ARLENE OKERLUND
'A penetrating, thorough and wholly convincing vindication of this unlucky queen'
Sarah Gristwood
£18.99
0 7524 3384 9

The Battle of Hastings 1066
M.K. LAWSON
'Deeply considered and provocative' **BBC History Magazine,** Books of the Year 2003
£25
0 7524 2689 3

 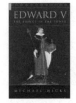

The Welsh Wars of Independence
DAIVD MOORE
'Beautifully written, subtle and remarkably perceptive... a major re-examination of a thousand years of Welsh history' **John Davies**
£25
0 7524 3321 0

Medieval England
From Hastings to Bosworth
EDMUND KING
'The best illustrated history of medieval England' **John Gillingham**
£12.99
0 7524 2827 5

A Companion to Medieval England
NIGEL SAUL
'Wonderful... everything you could wish to know about life in medieval England'
Heritage Today
£19.99
0 7524 2969 8

Edward V The Prince in the Tower
MICHAEL HICKS
'The first time in ages that a publisher has sent me a book that I actually want to read!'
David Starkey
£25
0 7524 1996 X

If you are interested in purchasing other books published by Tempus, or in case you have difficulty finding any Tempus books in your local bookshop, you can also place orders directly through our website:
www.tempus-publishing.com

TEMPUS — REVEALING HISTORY

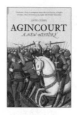

Anne Neville
Queen to Richard III
MICHAEL HICKS
'A masterful and poignant story'
Alison Weir
£18.99
0 7524 3663 5

The Vikings
MAGNUS MAGNUSSON
'Serious, engaging history'
BBC History Magazine
£9.99
0 7524 2699 0

William the Conqueror
DAVID BATES
'As expertly woven as the Bayeux Tapestry'
BBC History Magazine
£12.99
0 7524 2960 4

Agincourt: A New History
ANNE CURRY
'Overturns a host of assumptions about this most famous of English victories... *the* book on the battle' ***Richard Holmes***
£25
0 7524 2828 4

Hereward The Last Englishman
PETER REX
'An enthralling work of historical detection'
Robert Lacey
£17.99
0 7524 3318 0

The English Resistance
The Underground War Against the Normans
PETER REX
'An invaluable rehabilitation of an ignored resistance movement' ***The Sunday Times***
£17.99
0 7524 2827 6

Richard III
MICHAEL HICKS
'A most important book by the greatest living expert on Richard' ***Desmond Seward***
£9.99
0 7524 2589 7

The Peasants' Revolt
England's Failed Revolution of 1381
ALASTAIR DUNN
'A stunningly good book... totally absorbing'
Melvyn Bragg
£9.99
0 7524 2965 5

If you are interested in purchasing other books published by Tempus, or in case you have difficulty finding any Tempus books in your local bookshop, you can also place orders directly through our website:
www.tempus-publishing.com